A Practical Grammar

THE SCIENCE OF THE ENGLISH LANGUAGE

A

PRACTICAL GRAMMAR:

IN WHICH

WORDS, PHRASES, AND SENTENCES

ARE

CLASSIFIED ACCORDING TO THEIR OFFICES,

AND

THEIR VARIOUS RELATIONS TO ONE ANOTHER.

ILLUSTRATED BY A COMPLETE SYSTEM OF DIAGRAMS.

"Speech is the body of thought."

BY S. W. CLARK, A. M.,
PRINCIPAL OF CORTLAND ACADEMY.
"AUTHOR OF ANALYSIS OF THE ENGLISH LANGUAGE," "ETYMOLOGICAL CHART."

REVISED EDITION.

NEW YORK:
A. S. BARNES & BURR, 51 & 53 JOHN STREET.
SOLD BY BOOKSELLERS, GENERALLY, THROUGHOUT THE UNITED STATES.
1859.

[redacted]

PREFACE.

The Grammar of a Language, Quintilian has justly remarked, is like the foundation of a building; the most important part, although out of sight, and not always properly valued by those most interested in its condition.

In the opinion of many modern educators there is a tendency, on the part of all, to neglect this important branch of English Education—not so much from a conviction that the science is not important, as that there is a radical defect in the common method of presenting it to the attention of the Scholar. This was the sentiment of the Author when, some ten years since, he was called to the supervision of a Literary Institution, in which was established a department for the education of Teachers. Accordingly, recourse was had to oral instruction; and, for the convenience of Teachers, a manuscript Grammar was prepared, which embodied the principles of the science and the Author's mode of presenting it. These principles and this method have been properly tested by numerous and advanced classes during the seven years last past. The manuscript has in the mean time, from continued additions, unexpectedly become a book. It has received the favorable notice of Teachers, and its publication has been, by Teachers, repeatedly solicited. To these solicitations the Author is constrained to yield, and in the hope and belief that the work will "add to the stock of human knowledge," or at least tend to that result, by giving an increased interest to the study of the English language, it is, with diffidence, submitted to the public.

In revising the work for publication, an effort has been made to render it simple in style, comprehensive in matter—adapted to the capacities of the younger pupil, and to the wants of the more advanced scholar. It is confidently believed that the Method of teaching Grammar herein suggested, is the true method. The method adopted by most text-books may be well suited to the wants of foreigners in first learning our language. They need first to learn our Alphabet—the power and sounds, and the proper combinations of Letters—the definitions of words and their classification according to definitions.

But the American youth is presumed to know all this, and be able to catch the thought conveyed by an English Sentence; in fine, to be able to use practically the language, before he attempts to study it as a science. Instead, therefore, of beginning with the Alphabet, and wasting his energies on technical terms and ambiguous words, he should be required to deal with thought as conveyed by Sentences. Accord ingly, this introduction to the Science of Language begins with a Sentence, properly constructed, and investigates its structure by developing the offices of the Words which compose it; making the *office* rather than the *form* of a Word, determine the class to which it belongs.

As an important auxiliary in the analysis of Sentences, a system of DIAGRAMS has been invented and introduced in the work. It is not claimed for the DIAGRAMS that they constitute any essential part of the Science of Language;—nor do Geometrical Diagrams constitute such a part of the Science of Geometry; Maps, of Geography; or Figures, of Arithmetic. But it will not be denied that these are of great service in the study of those branches. Experience has established their importance. Let, then, the use of Diagrams, reduced as they are here, to a complete system, be adopted in the analyses of Sentences, and their utility will become as obvious in the science of Language, as it is in the science of Magnitude; and for precisely the same reason, that an abstract truth is made tangible; the eye is permitted to assist the mind; the memory is relieved, that the judgment may have full charter of all the mental powers.

Conscious that novelty, as such, should not bear sway in the investigations of Science, the Author has been careful neither to depart from the ordinary method of presenting the Science, for the sake of novelty, nor, from dread of novelty, to reject manifest improvements. The old Nomenclature is retained, not because a better could not be proposed, but because the advantages to be gained would not compensate for the confusion necessarily consequent to such a change. But the terms purely technical have been introduced *as a natural inference from facts previously deduced.* Principles and Definitions are preceded by such Remarks as have fully established their propriety. The inductive method of arriving at truth has been followed throughout—with that it stands or falls.

ADVERTISEMENT

TO THE FIFTEENTH EDITION.

IN sending forth this revised Edition of the PRACTICAL GRAMMAR, the Author takes occasion to render acknowledgments to his numerous professional brethren who have so favorably received the former editions, and also to express his gratitude for the various criticisms which its use has suggested. Especially is he gratified that, with frank and faithful notices of the omissions and other defects in the arrangement of the former Editions, there has been a unanimous approval of the SYSTEM and METHOD herein adopted. Accordingly, the work has been rewritten upon the basis of the former Edition.

In making the revision, an effort has been made to perfect the work in all its parts;—to supply defects—to simplify the arrangement—to bring the various parts more fully in harmony with the system—and to adapt it more completely to Class Exercises.

To Part I. important Additions have been made; the Elements of Sentences have been discussed more fully, and the DIAGRAMS are made to render the Analysis of Sentences more perspicuous. ANALYSIS discloses to the Student the right use of Words, according to established custom, thus furnishing the only appropriate key to the true Etymology of the Language.

In Part II. ETYMOLOGY is so presented as to furnish a proper foundation for Syntax;—the several *materials* are adapted to their various positions in the *structure* to be reared.

In Part III. careful attention has been given to make the other branches of the science of Language subserve SYNTAX and harmonize with it. In this effort consists the great improvement in the Grammar as now presented;—the Analytical is made to accompany the Synthetical.

Exercises in CRITICISM are inserted, in which common errors are noticed and corrected by proper references to Rules, Notes, and Observations in the text.

The extensive and constantly increasing circulation of the original work, encourages the hope that, with its present improvements, it will secure the desired approbation of a discerning public.

CORTLAND ACADEMY,
Homer, N. Y., March 1st, 1855.

THE ETYMOLOGICAL CHART.

THIS CHART presents, at one view, the entire Etymology of the English language. It is useful chiefly in reviews and in etymological parsing.

The large edition of the Chart—44 inches diameter—may be used more profitably, as, with it, the whole class may follow the reciting pupil—all having their attention directed to the same thing, at the same time. In the absence of a large Chart, the small ones* may be used—each student using his own.

It will be noticed that the Chart does not give the Definitions of the Classes and Modifications of words; but simply presents the principles of Etymology; showing, for example,

That a "Sentence" consists of "Principal Parts," and may have "Adjuncts." That the Principal Parts of a Sentence must be a "SUBJECT," a "PREDICATE," and (if Transitive) an "OBJECT." That the *Subject* may be a "WORD," a "PHRASE," or a "SENTENCE." That if the Subject is a *Word*, it is a "NOUN" or "PRONOUN"—if a *Noun*, it is "COMMON" or "PROPER"—if a *Pronoun*, it is "PERSONAL," "RELATIVE," "INTERROGATIVE," or "ADJECTIVE." That the Noun or Pronoun must be of the "NEUTER," "FEMININE," or "MASCULINE" Gender—of the "FIRST," "SECOND," or "THIRD" Person—of the "SINGULAR" or "PLURAL" Number—and that it must be in the "NOMINATIVE" Case.

If the Subject is a "*Phrase*," it is a SUBSTANTIVE Phrase—and may be (in form), "PREPOSITIONAL," "PARTICIPIAL," "INFINITIVE," or "INDEPENDENT"—and may be "TRANSITIVE" or "INTRANSITIVE."

If the Subject is a "*Sentence*," it is a "SUBSTANTIVE" Sentence—and may be "SIMPLE" or "COMPOUND," "TRANSITIVE" or "INTRANSITIVE."

Thus, a comparison of the Chart with the General Principles, on pages 175–180, will readily suggest to the skillful Teacher the proper method of using it in *review*.

The proper use of the Chart in *Etymological Parsing* is illustrated by EXERCISES, pp. 181–186.

---

* See "CLARK'S ANALYSIS OF THE ENGLISH LANGUAGE."

CONTENTS.

PART I.

PAGE

PART II.

ETYMOLOGY.

PART III.

SYNTAX.

PART IV.

PROSODY.

APPENDIX.

PART I

INTRODUCTORY EXERCISES.

God moves in a mysterious way,
His wonders to perform;
He plants his footsteps in the sea,
And rides upon the storm."

Quest. *Of whom* is something asserted in the lines above written

Ans. Something is said concerning "*God.*"

What is said of God?

A. God "*moves.*"

How does God move?

A. "*In a mysterious way.*"

What way?

A. "*Mysterious*" way.

What mysterious way?

A. "*A*" mysterious way.

"God moves in a mysterious way"—*why?*

A. "*To perform his wonders.*"

To perform *what* wonders?

A. "*His*" wonders.

Concerning whom is something more said?

A. Something more is said concerning "God."

Why do you think so?

A. Because, in this connection "He" means God.

What more is said of God?

A. He "*plants.*"

He plants *what?*

A. He plants "*footsteps.*"

He plants *what* footsteps?

A. "*His*" footsteps.

He plants his footsteps—*where?*

A "*In the sea.*"

In *what* sea?

A. In "*the*" sea.

***What more* is said of God?**

A. He "*rides.*"

He rides—*where?*

A. "*Upon the storm.*"

Upon *what* storm?

A. "*The*" storm.

In the lines written above what is the *use* or *office* of the word "God"?

A. It is used to tell *who* "moves."

What is the use of the word "*moves*"?

A. To tell what God *does.*

What is the use of "*in a mysterious way*"?

A. To tell *how* God moves

What is the use of "*a*"?

A. To tell *what* mysterious way.

What is the use of "*mysterious*"?

A. To tell *what kind* of way.

What is the use of "*his wonders to perform*"?

A. To tell *for what purpose* God moves.

What is the use of "*He*"?

A. To tell *who* "plants footsteps" and "rides."

What is the use of "*plants*"?

A. To tell *what* "He" *does.*

What is the use of "*his*"?

A. To tell *whose* footsteps.

What is the use of "*footsteps*"?

A. To tell *what* He plants.

What is the use of "*in the sea*"?

A. To tell *where* He plants footsteps.

What is the use of "*rides*"?

A. To tell *what* "He" *does.*

What is the use of "*upon the storm*"?

A. To tell *where* He rides.

REMARK.—The young Pupil has seen, in this exposition of the four lines written above, that *words have meaning,* and that when they are properly put together, they convey the thoughts of the person who wrote them, to those who read them.

ADDITIONAL EXERCISES FOR ANALYSIS.

1. "The | sun | rose | on the sea | ."
2. "A | mist | rose | slowly | from the lake | ."
3. "The | night | passed | away | in song | ."
4. "Morning | returned | in joy | ."
5. "The | mountains | showed | their | gray | heads | ."
6. "The | blue | face | of ocean | smiled | ."
7. "Day | declines | ;"
8. "Hollow | winds | are | in the pines | :"
9. "Darkly | moves | each | giant | bough, |
   O'er the sky's last crimson glow | ."
10. "Nature's | richest | dyes |
    Are floating | o'er Italian skies | ."

11. "A golden staff his steps supported."
12. "The dying notes still murmur on the string."
13. "A purple robe his dying frame shall fold."
14. "At the heaving billows, stood the meager form of Care."
15. "Oft the shepherd called thee to his flock."
16. "The comely tear steals o'er the cheek."
17. "The storms of wintry Time will quickly pass."
18. "Thus in some deep retirement would I pass
    The winter-glooms, with friends of pleasant soul."
19. "Then comes the father of the tempest forth,
    Wrapt in thick glooms."

20. ' Thy bounty shines in Autumn unconfined,
And spreads a common feast for all that live."
21. "Some in the fields of purest ether play
And bask and whiten in the blaze of day."
22. "On thy fair bosom, waveless stream,
The dipping paddle echoes far,
And flashes in the moonlight gleam."
23. "Who can observe the careful ant,
And not provide for future want."
24. Nature with folded hands seemed there,
Kneeling at her evening prayer.
25. ———————— "The woods
Threw their cool shadows freshly to the west."
26. "The clear dew is on the blushing bosoms
Of crimson roses, in a holy rest."
27. Spring calls out each voice of the deep blue sky.
28. Thou'rt journeying to thy spirit's home,
Where the skies are ever clear.
29. "A summer breeze
Parts the deep masses of the forest shade,
And lets a sunbeam through."
30. "The pines *grew red* with morning."
31. "Sin hath broke the world's sweet peace—unstrung
Th' harmonious chords to which the angels sung."
32. "And eve, along the western skies,
Spreads her intermingling dyes."
33. The blooming morning ope'd her dewy eye.
34. "No marble marks thy couch of lowly sleep;
35. But living statues there are seen to weep."
36. "A distant torrent faintly roars."
37. "His gray locks slowly waved in the wind
And glittered to the beam of night."

LANGUAGE.

DEFINITION 1.—*Language* is any means of communicating thought, feeling, or purpose.

OBS. 1.—Thoughts and feelings are indicated—

1. By certain expressions of the features, by gestures, and by other physical acts. This is called *Natural Language.*
2. By articulate sounds, or by written characters. This is called *Artificial Language.*

OBS. 2.—Natural language is common to all intelligent beings, and is understood by all without previous instruction.—Smiling, frowning, laughing, weeping, are instances of natural language.

OBS. 3.—Artificial language is invented by men.—Sounds are made to indicate thoughts by mutual or common consent. Generally, each nation has its peculiar language.

PRINCIPLE.—*Artificial Language* is SPOKEN and WRITTEN.

DEF. 2.—*Spoken Language* consists in vocal sounds, indicative of thought, of feeling, or of purpose.

DEF. 3.—*Written Language* consists in artificial characters, so arr[illegible]nged and combined as, by common consent, to represe[illegible] thought or emotion.

REM.—[illegible] customary to give to every science a *name*, by which it may be [illegible]guished from other sciences; accordingly, people have agreed to [illegible] the science which treats of [illegible]

GRAMMAR.

DEF. 4.—*Grammar* is the science of Language.

OBS. 1.—There are certain *General Princip*[illegible] Grammar which are common to all languages—Hence the term G[illegible]

OBS. 2.—But each particular language has some idioms [illegible] construction, peculiar to *itself.*—Hence the term PARTICULAR GRAM[illegible].

REM.—Every *Particular Grammar* should include all the principles of *General Grammar.*

DEF. 5.—*English Grammar* is the science which investigates the principles, and determines the proper construction of the English language.

REM.—The articulate sounds of language are indicated by Letters.

DEF. 6.—*A Letter* is a character used to indicate a sound, or to modify the sound of another letter.

OBS.—For observations on the properties and offices of Letters, see APPENDIX, Note A.

REM.—*Letters* are combined to form Words.

DEF. 7.—*A Word* is a Letter, or a combination of Letters, used as the *sign* of an idea.

EXAMPLES.—*God—mysterious—stood—slowly—Ah!—by—and.*

REM.—*Words* are combined to form *Phrases* and *Sentences.*

DEF. 8.—A *Phrase* is a combination of Words, not constituting an entire proposition, but performing a distinct office in the structure of a Sentence or of another Phrase.

EXAMPLES.— *At midnight, in his guarded tent,*
The Turk was dreaming *of the hour,*
When Greece, *her knee in suppliance bent,*
Should tremble *at his power.*

DEF. 9.—A *Sentence* is an assemblage of words, so combined as to assert an entire proposition.

EXAMPLES.—1. Night approaches.
2. Day is departing.
3. William is sleepy.
4. Socrates was a philosopher.
5. Virtue secures happiness.
6. John and George have arrived.
7. God created the heaven and the earth.
8. "The dying notes still murmur on the string."

WORDS.

CLASSIFICATION

REMARK.—In a Discourse, words are used—

1. As *Names* of beings, places, or things;
2. As *Substitutes* for names or facts;
3. As *Qualifiers* or *Limiters* of Names;
4. To *assert* an act, being, or state;
5. To *modify* an assertion or a quality;
6. To express *relations* of things or of thoughts;
7. To *introduce* or to *connect* Words and Sentences;
8. To express a *sudden* or an *intense emotion;* or,
9. For Rhetorical effect.

nence, by their uses—

PRINCIPLE.—*Words* are distinguished as,

1. *Nouns,*
2. *Pronouns,*
3. *Adjectives,*
4. *Verbs,*
5. *Adverbs,*
6. *Prepositions,*
7. *Conjunctions,*
8. *Exclamations,* and
9. *Words of Euphony.*

DEF. 10.—*A Word* used as the name of a being, a place, or a thing, is called

A Noun.

EXAMPLES.—*God—man—sea—way—wonders.*

DEF. 11.—A Word used fr [illegible] is called

A Pronoun.

EXAMPLES.—*I—thou—he—she—it—who—what—that.*

DEF. 12.—A Word used to qualify, or otherwise describe a Noun or a Pronoun, is c[illegible]

An Adjective.

EXAMPLES.—*Mysterious* [way]—*his* [wonders]—*the* [sea.]

DEF. 13.—A Word used to assert an *act*, *being*, or *state*, of a person or a thing, is called

A Verb.

EXAMPLES.—[God] *moves*—[He] *plants*—Day [*declines*].

DEF. 14.—A Word used to modify the signification of a Verb, an Adjective, or another Modifier, is called

An Adverb.

EXAMPLES.—"A mist ROSE *slowly* from the lake."
"The task was *exceedingly* DIFFICULT."
"He came between us *very* OFT."

DEF. 15.—A Word used to express a relation of words to each other, is called

A Preposition.

EXAMPLES.—"*At* MIDNIGHT *in* his guarded TENT,
The Turk WAS DREAMING *of* the HOUR."

DEF. 16.—A Word used to introduce a Sentence, or to connect Words and Phrases, is called

A Conjunction.

EXAMPLES.—"*And* I am glad *that* he has lived thus long."
"God created the HEAVEN *and* the EARTH."

DEF. 17.—A Word used to express a sudden or an intense emotion, is called

An Exclamation.

EXAMPLES.—*Alas!—oh! shocking!*

DEF. 18.—A Word used chiefly for the sake of *sound*, is called *A Word of Euphony.*

EXAMPLES.—"*There* are no idlers here."
"Now then, we are prepared to define our position."
"*Even* in our ashes live their wonted fires."

OBS.—For observations on "*Words of Euphony*," see Part II.

PHRASES.

CLASSIFICATION.

REMARK.—Phrases are used as *substitutes* for Nouns, Adjectives, and Adverbs; or they are independent in construction. Hence, in respect of their offices,

PRINCIPLE.—*Phrases* are distinguished as,

1. *Substantive,*
2. *Adjective,*
3. *Adverbial,*
4. *Independent.*

DEF. 19.—A *Substantive Phrase* is a phrase used as the Subject or the Object of a Verb, or the Object of a Preposition.

EXAMPLES.—"*To be,* contents his natural desire."
"*His being a minister,* prevented his rising to civil power."
"I doubted *his having been a soldier.*"
"The crime of *being a young man,* I shall attempt neither to palliate nor deny."

What "contents his natural desire"?
"*To be,*"—i. e., mere existence.
"I doubted"—*What?*
"His having been a soldier."
"The crime of"—*What?*
"Being a young man."

OBS.—Substantive Phrases perform *offices* similar to those of Nouns and Pronouns.

DEF. 20.—*An Adjective Phrase* is a phrase used to qualify or limit the application of a Noun or a Pronoun.

EXAMPLES.—"The time *of my departure* is at hand."
"*Forgetting the things that are behind,* I press forward.
What "time"?—"Of my departure."
"The dishes *of luxury* cover his table."
What dishes?—"Of luxury."

DEF. 21.—*An Adverbial Phrase* is a phrase used to modify the signification of a Verb, an Adjective, or an Adverb.

EXAMPLES.—"God moves *in a mysterious way.*"
"He is powerful *for evil*—impotent *for good.*"
"God moves"—*How?*
"In a mysterious way."
"Powerful"—*In what respect?*
"For evil."

DEF. 22.—*An Independent Phrase* is a phrase not grammatically connected with any other element.

EXAMPLES.—"*The hour having arrived,* we commenced the exercises."

OBS.—An Independent Phrase performs an office in its sentence rather *Logical* than *Grammatical.* Thus, in the sentence, "The hour having arrived, we commenced the exercises," the phrase "the hour having arrived," indicates the *time* of commencing the exercises; but it is not joined to the word "commenced" by any connecting word.

PRIN.—Phrases are distinguished also by their *forms,* as,

1. *Prepositional,*
2. *Infinitive,*
3. *Participial,*
4. *Independent.*

DEF. 23.—*A Prepositional Phrase* is a phrase introduced by a Preposition, having a *Noun* or a *Substitute* as its object of relation.

EXAMPLES.—"*In* a mysterious *way.*" "To me."
"A habit *of moving quickly* is another way *of gaining time.*"

DEF. 24.—*An Infinitive Phrase* is a phrase introduced by the Preposition TO, having a Verb as its object of relation.

EXAMPLES.—"*To love*"—"*To study*"—"*To be diligent.*"
"We ought not *to be satisfied* with present attainments."
"I sit me down *a pensive hour to spend.*"

DEF. 25.—*A Participial Phrase* is a phrase introduced by a *Participle*, having an Object or an Adjunct.

EXAMPLES.— "*Scaling yonder peak*,
I saw an eagle, *wheeling near its brow*."

DEF. 26.—*An Independent Phrase* is introduced by a *Noun* or a *Pronoun*, followed by a Participle depending upon it.

EXAMPLES.—"*The cars having left*, we chartered a coach."
"Thus talking, *hand* [*being*] *in hand*,
Alone they passed on to their blissful bower."

ANALYSIS OF PHRASES.

PRINCIPLE.—*A Phrase* consists of
Principal Elements, | *Adjunct Elements*.

DEF. 27.—The *Principal Elements* of a Phrase are the words necessary to its structure.

EXAMPLES.—"Rays | *of* limpid *light* | gleamed | *round* their *path*." |
"Birds sang | *amid* the sprouting *shade*." |
"Manhood is disgraced | *by* the *consequences* | *of* neglected *youth*." |

DEF. 28.—*The Adjuncts* of a Phrase are the words used to modify or limit the offices of other words in the Phrase.

EXAMPLES.—"Rays | of *limpid* light | gleamed | round *their* path." |
"Birds sang | amid *the whispering* shade." |
"See! Winter comes | to rule *the varied* year." |
"With what an awful, world-revolving power,
Were first the unwieldy planets lanched along
The illimitable void."

PRIN.—The *Principal Elements* of a Phrase consist of
The Leader, | *The Subsequent*.

DEF. 29.—The *Leader* of a Phrase is the word used to *introduce* the Phrase—generally connecting its Subsequent to the word which the Phrase qualifies.

EXAMPLES.—"*Like* a spirit | it came, | *in* the van | *of* a storm." |
"Enough remains, | *of* glimmering light |
To guide the wanderer's steps aright." |
"The previous *question* being demanded, | the debate closed."

OBS.—The Leader of a Phrase is *commonly* the first word *in position*—but not *always*; Adjuncts may precede. [See the last example.]

PRIN.—The *Leader* of a Phrase may be

A *Preposition*,	The *Preposition* TO,
A *Participle*,	A *Substantive*.

EXAMPLES.—"I am monarch *of* all I survey;
My right there is none *to* dispute."

"*Taking* a madman's sword | *to* prevent | his *doing* mischief, | can not be regarded | AS *robbing* him | ."

"The evening *star* having disappeared, | we returned to the castle."

DEF. 30.—A *Participle* is a word derived from a Verb, retaining the signification of its verb, while it also performs the office of some other "part of speech."

OBS.—For observations on Participles, see Part II.

DEF. 31.—The *Subsequent* of a Phrase is the Element which follows the Leader as its object of *action* or *relation*, or which depends on it in construction.

EXAMPLES.—At *parting* | , too, there was a long ceremony | in the *hall* | , buttoning up *great-coats* | , tying on woolen *comforters* | , fixing silk *handkerchiefs* over the *mouth* and up to the *ears*, and grasping sturdy *walking-canes* to support unsteady *feet*.

PRIN.—The *Subsequent* of a Phrase may be,

A *Word*, | A *Phrase*, | A *Sentence*.

EXAMPLES.—"Sweet was the sound, when oft | at evening's *close* |
Up yonder *hill* | the village murmur rose."

"A habit | of *moving quickly* | , is another way | of *gaining time* | "

"The footman, in his usual phrase,
Comes up with '*Madam, dinner stays*.'"

OBS. 1.—The *Subsequent* of a Phrase is sometimes suppressed.

EXAMPLE.—"These crowd *around*, to ask him of his health."

OBS. 2.—When any Element of a Phrase is suppressed, that part of the Phrase which is expressed—whether Leader, Subsequent, or Adjunct—is to be regarded as the *representative* of the whole Phrase, and, in the analysis of a Sentence, it should be construed as the whole Phrase would be if fully expressed.

EXAMPLES.—1. "These crowd *around*," i. e., *around him*.
2. William will come *home*, i. e., *to his home*.
3. Mary has come to school *early*, i. e., *at an early hour*.

"*Around*," as an Element in the Phrase, is a *Preposition*.

"*Around*," as an Element in the Sentence, is an *Adverb*—for it is a *representative* of an Adverbial Phrase.

"*Home*," as an Element in the *Phrase*, is a *Noun*.

"*Home*," as an Element in the *Sentence*, is an *Adverb*—for it is a *representative* of an Adverbial Phrase.

"*Early*," as an Element in the *Phrase*, is an *Adjective*.

"*Early*," as an Element in the *Sentence*, is an *Adverb*—for it is a *representative* of an Adverbial Phrase.

SENTENCES.

ANALYSIS AND CLASSIFICATION.

REMARK.—As a Word is a physical representative of an idea, so a Sentence is a mechanical structure embodying a Preposition. A Sentence may be resolved into its Elements.

DEF. 32.—*The Elements* of a sentence are the parts which enter into its structure.

REM.—In the structure of Sentences, certain *general principles* are involved, which are common to all languages.

1. We have *that of which something is declared*. This is called the *Subject* of the Sentence.

2. There must be a word or words used to *declare*—positively negatively, or interrogatively—something of the subject. This is called the *Predicate*.

These two parts are essential to the structure of a Sentence.

3. The Predicates of some Sentences assert acts which pass over to an Object.

4. There are often other Elements, used to *qualify*, to *limit*, or to *modify* the various parts of Sentences. These are called *Adjunct Elements.*

PRIN.—*The Parts* of a Sentence are distinguished as
Principal Elements and
Adjunct Elements.

DEF. 33.—*The Principal Elements* of a Sentence are the parts which make the unqualified assertion.

EXAMPLES.—*Birds fly*—The *sun shines.*
"The *night passed* away in song."
"The *mountains showed* their gray *heads.*"
"Thy *bounty shines* in Autumn unconfined,
And *spreads* a common *feast* for all that live."
"The *king* of shadows *loves* a shining *mark.*"
"In the beginning, *God created* the *heaven* and the *earth.*"

DEF. 34.—*The Adjunct Elements* of a Sentence are such as describe or modify other elements.

EXAMPLES.—"*The* | night passed | *away* | *in song.*"
"*The* king | *of shadows* | loves | *a* | *shining* mark."
"*There* | *in his noisy mansion,* | *skilled to rule,* |
The | *village* | master | taught | *his* | *little* | school." |
"Lend *me your* songs, ye nightingales."
"O Liberty! I wait *for thee.*"

REM.—There are still other words, which are neither Principal Elements nor Adjuncts,—words which are sometimes used in connection with the Sentence, but which do not constitute an integral part of it. Hence,

DEF. 35.—Words accompanying a Sentence without entering into its structure, are called
Attendant Elements.

EXAMPLES.—"Lend me your songs, ye *nightingales!*"
"*O Liberty!* I wait for thee."

"*There* are no idlers here."
"I sit *me* down, a pensive hour to spend."
"*Even* in our ashes live their wonted fires."
"*Friends, Romans, Countrymen!* lend me your ears."

ELEMENTS OF SENTENCES.

PRINCIPAL ELEMENTS.

PRIN.—The Principal Elements of a Sentence, are,

The Subject, | *The Predicate,* | *The Object.*

OBS.—Every Sentence must have, at least, one *Subject* and one *Predicate*, expressed or understood.

DEF. 36.—*The Subject* of a Sentence is that of which something is asserted.

OBS.—The Subject of a Sentence is a *Noun*, or a *Word*, a *Phrase*, or a *Sentence* used for a Noun.

EXAMPLES.

1. *A Noun.*—*Birds* fly—"*Knowledge* is power."
"*Truth* crushed to earth, will rise again."
2. *A Pronoun.*—*We* come—*They* are satisfied.
"*They that* seek me early, shall find me."
3. *A Phrase.*—*To do good*, is the duty of all men.
"*His being a minister*, prevented his rising to civil power."
4. *A Sentence.*—"*At what time he took orders*, doth not appear."
"*That all men are created equal*, is a self-evident truth."

DEF. 37.—*The Predicate* of a Sentence is the Word or Words that express what is asserted of the subject.

OBS.—The Predicate consists of a *Verb*, with or without another *Verb*, a *Participle*, an *Adjective*, a *Noun*, a *Pronoun*, or a *Preposition*.

EXAMPLES.

1. A *Verb only.*—*Birds* fly—Quadrupeds *run*.
"Here *sleeps* he now alone."
2. *Two Verbs.*—We *shall go*—I *do remember*.
"Ye *shall* not in the lofty pine
Disturb the sparrow's nest."

3. *A Verb* and a *Participle.*—John *was injured*—Willie *is reading.*
"Thou art perched aloft on the beetling crag."

4. A *Verb* and an *Adjective.*—James *became poor*—Warner *is sleepy*
"And the waves *are white* below."

5. A *Verb* and a *Noun.*—God *is love*—We *are friends.*
The proper *study* of mankind *is* man.

6. A *Verb* and a *Pronoun.*—It *is I*—*Who are* you?
"*Thine is* the kingdom."

7. A *Verb* and a *Preposition.*—Its idle hopes *are o'er.*
That business *has been attended to.*

REMARKS.—The Predicate is varied not only in *form*, but also in its functions.

1. It may assert an *act*—as, William *walks*
2. It may assert *being*—as, God *exists.*
3. It may assert *quality*—as, Sugar *is sweet.*
4. It may assert *possession*—as, "*Thine is* the kingdom."
5. It may assert *identity*—as, It *is I.*
6. It may assert *condition*—as, Its idle hopes *are o'er.*
7. It may assert *change* of condition—as, "His palsied hand *waxed strong.*"

OBS. 1.—The term "*Predicate*" has two applications—a *Logical* and a *Grammatical.* The *Logical Predicate* includes the *Grammatical Predicate* and its *Object.* Thus, in the sentence,

"The king of shadows loves a shining mark,"

"*Loves a shining mark,*" is the Logical Predicate;
"*Loves*" is the Grammatical Predicate.

OBS 2.—In Sentences that have no Objects, the *Logical* and the *Grammatical* Predicates are identical. Thus, in the sentence,

"The oaks of the mountains fall,"

"*Fall*" is both the *Logical* and the *Grammatical* Predicate.

OBS. 3.—The *Modified* Predicate includes the *Grammatical Predicate* and its *Adjuncts.* Thus, in the sentence,

"Low winds are in the pines,"

"*Are in the pines*" is the *Modified* Predicate of "winds."
"*Are*" is the *Grammatical Predicate.*

REM.—The *Object* of a Sentence, being distinct from the Grammatical Predicate, is properly regarded as a distinct Element in the structure of such Sentences as contain Objects. Hence,

DEF. 38.—The *Object* of a Sentence is the Word or Words on which the act, expressed by the Predicate, terminates.

OBS.—The Object of a Sentence is a *Noun*, or a *Word*, a *Phrase*, or a *Sentence* used for a Noun.

EXAMPLES.

1. A *Noun*.—John saws *wood*—Birds build *nests*.
   "Shall joy light the face of the Indian?"
   "The king of shadows loves a shining mark."
2. A *Pronoun*.—I have seen *him*—*Whom* seekest thou?
   "Oft the shepherd called thee to his flock."
   "We buried him darkly, at dead of night."
3. A *Phrase*.—"I regret *his being absent*."
   "His being a minister, prevented *his rising to civil power*."
4. A *Sentence*.—"The fool hath said in his heart, *There is no God*."
   "And God said, *Let there be light*."
   "God never meant *that man should scale the heavens*
   By strides of human wisdom."

ADJUNCT ELEMENTS.

REM.—If I say, *Students deserve approbation*, I make an "unqualified assertion," applicable to all "students," and to the "approbation" of all persons. But, if I say *Diligent* Students deserve *the* approbation *of their Teacher*, I speak of only a particular class of Students,—and of approbation as limited to a particular source; for the Word "*Student*," is limited by the word "*diligent*;" and the Word "*approbation*," is limited by the Word "*the*," and by the Phrase "*of their Teacher*." These limiting Words and Phrases are necessary, not *to make the Sentence*, but *to perfect the sense*; they are *joined to* other words, and are therefore called *adjuncts*.

PRIN.—*An Adjunct Element* may be

A *Word*, | A *Phrase*, | A *Sentence*.

EXAMPLES.

(*a*) A *Word*.—1. We were walking *homeward*.
2. We shall arrive *soon*.
3. "*Brilliantly*
The glassy waters mirror *back His* smiles."

4. "*Darkly* waves *each giant* bough."
5. "*A purple* robe *his dying* frame shall fold."

(*b*) A *Phrase.*—1. We were walking *towards home.*
2. We shall arrive *in a short time.*
3. Sons *of sorrow* echoed notes *of sadness.*
4. I came *to bury Cæsar.*
5. "*Scaling yonder peak,*
I saw an eagle *wheeling near its brow.*"

(*c*) *A Sentence.*—1. Students, *who study,* will improve.
2. Students will improve, *if they study.*
3. They kneeled *before they fought.*
4. "The sweet remembrance of the just,
Shall flourish *when he sleeps in dust.*"

ANALYSIS.

"*How* | *dear* | *to my heart* | are | *the* | scenes | *of my childhood,* |
| When | *fond* | recollection | presents | them | *to view.*"

"*How,*"	limits	"dear,"	Hence, an Adjunct Word.
"*To my heart,*"	"	"are dear,"	Hence, an Adjunct Phrase.
"*My,*"	"	"heart,"	Hence, an Adjunct Word.
"*The,*"	"	"scenes,"	Hence, an Adjunct Word.
"*Of my childhood,*"	"	"scenes,"	Hence, an Adjunct Phrase.
"*My,*"	"	"childhood,"	Hence, an Adjunct Word.
"*When fond recollection presents them to view,*"	"	"*are dear,*"	Hence, an Adjunct Sentence.
"*Fond,*"	"	"recollection,"	Hence, an Adjunct Word.
"*To view,*"	"	"presents,"	Hence, an Adjunct Phrase.

REM.—Adjuncts are used to *limit or describe things,* or to modify *acts* or *qualities.* Hence,

PRIN.—*Adjuncts* are distinguished as

ADJECTIVES OF ADVERBS.

OBS. 1.—*Adjective Adjuncts,* whether Words, Phrases, or Sentences, are such as answer to the questions, *What? What kind? Whose? How many?* &c. They are attached, in construction, to *Nouns* and *Pronouns.*

OBS. 2.—*Adverbial Adjuncts*—Words, Phrases, or Sentences—are such as answer to the questions, *How? Why? Where? Whence? Whether?* &c. They are attached to *Verbs,* to *Adjectives,* and to *Adverbs.*

OBS. 3.—Words, Phrases, and Sentences, having no *Grammatical connection* with other Elements in a Sentence, often perform *Adjunct offices*, by *limiting* or modifying the application of other Elements. Such are properly called *Logical Adjuncts.*

EXAMPLES.

(*a*) *Words.*—1. Webster, the *Statesman*, is remotely related to Webster, the *Lexicographer.*

2. Clay—*Cassius M.*—had more honorable benevolence than political sagacity.

(*b*) *Phrases.*—1. "*Napoleon having fallen*, there is no more cause for alarm."

2. "Thus talking, *hand in hand*, alone they passed on to their blissful bower."

(*c*) *Sentences.*—"I solemnly declare—*and I do not speak unadvisedly*—that the measures adopted by the passage of those resolutions will hasten the dissolution of the Union."

REM.—The words "*Statesman*" and "*Lexicographer*" are used to distinguish the two "Websters;" "*Cassius M.*," to determine which "Clay" is spoken of:—the Phrase "*Napoleon having fallen*," to tell why there is no more cause for alarm; and "*I do not speak unadvisedly*," is a Sentence thrown in to add force to the Principal Sentence. Hence we have *Grammatical Adjuncts* and *Logical Adjuncts.*

EXERCISES IN ANALYSIS.

SENTENCES WITHOUT ADJUNCTS.

Birds fly.

1.

(*a*)

Quest. *Of what* is something here said?

Ans. Something is said of "*Birds.*"

What is said of "Birds"?

A. They *fly.*

These two Words thus placed, form what?

A. A *Sentence*, for they constitute "an assemblage of words, so arranged as to assert an entire proposition."

(*b*)

Birds fly.

Quest. In this Sentence, *for what* is the Word "Birds" used?

Ans. To tell *what* "fly."

For what is the Word "fly" used?

A. To tell *what* "Birds" *do.*

(*c*)

Birds fly.

"Every Sentence must have a *Subject* and a *Predicate.*"

Quest. In this Sentence, what is the *Subject?*

Ans. "*Birds*"—for it "is that of which something is asserted."

What is the *Predicate?*

A. "*Fly*"—for "it is the word that expresses what is asserted of the Subject."

☞ Thus, analyze the following additional

EXAMPLES.

1. Fishes swim.
2. Horses gallop.
3. Lightnings flash.
4. Thunders roll.
5. Girls sing.
6. Boys play.
7. Waters are running.
8. Mary is reading.
9. Winter has come.
10. Resources are developed.
11. Wheat has been sown.
12. Mountains have been elevated.
13. Lessons should have been studied.
14. Recitations could have been omitted.
15. He might have been respected.

REM.—In the last example, the four words "might have been respected," constitute the Predicate of "he."

REM. 2.—The Pupil will notice that, when the Predicate consists of more than one word, the *last word* makes the *Principal Assertion;* the other words perform subordinate offices. Thus, in Example 13, "Should" denotes *obligation;* "Should have" denote *obligation* and *time;* "Should have been" denote *obligation, time,* and *voice.* These are subordinate to the principal assertion expressed by the word "Studied."

John is sleepy.

2.

A *Sentence*—because it is "an assemblage of Words, so arranged as to assert an entire proposition."

ANALYSIS.

"*John*" is the Subject—for it is the name of the person "concerning whom something is asserted."

"*Is sleepy*," is the Predicate—for these two words "express what is affirmed of the Subject."

REM.—In a limited sense, a Verb may be said to qualify or describe its subject.

EXAMPLES.—*John sleeps.*

Here, "*sleeps*" describes a condition of "John."

John is sleeping.

Here, "*is sleeping*" asserts a condition of "John."

John is sleepy.

In this Sentence, "*is sleepy*" asserts a condition as definitely as do the Words, "*is sleeping*"; and the genius of the language requires the Word "sleeping" to be added to the Verb "is," in order to express the fact intended; so the other fact concerning "John" requires the Word "sleepy" to be added to the Verb "is." The Sentence is not, *sleeping John is*—*i. e.*, exists; nor is the other, *sleepy John is*—*i. e.*, exists; but "*John is sleeping*," and "*John is sleepy*." "Sleeping" is a Participle, in predication with "*is*." "Sleepy" is an Adjective, in predication with "*is*."

☞ Let the Pupil, in like manner, construe and place in Diagrams the following additional

EXAMPLES.

1. William is diligent.
2. James was weary.
3. Flowers are beautiful.
4. Mountains are elevated.
5. Velvet feels smooth.
6. Robert has become poor.
7. I felt languid.
8. Soldiers waxed valiant.
9. "His palsied hand wax'd strong."—*Wilson.*
10. "All earth-born cares are wrong."—*Anon.*

God is love.

3.

A *Sentence*, ... See Definition.

ANALYSIS

"God,"—the *Subject*, ... See Definition.

"Is love,"—the *Predicate*, . . . See Definition.

NOTE.—"*God*," is the name of a Being—"*Love*," is the name of an *attribute* of that Being. "*Is love*," asserts a fact concerning God; and that fact can not well be expressed without these two Words thus combined.

ADDITIONAL EXAMPLES.

1. We are slaves.
2. Men are animals.
3. Thou art Peter.
4. John is [a] friend.
5. Ye are benefactors.
6. I am [a] student.
7. William and John are brothers.
8. We are friends and neighbors.

Virtue secures happiness.

4.

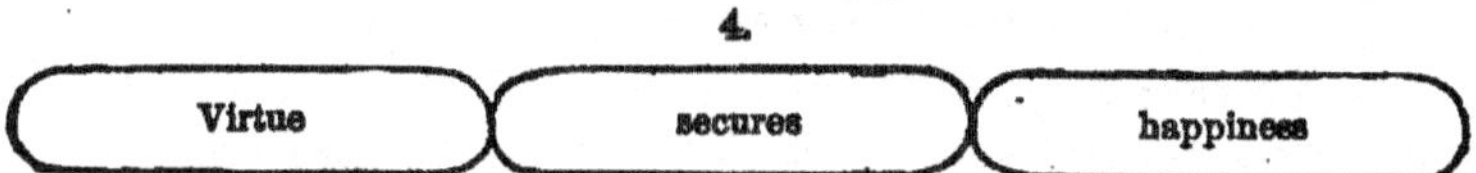

A *Sentence*, ... See Definition.

ANALYSIS.

"Virtue,"—the *Subject*, ... See Definition.

"Secures,"—the *Predicate*, . . . See Definition.

"Happiness,"—the *Object*, ... See Definition.

ADDITIONAL EXAMPLES.

1. Birds build nests.
2. Clouds furnish rain.
3. Science promotes happiness.
4. Sin produces misery.
5. Conscience demands obedience.
6. Napoleon obtained renown.
7. Washington secured admiration.
8. Howard alleviated suffering.
9. Columbus discovered America.
10. Fulton invented steamboats.
11. David enlarged Jerusalem.
12. Cæsar conquered Gaul.
13. John preached repentance.
14. Master taught school.
15. Students need instruction.
16. Railroads facilitate travel.

SENTENCES WITH ADJUNCTS.

"Our national resources are developed by an earnest culture of the arts of peace."

4.

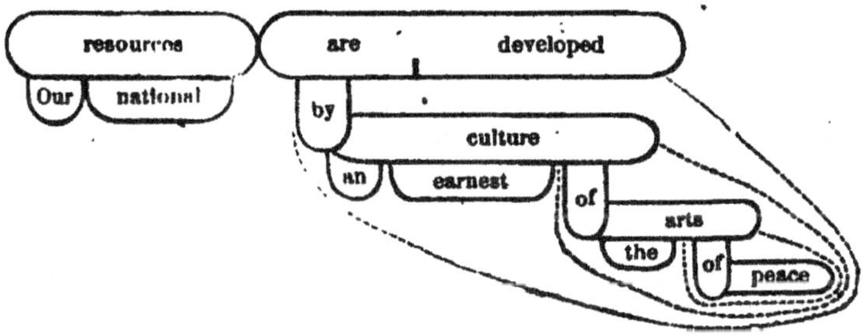

(a)

Quest. Concerning what is an assertion here made?

Ans. Concerning "*resources.*"

What is asserted of "resources"?

A. Resources "*are developed.*"

What resources are developed?

A. "*National*" resources.

What national resources?

A. "*Our*" national resources.

How are our national resources developed?

A. "*By an earnest culture of the arts of peace.*"

By *what* culture?

A. By "*earnest*" culture.

What earnest culture?

A. "*An*" earnest culture.

What *special* culture?

A. Culture "*of the arts of peace.*"

Of *what* arts?

A. "*The*" arts "*of peace.*"

(*b*)

Quest. **In the above sentence, what is the use of 'our"?**

Ans. To define some particular *national resources.*

What is the use of "national"?

A. To tell *what* resources?

What is the use of "resources"?

A. To tell what *are developed.*

What s the use of "are developed"?

A. To tell what is said of *resources.*

What is the use of "by an earnest culture of the arts of peace"?

A. To tell how resources *are developed.*

What is the use of "an"?

A. To tell what earnest *culture.*

What is the use of "earnest"?

A. To tell what *culture.*

What is the use of "of the arts of peace"?

A. To tell what species of *culture.*

What is the use of "the"?

A. To tell what *arts.*

What is the use of "of peace"?

A. To tell what species of *arts.*

(*c*)

Ques. **What are the principal elements of this Sentence?**

Ans. "*Resources are developed.*" They "express the unqualified assertion."

What* is the *Subject?

A. "*Resources.*" It is the name of "that of which something is asserted."

What is the *Predicate?*

A. "*Are developed.*" Those words "express what is affirmed of the Subject."

What are the Adjunct Elements of the Sentence?

A. "Our" and "National" are Word Adjuncts of "Resources;" and "by an earnest culture of the arts of peace" is a Phrase Adjunct of "are developed."

QUESTIONS FOR REVIEW.

AGE

15.—What is *Language?*..............................See Def. 1.
What language is *Natural?*—What, Artificial?........See Obs. 1.
Artificial language is how distinguished?.............See Prin.
What is *Spoken Language?*..........................See Def. 2.
What is *Written Language?*.........................See Def. 3.
What is Grammar?...................................See Def. 4.
16.—What is *English* Grammar? ....See Def. 5.
What is a *Letter?*—a *Word?*—a *Phrase?*........See Def. 6, 7, 8.
What is a *Sentence?* ....See Def. 9.
17.—By their uses, how are words *classified?*.............See Prin.
What is a *Noun?*—a *Pronoun?*—an *Adjective?*..See Def. 10, 11, 12.
18.—What is a *Verb?*—an *Adverb?*—a *Preposition?* ..See Def. 13, 14, 15.
What is a *Conjunction?*—an *Exclamation?*—a *Word of Euphony?*...................... See Def. 16, 17, 18.
19.—By their *offices*, how are Phrases *classified?* ....See Prin.
What is a *Substantive Phrase?*—an *Adjective Phrase?*.See Def. 19, 20.
20.—What is an *Adverbial Phrase?*—an *Independent Phrase?*..Def. 21, 22.
By their forms, how are Phrases *classified?*...........See Prin.
What is a *Prepositional Phrase?*—an *Infinitive Phrase?*..Def. 23, 24.
21.—What is a *Participial Phrase?*—an *Independent Phrase?*.Def. 25, 26.
What are the distinct *Elements* of Phrases? ....See Prin.
What are *Principal* " " ....See Def. 27.
What are *Adjunct* " " ....See Def. 28.
The Principal Elements *consist* of what?..............See Prin.
22.—What is the *Leader* of a Phrase?—it may *consist* of what?..Def. 29.
What is the *Subsequent* of a Phrase?—it may consist of what?.Def. 31.
23.—What are the *Elements of a Sentence?*—How distinguished?.Def. 32.
24.—What are *Principal Elements?*—What, *Adjunct* Elements? .... See Def. 33, 34.
What are called *Attendant* Elements?................See Def. 35.
25.—The Principal Elements of a Sentence *consist* of what?..See Prin.
What is the *Subject* of a Sentence?—it may *consist* of what?.Def. 36
What is the *Predicate?*—it may *consist* of what?......See Def. 37

DIAGRAMS.

Rem.—The *office* of an Element in a Sentence, determines its *position* in the Diagram, according to the following

GENERAL RULES.

(A)

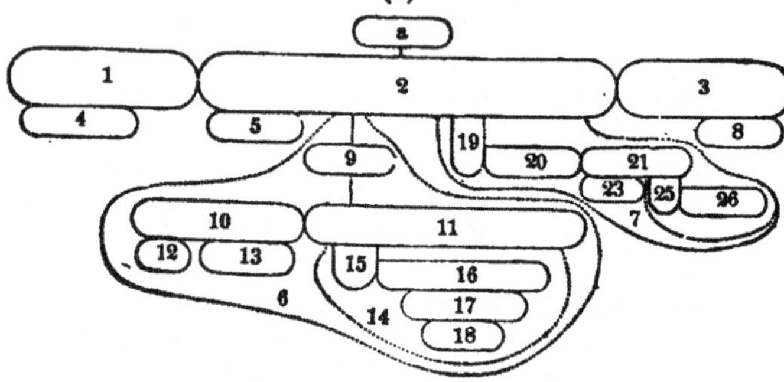

(B.)

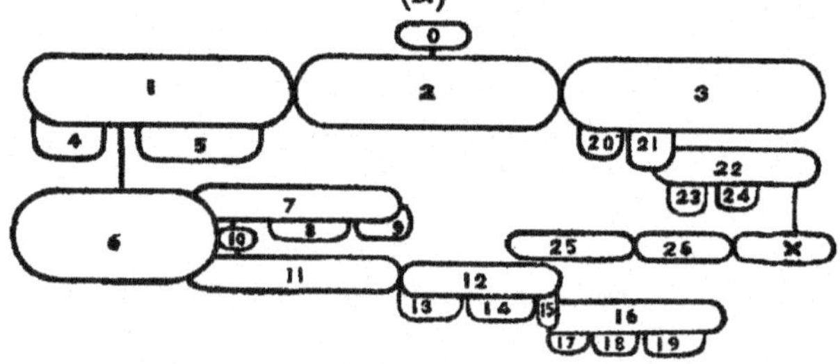

RULE 1.—The *Principal Elements* of a Sentence are placed uppermost, and on the same horizontal line;—as (1), (2), (3), Diagrams (A) and (B).

RULE 2.—The *Subject* of a Sentence takes the first place;—as, (1) and (10), Diagrams (A), and (1), (6), and (25) B.

RULE 3.—The *Predicate* of a Sentence is placed to the right of the Subject—attached;—as, (2), and (11), A, and (2), (7), (11), and (26), B.

Rule 4.—The *Object* of a Sentence is placed to the right of the Predicate—attached;—as, (3), A, and (3), (12), and (×) B.

Rule 5.—An *Adjunct* of a Sentence is placed beneath the Word which it limits or modifies—attached; as, (4), (5), (6), (7), (12), (13), (14), (17), (18), (23), A, and (4), (5), (8), (9), (17), (18), (19), (20), (23), (24), B.

Rule 6.—If the Adjunct is a *Phrase*, its Leader is attached to the Word which it limits;—as, (15), (19), (25), A, and (15), (21), B.

Rule 7.—If the Adjunct is a *Sentence*, it is attached by a line to the Word which the Adjunct Sentence limits; as, the Adjunct Sentence within the dotted line (6), is attached by the line from (2), to (9), A, and (6 to 19 inclusive) is attached to (1), B.

Rule 8.—A *Logical Adjunct* is placed beneath the Word which it describes, but not attached. [See page 39.]

Rule 9.—The *Subsequent* of a Phrase is placed to the right of its Leader—attached;—as, (20 and 21), to the right of (19),—(26), to the right of (25),—(16) of (15) A, and (22) of (21),—(16), of (15) B.

Rule 10.—A *Conjunction* used to introduce a Sentence, is placed above the Predicate of the Sentence which it introduces;—as, (*a*), used to introduce the Sentence (1, 2, 3), A, and (9), introducing the Adjunct Sentence (10, 11), (A), and (*a*) introducing the Sentence (1, 2, 3), B.

Rule 11.—A Conjunction used to *connect* Words, Phrases, or Sentences, similar in construction, is placed between the Elements connected;—as, (10), connecting (11) to (7), B. [See also Diagram, page 41.]

Rule 12.—A *Relative Pronoun* or a *Possessive Adjective* used to introduce an Adjunct Sentence, is attached to the "antecedent" by a line;—as (6) attached to (1) and (×) attached to (22) B.

CLASSIFICATION OF SENTENCES.

Remarks.—Some Sentences assert the *being, condition,* or *state* of a person or of a thing—or an act which does not pass over to an Object.

Others assert acts which terminate on an Object.

Some Sentences assert but one fact—others assert more than one.

Some assert an Independent or a Principal Proposition—others a secondary or qualifying proposition. Hence,

Prin.—Sentences are distinguished as

Intransitive or *Transitive,*
Simple or *Compound,*
Principal or *Auxiliary.*

Def. 43.—An *Intransitive Sentence* is a Sentence that asserts *condition, being,* or *state*—or an *act* which does not terminate on an Object.

EXAMPLES.

1. William sleeps.
2. Errors abound.
3. Mary is cheerful.
4. God is love.
5. Mountains are elevated.
6. Fishes swim.
7. "On some fond breast the parting soul relies."
8. "Now fades the glimmering landscape on the sight."
9. "Satyrs and sylvan boys were seen,
Peeping from forth their valleys green."

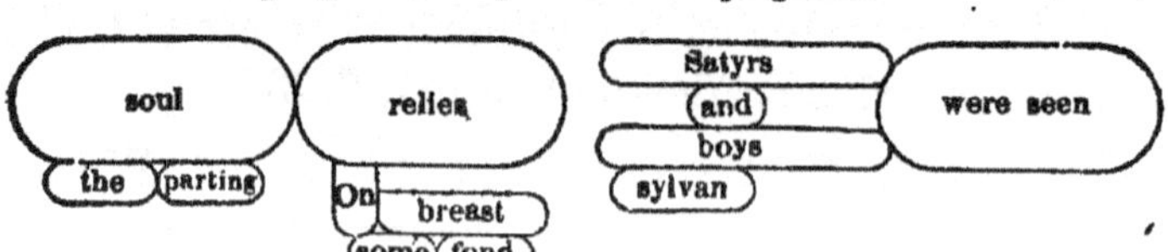

Obs.—An Intransitive Sentence contains one or more Subjects and Predicates,—but no Object.

DEF. 44.—A *Transitive Sentence* is a Sentence that asserts an *act* which terminates on an Object.

EXAMPLES.—1. Virtue secures happiness.
2. Industry promotes health and wealth.
3. "I thank thee, Roderick, for the word."
4. "The King of Shadows loves a shining mark."
5. "And the eye and the heart hailed its beautiful forms."

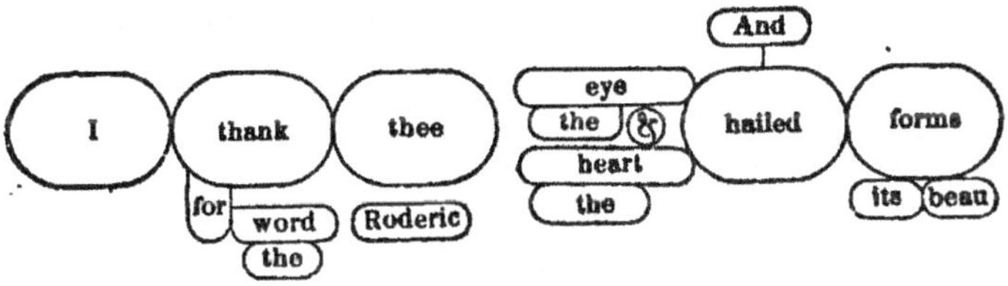

OBS.—A Transitive Sentence has at least one *Subject*, one *Predicate*, and one *Object*.

DEF. 45.—A *Simple Sentence* is a Sentence that asserts but one proposition.

EXAMPLES.—1. William sleeps.
2. Mary is cheerful.
3. Virtue secures happiness.
4. "Now fades the glimmering landscape on the sight."
5. "The King of Shadows loves a shining mark."

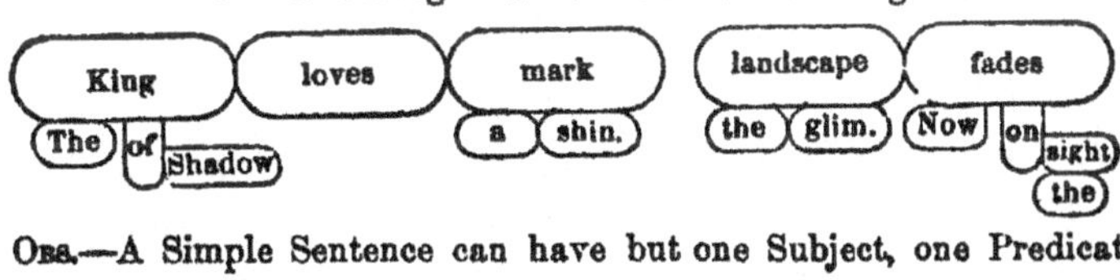

OBS.—A Simple Sentence can have but one Subject, one Predicate, and—when Transitive—one Object.

DEF. 46.—A *Compound Sentence* is a Sentence that asserts more than one proposition.

EXAMPLES.—1. *Anna* and *Mary* study Latin.
2. Temperance *elevates* and *ennobles* man.
3. Robert studies *Grammar* and *Arithmetic*.
4. "Slowly and sadly they climb the distant mountain,
And read their doom in the setting sun."

DEF. 46 (*b*).—In a Compound Sentence, the Principal Elements which are compounded, are called *Clauses.*

OBS.—The Compound clauses may be,

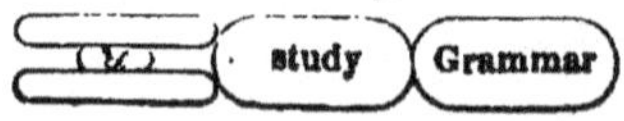

1. The *Subjects only*— *Warner* and *Arthur* study Grammar.

2. The *Predicates only*—Warner *studies* and *recites* Grammar.

3. The *Objects only* — Warner studies *Grammar* and *Arithmetic.*

4. The *Subjects* and the *Predicates*— *Warner* and *Arthur study* and *recite* Grammar.

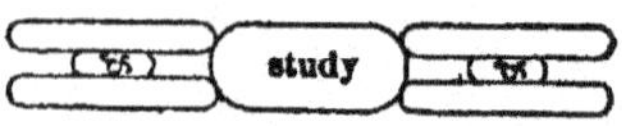

5. The *Subjects* and the *Objects*— *Warner* and *Arthur* study *Grammar* and *Arithmetic.*

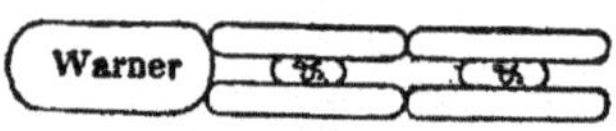

6. The *Predicates* and the *Objects*—Warner *studies* and *recites Grammar* and *Arithmetic.*

7. The *Subjects,* the *Predicates,* and the *Objects*— *Warner* and *Arthur study* and *recite Grammar* and *Arithmetic.*

OBS.—A Compound Sentence may have more than two clauses.

EXAMPLES.

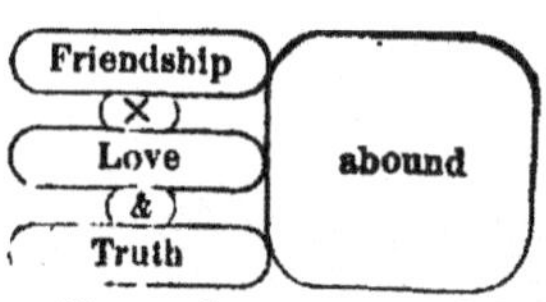

Friendship, Love, and *Truth* abound.

"Oxygen, Carbon, Hydrogen, and Nitrogen constitute the chief elements of organized matter."

REM.—Sentences which have Compound Predicates, often have Objects applicable to only a part of them. Hence,

DEF. 46 (*c*).—A *Compound Sentence,* having one or more Transitive, and one or more Intransitive Predicates, is called a *Mixed Sentence.*

EXAMPLES.

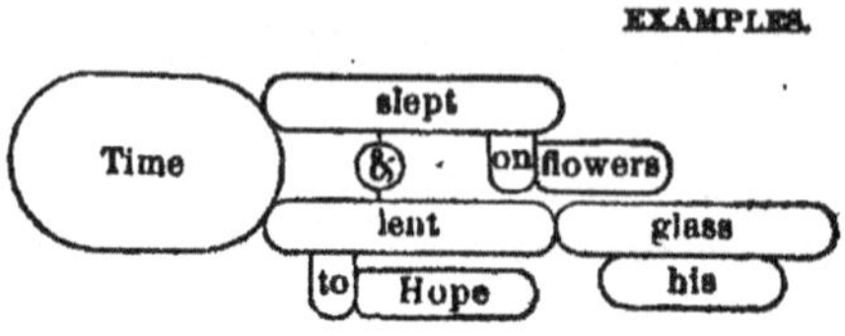

1. "*Time slept* on flowers, and *lent* his glass to Hope."

REM.—"Slept" is Intransitive; "lent" is transitive.

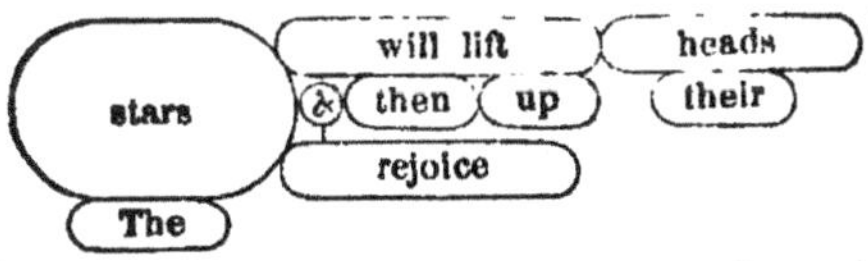

2. The *stars will* then *lift* up their *heads* and *rejoice.*

3. "I *will* never *pant* for public honors,
Nor *disturb* my *quiet* with the affairs of state."

4. "Who *can observe* the careful *ant,*
And not *provide* for future want."

Def. 47.—A *Principal Sentence* asserts an independent or a principal proposition.

EXAMPLES.

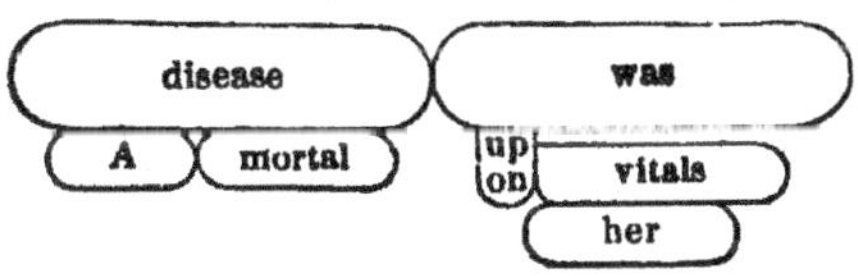

1. A mortal disease was upon her vitals.

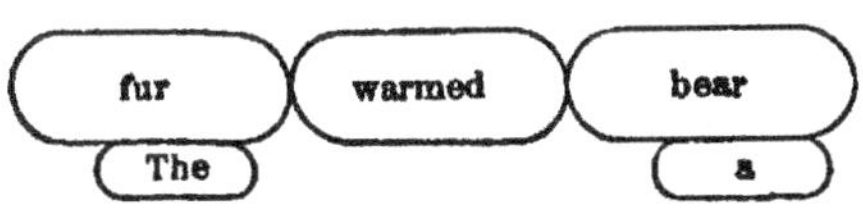

2. "The fur warmed a bear."

3. "He hath brought many captives to Rome."

Def. 48.—An *Auxiliary Sentence* is a Sentence that is used as an *Element* in the structure of another Sentence or of a Phrase.

EXAMPLES.

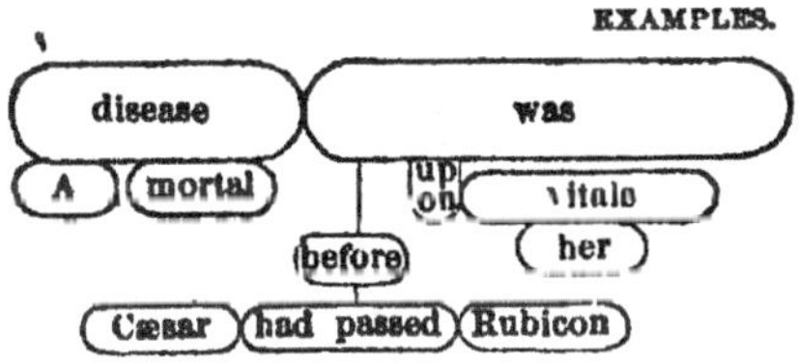

1. "A mortal disease was upon her vitals *before Cæsar had passed the Rubicon.*"

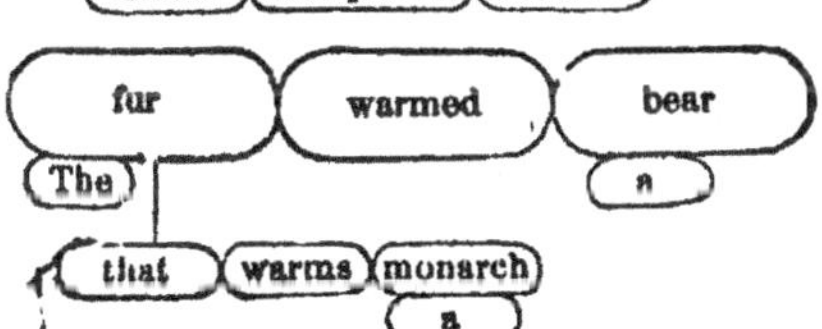

2. "The fur *that warms a monarch,* warmed a bear."

Remark.—"That warms a monarch" is an Adjunct of "fur."

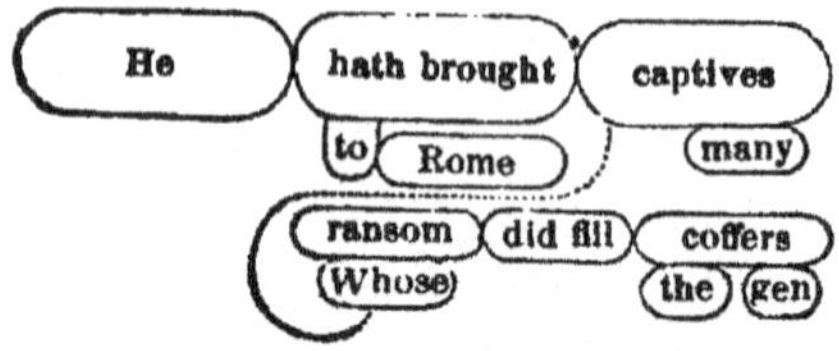

3. "He hath brought many captives to Rome,
Whose ransom did the general coffers fill."

4. "Sweet was the sound, *when* oft, at evening's close,
Up yonder hill the village *murmur rose.*"
5 "The bounding steed *you* pompously *bestride*,
Shares with his lord the pleasure and the pride."
6. "Thou hadst a voice whose *sound was* like the sea."

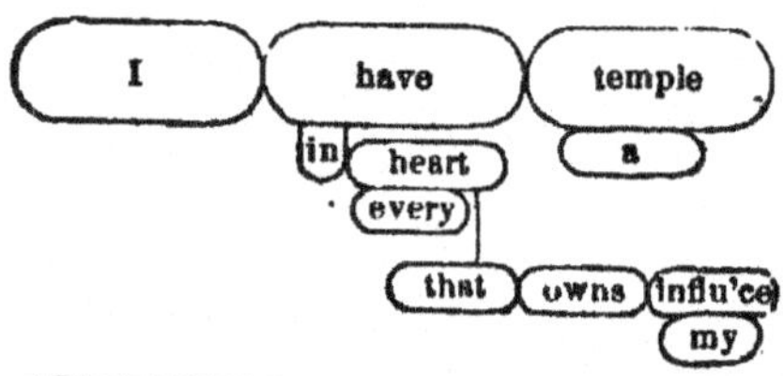

7. "I have a temple in every heart *that owns my influence.*"

REMARK.—"That owns my influence" describes "heart."

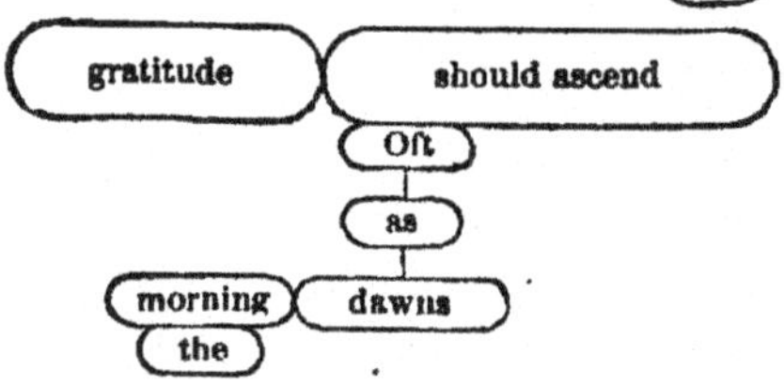

8. "Oft as the *morning dawns* should gratitude ascend."

REMARK.—"Oft" modifies "should ascend." "As the morning dawns" limits "oft."

9. "To him *that wishes for me*, I am always present."
10. "These lofty trees wave not less proudly,
That their ancestors moulder beneath them."

OBS.—A Principal Sentence and its Auxiliary Sentences constitute a *Complex Sentence.* [See EXAMPLES (1), (2), above.]

REM.—An Auxiliary Sentence is an Adjunct of a Word, a Phrase, or a Sentence going before in construction; or it is used as a substitute for a Noun. Hence,

PRIN.—*Auxiliary Sentences* are distinguished as

Substantive,
Adjective, and
Adverbial.

Def. 49.—A *Substantive Sentence* is used as the *Subject* or the *Object* of a Sentence; or as the *Object* of a Phrase.

EXAMPLES.

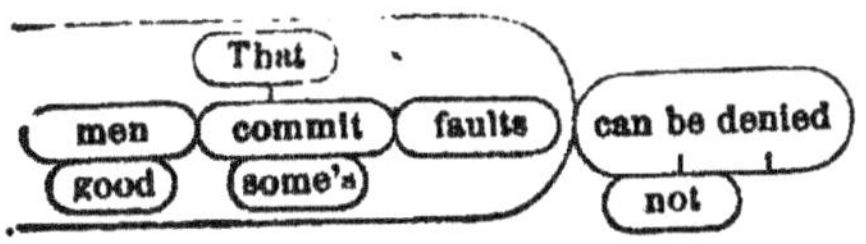

1. "*That good men sometimes commit faults*, cannot be denied."

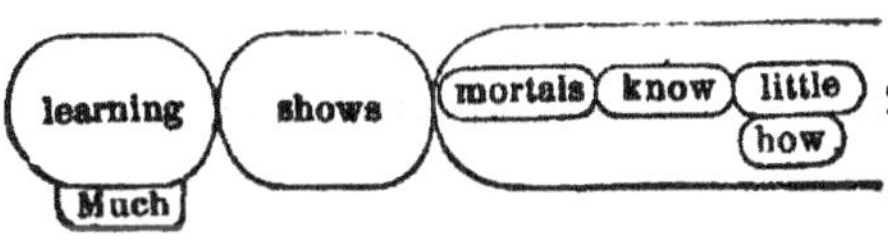

2. Much learning shows *how little mortals know.*

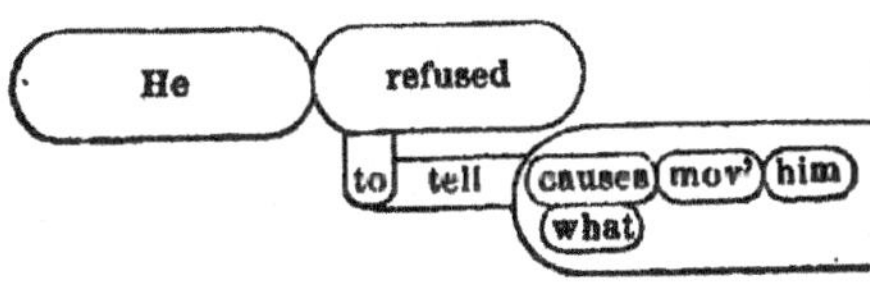

3. He refused to tell *what causes moved him.*

4. "*That all men are created equal*, is a self-evident truth"
5. "Yet Brutus says *he was ambitious.*"

Def. 50.—An *Adjective Sentence* is a Sentence that is used as an Adjunct of a Substantive.

EXAMPLES.

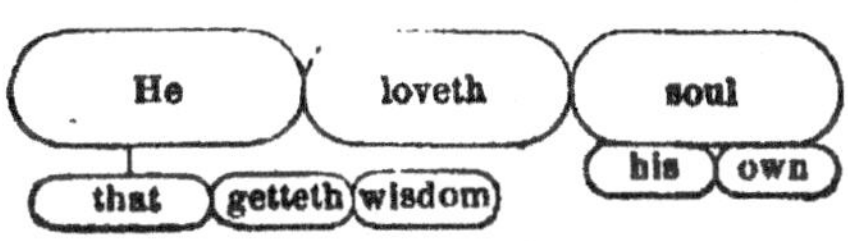

1. "He *that getteth wisdom* loveth his own soul."

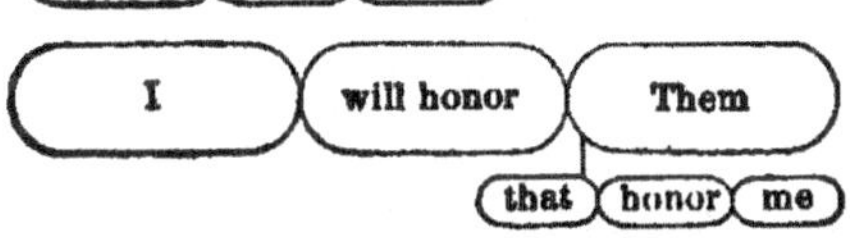

2. Them *that honor me*, I will honor.

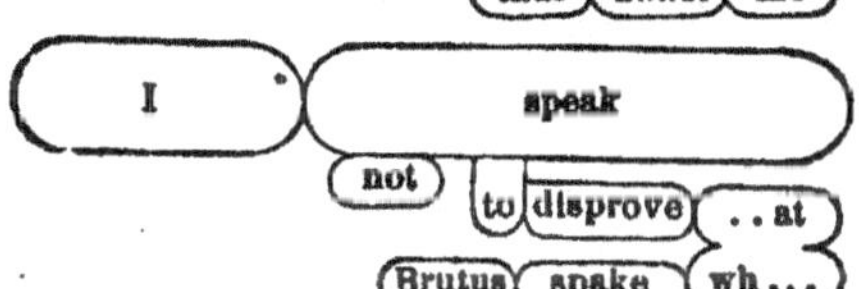

3. I speak not to disprove *what* [that which] *Brutus spake.*

4. "That life is long *which answers life's great end.*"
5. "The man of wealth and pride,
   Takes up a space *that many poor supplied.*"
6. "Here I come to tell *what I do know.*"

DEF. 51.—An *Adverbial Sentence* is a Sentence that is used as an Adjunct of a *Verb*, a *Participle*, an *Adjective*, or another *Adverb*.

EXAMPLES.

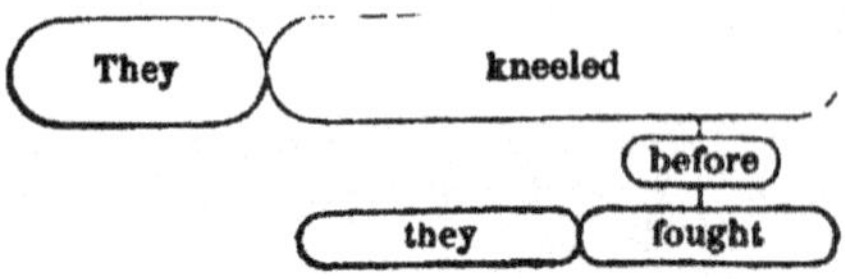

1. "They kneeled before they fought."

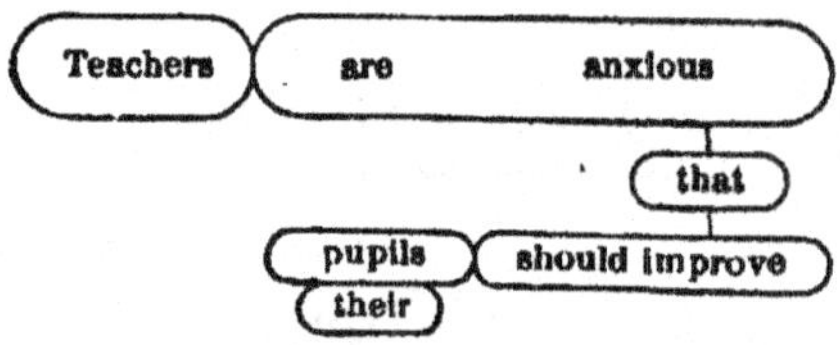

2. "Teachers are anxious *that their pupils should improve.*"

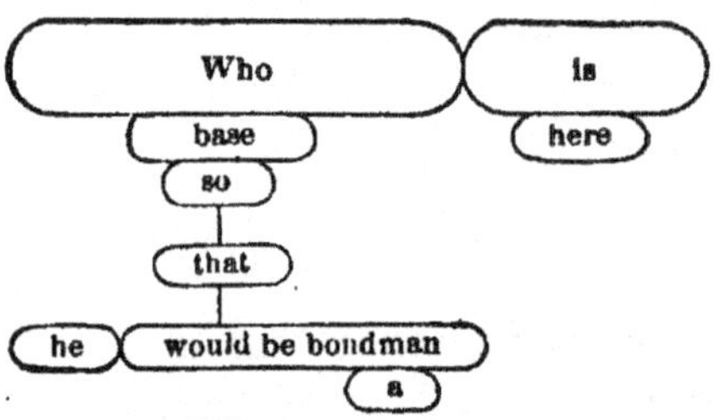

3. "Who is here so base *that he would be a bondman?*"

REMARK.—"Base" describes "who;" "so" modifies "base;" "that he would be a bondman" limits "so'

4. "*Where wealth and freedom reign*, contentment fails."
5. "How dear to my heart are the scenes of my childhood,
When fond recollection presents them to view."
6. "These lofty trees wave not less proudly
That their ancestors moulder beneath them."

OBS.—A Sentence is sometimes a *Logical Adjunct* of some Word in a Principal Sentence.

EXAMPLES.

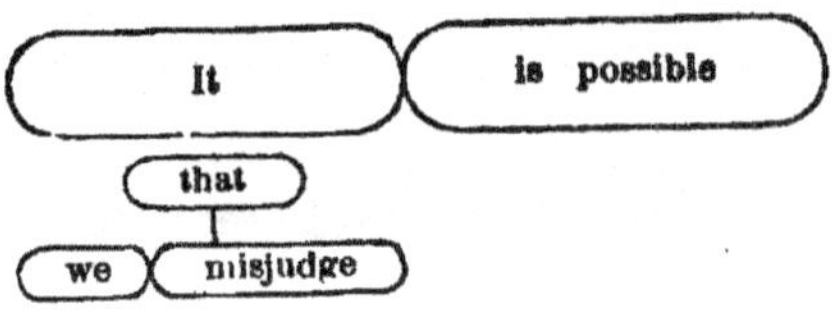

1. It is possible *that we misjudge.*

NOTE.—"That we misjudge" is a Sentence, used to limit the application of the Word "it." Hence, the *Sentence* is an Adjunct of the Word It is called a *Logical Adjunct* because there is no *Grammatical* connection between the two Sentences

RECAPITULATION OF DIAGRAMS.

1. FOR SENTENCES.

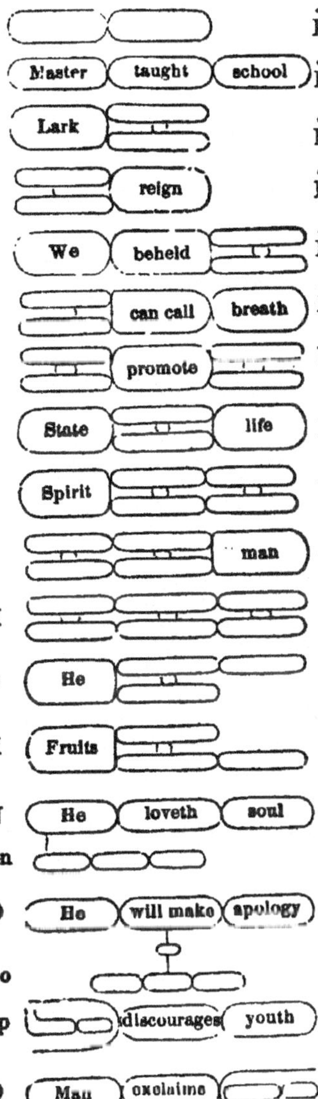

A ....a Simple Sentence—Intransitive. EXAMPLE.—"*Landscape fades.*"

B .....a Simple Sentence—Transitive. Ex.—"*Master taught school.*"

C .a Compound Sentence—Intransitive. Ex.—"*Lark ascends and sings.*"

D .a Compound Sentence—Intransitive Ex. "*Wealth and freedom reign.*" [G. 22.]

E ..a Compound Sentence—Transitive. Ex.—"*We beheld moon and stars.*"

F ..a Compound Sentence—Transitive. Ex.—"*Urn* or *bust can call breath.*"

G ..a Compound Sentence—Transitive. Ex.—"*Liberty and union promote peace and safety.*"

H ..a Compound Sentence—Transitive. Ex.—"*State conforms and models life.*"

I ..a Compound Sentence—Transitive. Ex.—"*Spirit unfurls light* and *wheels course.*"

J ..a Compound Sentence—Transitive. Ex.—"*Wisdom* and *virtue elevate* and *ennoble man.*"

K ..a Compound Sentence—Transitive. Ex.—"*Youth and beauty tread, ring and shout raptures.*" [G. 26.]

L .....a Compound Sentence—Mixed. Ex. "*He breathes fragrance* and *sleeps.*"

M .....a Compound Sentence—Mixed. Ex.—"*Fruits ripen and yield repasts.*"

COMPLEX SENTENCES.

N ....the Principal Sentence. Ex.—"*He loveth soul.*"

N-n .....Auxiliary Sentence—Adjective. Ex.—"*That getteth wisdom.*"

O ....the Principal Sentence. Ex.—"*He will make apology.*"

O-o .....Auxiliary Sentence—Adjective. Ex.—"*If John has injured you.*"

P-p ..a Sentence having a Phrase for its Subject. Ex.—"*Finding fault discourages youth.*"

Q ..a Sentence having a Sentence for its Object. Ex. "*Man exclaims, they come.*" [p. 14.]

2. PHRASES.

Leader—Subsequent.

R 

........a Prepositional Phrase—Simple.
EXAMPLE.—"*Of Java.*"

R 2 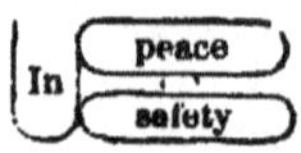

.... a Prepositional Phrase—Compound.
Ex.—"*In peace and safety*"

S 

..a Participial Phrase—Simple, Transitive.
Ex.—"*Gaining time.*" [See page 31.]

T 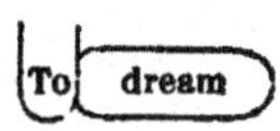

...... an Infinitive Phrase—Intransitive
Ex.—"*To dream.*"

T 2 

.. ...an Infinitive Phrase—Transitive.
Ex.—"*To give gifts.*"

U 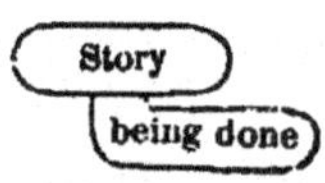

....an Independent Phrase—Intransitive.
Ex.—"*Story being done.*" [See page 26.]

U 2 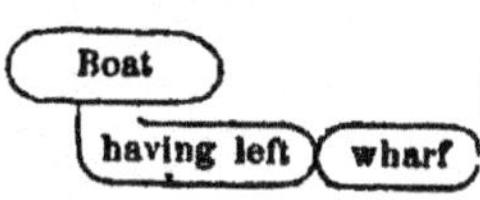

.....an Independent Phrase—Transitive.
Ex.—"*Boat having left wharf.*" [See p. 36.]

COMPLEX PHRASES.

V 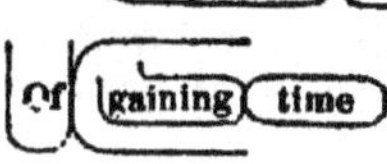

..a Participial Phrase the Object of a Preposition.
Ex.—*Of gaining time.* [See page 30.]

W 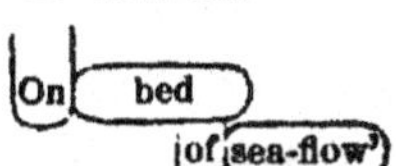

Principal Phrase Prepositional, or Infinitive.
Auxiliary Phrase Prepositional, or Infinitive.
Ex.—"*On bed of sea-flowers.*" [See p. 31.]

X 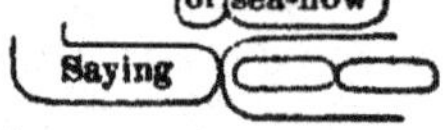

..a Participial Phrase, having a Sentence for its Subsequent.
Ex.—"*Saying, we will reply.*"

Y 

....Adjunct Word—Adjective or Adverb.

Z 

....Compound Adjunct.

REM.—1. With the exception of the last two, the above Diagrams are adapted to the *Principal Elements* of a Sentence or of a Phrase. In the exercises which follow, these Elements are variously modified by Adjunct Words, Phrases, and Sentences.

2. The whole Predicate—consisting of one, two, three, four, and sometimes five words, is placed in one Diagram—as exhibited on the following pages.

QUESTIONS FOR REVIEW.

PAGE

38.—*Why* are Sentences classified?....................See Remark.

How are Sentences classified?....................See Principle.

What is an *Intransitive Sentence?* ....See Def. 43.

May Intransitive Sentences be *either* Simple or Compound?..See Obs.

Make Intransitive Sentences, ...*Simple.*

Make " " ....*Compound.*

39.—What is a *Transitive Sentence?* ....See Def. 44.

Make Transitive Sentences, ...*Simple.*

Make " " ....*Compound.*

What is a *Simple Sentence?*......................See Def. 45.

Make Simple Sentences, ...*Intransitive.*

Make " ....*Transitive.*

What is a *Compound Sentence?* ....See Def. 46.

Make Compound Sentences,.........*Intransitive.*

Make " " ....*Transitive.*

40.—What are *Clauses* of a Sentence?..................See Def. 46 (*b*).

What Elements in a Sentence may be compounded?..See Obs. (1–7).

Make Sentences having compound *Subjects.*

Make " " " *Predicates.*

Make " " " *Objects.*

How numerous may be the *Clauses* of a Sentence?

What is a *Mixed Sentence?* ....See Def. 46 (*c*).

Make Mixed Sentences—1st Clause Transitive.

Make " " 2d Clause Transitive.

41.—What is a *Principal Sentence?*....................See Def. 47.

What is an *Auxiliary Sentence?* ....See Def. 48.

What is a *Complex Sentence?*......................See Obs.

Make Compound Sentences.

42.—What are the *offices* of Auxiliary Sentences?.........See Rem.

By their offices, how are Auxiliary Sentences *distinguished?*..See Prin.

43.—What is a *Substantive Sentence?* ....See Def. 49.

Make a Substantive Sentence that shall be *Subject* of a Principal Sentence.

Make a Substantive Sentence that shall be *Object* of a Principal Sentence.

What is an *Adjective Sentence?* ....See Def. 50.

Make Adjective Sentences.

44.—What is an *Adverbial Sentence?*....................See Def. 51.

Make Adverbial Sentences.

EXERCISES IN ANALYSIS.

REM.—1. In the following Exercises, will be found Sentences of every grade—from the most simple to the most complex. The Teacher will find exercise for his judgment and discretion in assigning the Sentences to his pupils (for analysis) according to their several capacities.

2. The Teacher will find it interesting and profitable to his Pupils, to assign to each, at least one Sentence, to be placed in its appropriate Diagram—drawn on the black-board *ex tempore*, or on paper by appointment at a previous recitation.

SIMPLE SENTENCES.—*Intransitive.*

1. "*Now fades the glimmering landscape on the sight.*"

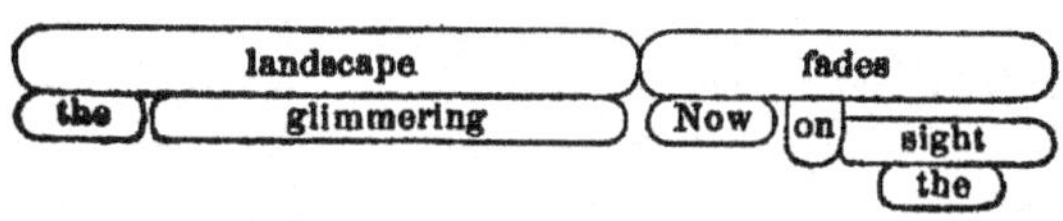

A *Simple Sentence*—Intransitive, ... See Def.

ANALYSIS.

PRINCIPAL ELEMENTS. { The *Subject*, . . "Landscape."
The *Predicate*, . "Fades."

ADJUNCT ELEMENTS. { *Of the Subject*, { "The," . . . . . a Word.
"Glimmering," a Word.
Of the Predicate, { "Now," . . . . . . a Word.
"On the sight," a Phrase.

CONSTRUCTION.

Elements.	*Office.*	*Class.*
Now,	tells *when* "landscape fades,"	Hence, an Adverb.
Fades,	tells *what* "landscape" *does*,	Hence, a Verb.
The,	tells *what* "landscape,"	Hence, an Adjective.
Glimmering,	tells *what* "landscape,"	Hence, an Adjective
Landscape,	tells *what* "fades,"	Hence, a Noun.
On the sight,	tells *where* "landscape *fades*,"	Hence, an Adverb

Other EXAMPLES *applicable to the same Diagram.*

2. The studious pupil seldom fails in his recitation.
3. The arrogant pedant was quickly banished from the company.
4. Such bright examples seldom fail, ultimately, to please.
5. That bright meteor flashed brilliantly athwart the heavens.
6. The young aspirant never succeeded in his effort.
7. Our brightest students are also foremost in their sports.

☞ Let each Pupil make a Sentence adapted to the same Diagram.

ADDITIONAL EXAMPLES.

Principal Elements similar—Adjuncts dissimilar.

8. "The big tear then startled from his eye."
9. "Morni's face brightened with gladness."
10. "His aged eyes look faintly through tears of joy."
11. "We came to the halls of Selma."
12. "We sat around the feasts of shells."
13. "Fingal rose in his place."
14. "The sword of Trenmor shook by his side."
15. "The gray-haired hero moved before."
16. "On the pathway of spirits
    She wanders alone."
17. "The song of the wood-dove has died on our shore."
18. "And on the stranger's dim and dying eye
    The soft, sweet pictures of his childhood lie."
19. "His hair falls round his blushing cheek, in the wreaths of waving light."
20. "A flood of glory bursts from all the skies."
21. "The long, bright days of summer quickly passed."
22. "The dry leaves whirled in Autumn's rising blast."
23. "The garden rose may richly bloom,
    In cultured soil and genial air,
    To cloud the light of Fashion's room,
    Or droop in Beauty's midnight hair."
24. "On Horeb's rock the prophet stood,—
25. The Lord before him passed;
26. A hurricane, in angry mood,
    Swept by him, strong and fast;
27. The forest fell before its force;
28. The rocks were shivered in its course;
29. God was not in the blast."

SIMPLE SENTENCES.—*Transitive.*

1. "*The king of shadows loves a shining mark.*"

A *Simple Sentence—Transitive,* . . . . See Def.

ANALYSIS.

PRINCIPAL ELEMENTS.
- The *Subject,* . . . . "King."
- The *Predicate,* . . "Loves."
- The *Object,* . . . . "Mark."

ADJUNCT ELEMENTS.
- *Of the Subject,*
  - "The," . . . . . a Word.
  - "Of shadows," a Phrase
- *Of the Predicate,*
- *Of the Object,*
  - "A," . . . . a Word.
  - "Shining," . . a Word

Elements.	*Office.*	*Class.*
The,	to tell *what* "king,"	an Adjective.
King,	to tell *who* "loves mark,"	a Noun.
Of shadows,	to tell *what* "king,"	an Adjective.
Loves,	to tell *what* the king does,	a Verb.
A,	to tell *what* "mark,"	an Adjective
Shining,	to tell *what* "mark,"	an Adjective
Mark,	to tell *what* the king "loves,"	a Noun.

Other EXAMPLES *applicable to the same Diagram.*

2. The science of Geology illustrates many astonishing facts.
3. A love for study secures our intellectual improvement.
4. The habit of intemperance produces much lasting misery.
5. A desire for improvement should possess all our hearts.
6. The use of tobacco degrades many good men.
7. A house on fire presents a melancholy spectacle.
8. A man of refinement will adopt no disgusting habits.

☞ Let each Pupil make a Sentence for the same Diagram.

ADDITIONAL EXAMPLES, *containing one Subject, one Predicate, and one Object with or without Adjuncts.*

9. "He mixes his words with his echoing shield."
10. "He seized my hand in silence."
11. "In his youth he may have displayed a different character."

1. "*Knowledge reaches or may reach every home.*"

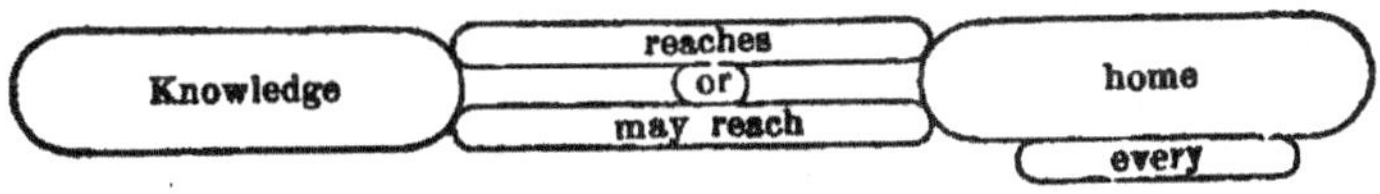

ANALYSIS.

PRINCIPAL ELEMENTS.	The *Subject*,	"Knowledge."
	The 1*st Predicate*,	"Reaches."
	The 2*d Predicate*,	"May reach."
	The *Object*,	"Home."
ADJUNCT ELEMENTS.	*Of the Subject*, ..	———
	Of the Predicate, .	———
	Of the Object, ...	"Every."

ADDITIONAL SENTENCES,

Having the PRINCIPAL ELEMENTS *similar in construction.*

2. "By thus acting, *we cherish* and *improve both.*"
3. "Whose patent arm perpetuates existence or destroys."
4. "For which we shunned and hated thee before."
5. "Hope, like a cordial, innocent though strong,
Man's heart at once inspirits and serenes."
6. "Hence every state, to one loved blessing prone,
Conforms and models life to that alone."
7. "When mighty Alfred's piercing soul,
Pervades and regulates the whole."
8. "Temperance fortifies and purifies the heart."
9. "Bright angels viewed with wondering eyes,
And hailed the incarnate God."
10. "Who does not receive and entertain a polite man with still greater cheerfulness?"
11. "And oft that blessed fancy cheers,
And bears my heart above."
12. "That voice of more than Roman eloquence, urged and sustained the Declaration of Independence."
13. "The pewter plate on the dresser, caught and reflected the flame."

Compound Sentences.—*Transitive.*

1. "*In the beginning, God created the heaven and the earth.*"

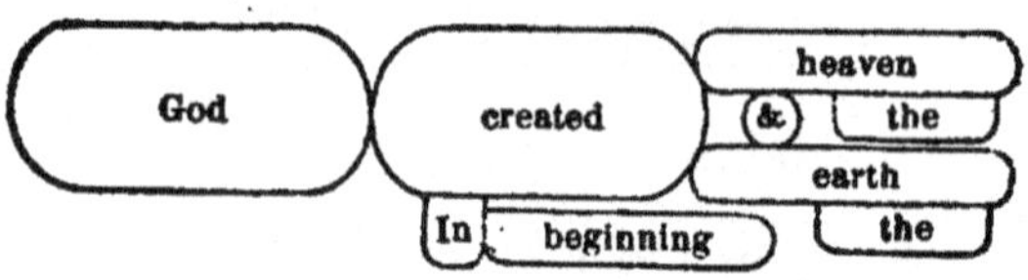

ANALYSIS.

Principal Elements.
- The *Subject*, ... "God."
- The *Predicate*, ... "Created."
- The *Objects*, ... "Heaven" and "Earth."

Adjunct Elements.
- *Of the Subject*, ... ———
- *Of the Predicate*, . . "In the beginning."
- *Of the 1st Object*, . . "The."
- *Of the 2d Object*, . . "The."

CONSTRUCTION.

Elements.	*Office.*	*Class.*
"In the beginning,"	tells *when* [God] "*created,*"	Hence, an Adverb.
"God,"	tells *who* "created heaven and earth,"	Hence, a Noun.
"Created,"	tells *what* "God" *did,*	Hence, a Verb.
The,	tells *what* "heaven,"	Hence, an Adjective.
Heaven,	tells *what* "God created,"	Hence, a Noun.
And,	joins "heaven and earth,"	Hence, a Conjunction.
The,	tells *what* "*earth,*"	Hence, an Adjective.
Earth,	tells *what* "God created,"	Hence, a Noun.

Additional Examples, *for the same Diagram.*

2. William loves his study and his play with equal attachment.
3. God, in the creation, has displayed his wisdom and his power.
4. Men gather the tares and the wheat with equal care.
5. We, at all times, seek our honor and our happiness.
6. Students require of the teacher much instruction and some patience.
7. He educated his daughter and his son at great expense.

1. " *Can storied urn or animated bust,*
Back to its mansion call the fleeting breath."

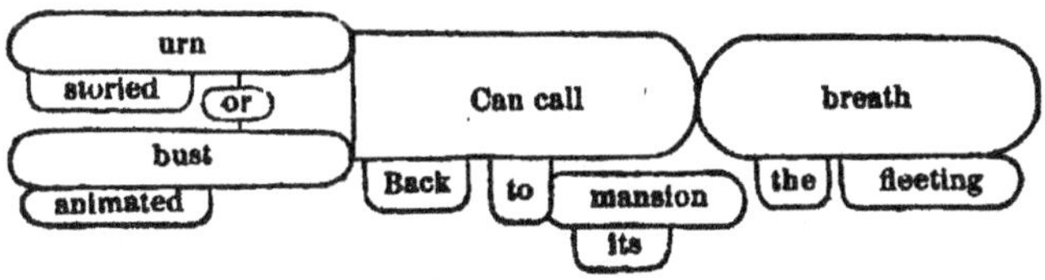

ANALYSIS.

PRINCIPAL ELEMENTS.
- 1st *Subject*, ... "Urn."
- 2d *Subject*, ... "Bust."
- The *Predicate*, . "Can call."
- The *Object*, . . . "Breath."

ADJUNCT ELEMENTS.
- *Of the* 1st *Subject*, . . "Storied."
- *Of the* 2d *Subject*, . . "Animated."
- *Of the Predicate*, . . "Back" "To its mansion."
- *Of the Object*, ... "The" "Fleeting."

ADDITIONAL SENTENCES,

In which the PRINCIPAL ELEMENTS *are similar.*

2. "Illuminated *reason* and regulated *liberty shall* once more *exhibit man* in the image of his Maker."
3. "The hunter's *trail* and the dark *encampments startled* the wild *beasts* from their lairs."
4. "Their *names*, their *years*, spelled by the unlettered muse,
The *place* of fame and elegy *supply*."
5. "Thy praise
The widows' sighs and orphans' tears embalm."
6. "Hill and valley echo back their songs."
7. "Then Strife and Faction rule the day."
8. "And Pride and Avarice throng the way."
9. "Loose Revelry and Riot bold,
In freighted streets their orgies hold."
10. "Here Art and Commerce, with auspicious reign,
Once breathed sweet influence on the happy plain."

1. "*The Lord uplifts his awful hand,*
And chains you to the shore."

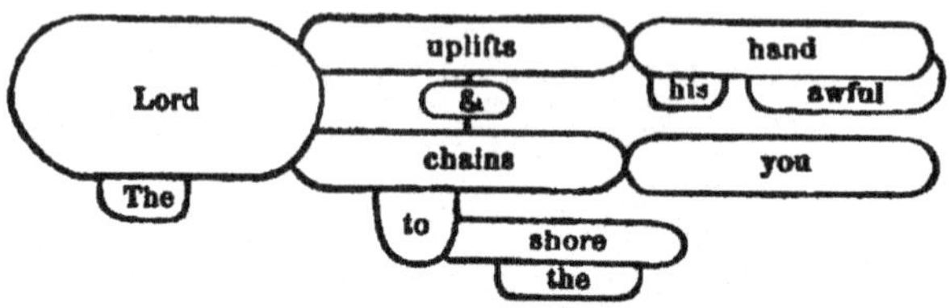

ANALYSIS.

PRINCIPAL ELEMENTS.	The *Subject*	"Lord."
	The 1*st Predicate*, ..	"Uplifts."
	The 2*d Predicate*, ..	"Chains."
	The 1*st Object*, ...	"Hand."
	The 2*d Object*, ...	"You."

ADJUNCT ELEMENTS.	Of the *Subject*, ...	"The."
	Of the 1*st Predicate*, ...	———
	Of the 2*d Predicate*, ...	"To the shore."
	Of the 1*st Object*, ...	"His" "Awful."
	Of the 2*d Object*, ...	———

ADDITIONAL EXAMPLES,

In which the PRINCIPAL ELEMENTS *are similar.*

2. "He heard the King's command,
And saw that writing's truth."
3. "For misery stole me at my birth,
And cast me, helpless, on the wild."
4. "That the page unfolds,
And spreads us to the gaze of God and men."
5. "Now twilight lets her curtain down,
And pins it with a star."
6. "They fulfilled the great law of labor in the letter, but broke it in the spirit."
7. "Then weave the chaplet of flowers, and strew the beauties of Nature about the grave."
8. "He marks, and in heaven's register enrolls
The rise and progress of each option there."

1. "*And the eyes of the sleeper waxed deadly and chill.*"

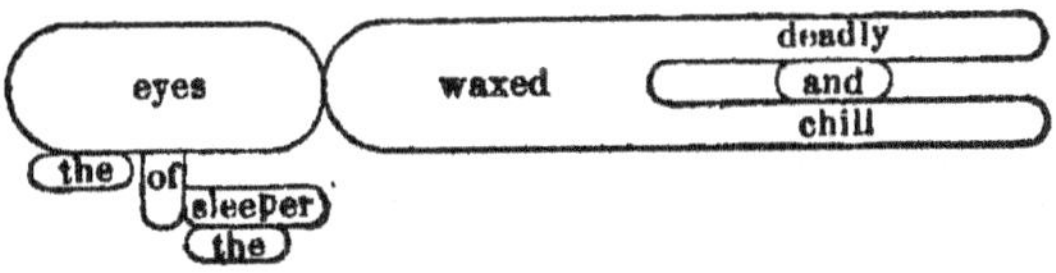

ANALYSIS.

PRINCIPAL ELEMENTS.	The *Subject*. . . .	"Eyes."	
	The *Predicate*, .	"Waxed deadly and chill."	
ADJUNCT ELEMENTS.	*Of the Subject*,	"The,"	a Word.
		"Of the sleeper,"	a Phrase.
	Of the Predicate,	———	

NOTE.—The words "deadly" and "chill" describe "eyes," and are therefore ADJECTIVES; but they describe by *making* (in connection with "waxed") *an assertion*. Hence they are ADJECTIVES IN PREDICATION—they constitute a part of the Predicate.

ADDITIONAL SENTENCES,

Having Adjectives or Participles in Predicate.

2. "Age is *dark* and *unlovely*."
3. "*Bloodless* are these limbs and cold."
4. "Now, therefore, be not grieved nor angry with yourselves."
5. "I am perplexed and confounded."
6. "They became agitated and restless."
7. "Rude am I in speech, and little blest
   With the set phrase of peace."
8. "What bark is plunging mid the billowy strife,
   And dashing madly on to fearful doom."
9. "The wares of the merchant are spread abroad in the shops, or stored in the high-piled warehouses."
10. "How finely diversified, and how multiplied into many thousand distinct exercises, is the attention of God!"
11. "Contentment is serious but not grave."
12. "The promises of Hope are sweeter than roses in the bud, and far more flattering to expectation."
13. "For cold and stiff and still are they
   Who wrought thy walls annoy"

1. "*Time slept on flowers and lent his glass to hope.*"

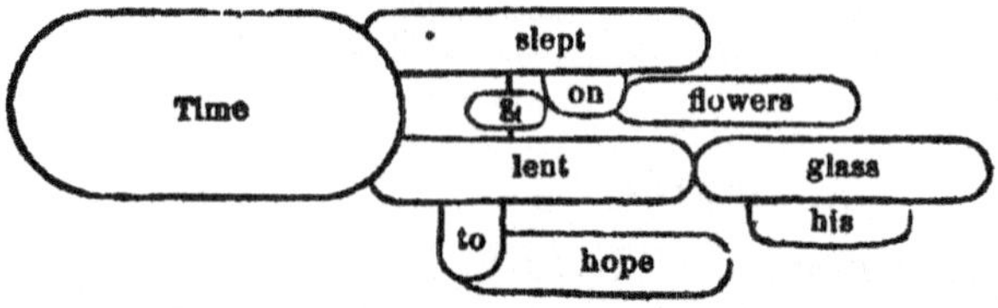

ANALYSIS.

PRINCIPAL ELEMENTS.
- The *Subject*, . . . "Time,"
- The *Predicates*, "Slep," . . . . Intransitive and "Lent," . . . . Transitive.
- The *Object*, ... "Glass,"

ADJUNCT ELEMENTS.
- Of the *Subject*, ... ———
- Of the 1*st Predicate*, "On flowers," a Phrase.
- Of the 2*d Predicate*, "To hope," . a Phrase.
- Of the *Object*, ... "His," . . . . . a Word.

ADDITIONAL SENTENCES, *adapted to the same Diagram.*

2. We sigh for change, and spend our lives for naught.
3. William goes to school, and pursues his study with zeal.
4. James stays at home, and spends his time at play.
5. We shall pass from earth, and yield our homes to others.
6. Fruits ripen in Autumn, and yield us rich repasts.

Other COMPLEX SENTENCES, *with variable Adjuncts.*

7. "For Spring shall return, and a lover bestow."
8. "The waves mount up and wash the face of heaven."
9. "In silence majestic they twinkle on high,
And draw admiration from every eye."
10. "Its little joys go out one by one,
And leave poor man, at length, in perfect night."
11. "But the black blast blows hard,
And puffs them wide of hope."
12. "Wreaths of smoke ascend through the trees,
And betray the half-hidden cottage."

COMPLEX SENTENCES.

1. The Auxiliary Sentences.—Substantive.

1. "*That all men are created equal is a self-evident truth.*"

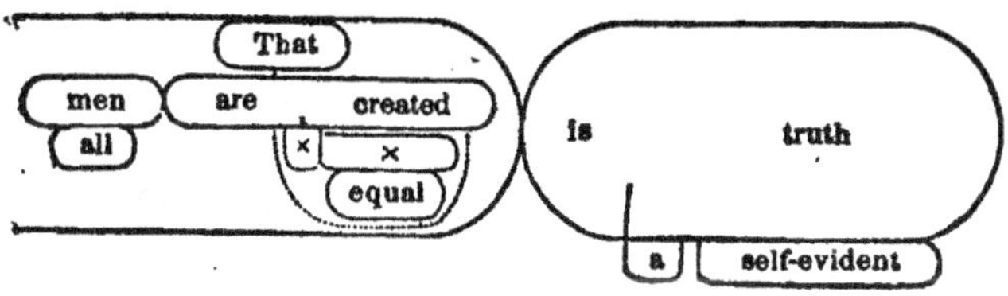

ANALYSIS.

PRINCIPAL ELEMENTS	The *Subject*,	"That all men are created equal."	a Sentence
	The *Predicate*, .	"Is," "Truth."	a Verb and a Noun.
ADJUNCT ELEMENTS.	*Of the Subject*, . .	———	
	Of the Predicate,	"A" "Self-evident."	

ANALYSIS *of the Auxiliary Sentence*.

PRINCIPAL ELEMENTS.	The *Subject*, . . .	"Men."	
	The *Predicate*, .	"Are created."	
ADJUNCT ELEMENTS.	*Of the Subject*, . .	"All," .	a Word.
	Of the Predicate,	"Equal."*	

ADDITIONAL COMPLEX SENTENCES,

Having SUBSTANTIVE SENTENCES *for their* SUBJECTS.

2. "'I can not,' has never accomplished anything."
3. "'I will try,' has done wonders."
4. "That friendship is a sacred trust,
   That friends should be sincere and just,
   That constancy befits them,
   Are observations on the case,
   That savor much of commonplace."

* A word *substituted* for the Adverbial Phrase, "[*with*] *equal* [*rights*]."

1. "But Brutus says *he was ambitious.*"

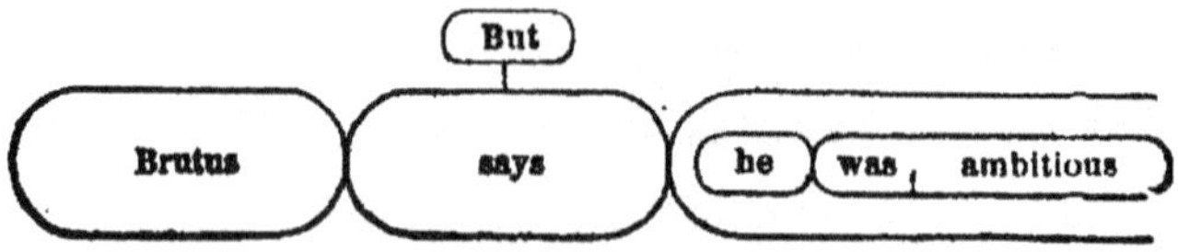

ANALYSIS.

PRINCIPAL ELEMENTS.	The *Subject*,	"Brutus,"	a Word.
	The *Predicate*,	"Says,"	a Word.
	The *Object*, ..	"He was ambitious,"	a Sentence.

ADJUNCT ELEMENTS.—None.

ADDITIONAL COMPLEX SENTENCES,

Having SUBSTANTIVE SENTENCES *for their* OBJECTS.

2. "Go to the raging sea, and say, '*Be still.*'"
3. "But tell not Misery's son *that life is fair.*"
4. "'And this to me?' he said."
5. "Cæsar cried, 'Help me, Cassius, or I sink.'"
6. "While man exclaims, 'See all things for my use,'
7. 'See man for mine,' replies a pampered goose."
8. "'Will you walk into my parlor?'
   Said a spider to a fly."
9. "He knew not that the chieftain lay,
   Unconscious of his son."
10. "He shouted but once more aloud,
   'My father! must I stay?'"
11. "We bustle up with unsuccessful speed,
   And in the saddest part cry, '*Droll, indeed!*'"
12. "Then Agrippa said unto Paul, 'Almost thou persuadest me to be a Christian.'"
13. "A celebrated writer says, 'Take care of the minutes and the hours will take care of themselves.'"
14. "The little birds, at morning dawn,
   Clothed in warm coats of feather,
   Conclude that they away will roam
   To seek for milder weather."
15. "I tell thee thou art defied."

AUXILIARY SENTENCES.—ADJECTIVE.

1. "*But they that fight for freedom, undertake*
The noblest cause mankind can have at stake."

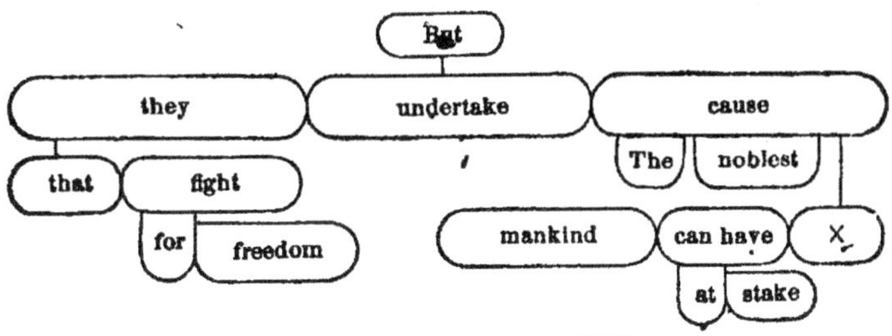

A COMPLEX SENTENCE.

ANALYSIS *of the* PRINCIPAL SENTENCE.

PRINCIPAL ELEMENTS. { The *Subject*, . . "They," / The *Predicate*, "Undertake," / The *Object*, . . . "Cause." } Simple Transitive.

ADJUNCT ELEMENTS. {
Of the Subjcet, { "That fight for freedom," } a Sentence.
Of the Predicate, ———
Of the Object, . { "The,". . . . . . . a Word. / "Noblest,". . . . a Word. / "[That] mankind can have at stake," } a Sentence. }

ANALYSIS *of the* FIRST AUXILIARY SENTENCE.

PRINCIPAL ELEMENTS. { The *Subject*, ... "That." / The *Predicate*, ... "Fight."

ADJUNCT ELEMENTS. { *Of the Subject*, . . ——— / *Of the Predicate*, . "For freedom," . a Phrase.

ANALYSIS *of the* SECOND AUXILIARY SENTENCE.

PRINCIPAL ELEMENTS. { The *Subject*, . . . "Mankind." / The *Predicate*, . . "Can have." / The *Object*, . [That] understood.

ADJUNCT ELEMENTS. { *Of the Subject*, . . ——— / *Of the Predicate*, . "At stake," . . . .a Phrase. / *Of the Object*, . . . ———

Thus analyse and place in the same Diagram the following

ADDITIONAL SENTENCES:

3. And students who love to study merit the highest honors which teachers can give them.
4. And actions which were founded in justice, produced the good results which we had in view.
5. "But such as seek for truth shall find the richest boon which God to man can give."
6. "And I who bleed for thee,
   Shall claim the brightest gift
   Which thou canst yield to me."
7. But he who wins at last,
   Shall love the very toils
   Which fortune round him cast.

THE ADJUNCTS VARY.

8. "He that walketh uprightly walketh surely."
9. "There is something in their hearts which passes speech."
10. "He is in the way of life that keepeth instruction."
11. "I love the bright and glorious sun
    That gives us light and heat,"
12. "I love the pearly drops of dew
    That sparkle 'neath my feet."
13. "I love to think of him who made
    These pleasant things for me."
14. "The boy stood on the burning deck,
    Whence all but him had fled:
15. The flames that lit the battle's wreck,
    Shone round him o'er the dead."
16. "I love to hear the little birds
    That carol on the trees."
17. "Poverty and shame shall be to him that refuseth instruction."
18. "Wisdom resteth in the heart of him that hath understanding."
19. "Understanding is a wellspring of life to him that hath it."
20. "But the noblest thing that perished there
    Was that young faithful heart."
21. Thou hast green laurel leaves that twine
    Into so proud a wreath.
22. Thou hast a voice whose thrilling tones
    Can bid each life-pulse beat.

23. "Around Sebago's lonely lake
There lingers not a breeze to break
The mirror which its waters make."

24. "Cold in the dust this perished heart may lie,
But that which warmed it once shall never die."

25. "He that by usury and unjust gain increaseth his substance, shall gather it for him that will pity the poor."

☞ Let the Pupil place Sentence (25) in the subjoined Diagram.

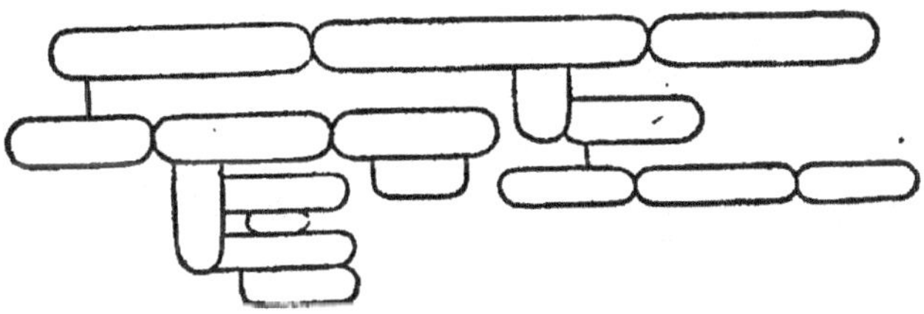

"*Our proper bliss depends on what we blame.*"

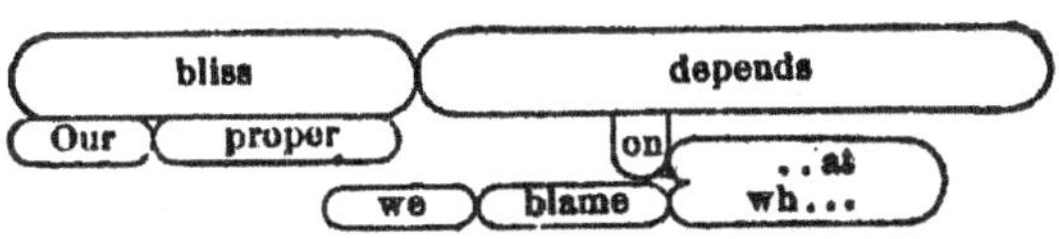

A Complex Sentence.—The Auxiliary qualifies a Phrase.

Elements.	*Offices.*
"Our,"	Adjunct of "bliss."
"Proper,"	Adjunct of "bliss."
"Bliss,"	Subject of "depends."
"Depends,"	Predicate of "bliss."
"On what we blame,"	Adjunct of "depends.
"What," { [That],	Object of "on."
[Which],	Object of "blame."
'We,"	Subject of "blame."
Blame,'	Predicate of "we."

Additional Examples.

2. "What thou dost not know thou canst not tell."
3. "I speak not to disprove what Brutus spoke."
4. "Seek not to know what is improper for thee."
5. "But here I stand and speak what I do know."

Auxiliary Sentences.—Adverbial.

"And when its yellow luster smiled
O'er mountains yet untrod,
Each mother held aloft her child,
To bless the bow of God."

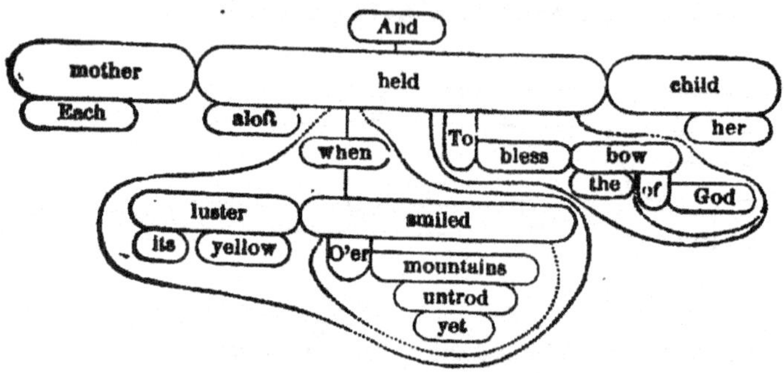

A COMPLEX SENTENCE.

ANALYSIS *of the* PRINCIPAL SENTENCE.

PRINCIPAL ELEMENTS.	The *Subject*, ... "Mother."		Simple Transitive.
	The *Predicate*, . . . "Held."		
	The *Object*, ... "Child."		
ADJUNCT ELEMENTS.	*Of the Subject*, . . "Each," . . .		a Word.
	Of the Predicate,	"Aloft,"	a Word.
		"When its yellow luster smiled o'er mountains yet untrod,"	a Sentence (Adverbial)
		"To bless the bow of God,"	a Phrase.
	Of the Object, . . . "Her,"		a Word.

Elements.	*Offices.*
"And,"	Introduces the *Principal Sentence.*
"When its y[illegible] luster smiled O'e[illegible]ins yet untrod,"	. . . . Adjunct of "held."
E[illegible]	Adjunct of "mother."
"[illegible]	Subject of "held."
"Held,"	Predicate of "mother."

"Aloft," ....Adjunct of "held."
"Her," ....Adjunct of "child."
"Child," ....Object of "held."
"To bless the bow of God," ....Adjunct of "held."

"When," ....Introduces the *Auxiliary Sentence*
"Its," ....Adjunct of "luster."
"Yellow," ....Adjunct of "luster."
"Luster," ....Subject of "smiled."
"Smiled," ....Predicate of "luster."
"O'er mountains yet untrod," ....Adjunct of "smiled."

ANALYSIS *of the* ADJUNCT PHRASES.

"To,"....Introduces the Phrase—connects "bless" with "held."
"Bless," ....Object of "to."
"The," ....Adjunct of "bow."
"Bow," ....Object of "bless."
"Of God," ....Adjunct of "bow."

"Of,"....Introduces the Phrase—connects "God" with "bow."
"God," ....Object of "of."

"O'er," Introduces the Phrase—connects "mountains" with "smiled."
"Mountains," ....Object of "o'er."
"Yet," ....Adjunct of "untrod."
"Untrod," ....Adjunct of "mountains."

☞ *Thus analyze the following* ADDITIONAL EXAMP[illegible]

2. "Wherefore is there a price in the hand of a fool t[illegible] wisdom, seeing he hath no heart to it."
3. "Yet do I feel my soul recoil within me,
As I contemplate the dim gulf of death."
4. "If we have *whispered* truth,
Whisper no longer."
5. "Speak as the tempest does,
Sterner and stronger."
6. "The hoary head is a crown of glory, if it [illegible] the way of righteousness."
7. "Their advancement in life and in education [illegible] each ought to have been a ge[illegible]"

8 “The sweet remembrance of the just,
Shall flourish when he sleeps in dust.”

9. “But, when he caught the measure wild,
The old man raised his head and smiled.”

10. “There are sumptuous mansions with marble walls,
Where fountains play in the perfumed halls.”

11. “The earth hath felt the breath of spring,
Though yet on her deliverer's wing
The lingering frosts of winter cling.”

EXAMPLES

Of SUBSTANTIVE, ADJECTIVE, *and* ADVERBIAL SENTENCES.

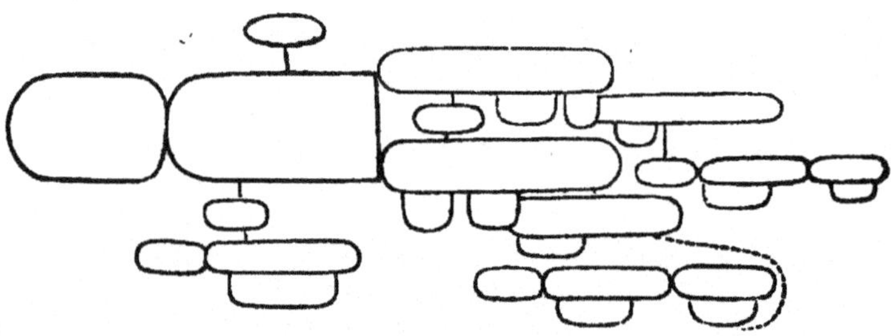

☞ Let the Pupil name the Sentence below adapted to this Diagram, and place it in an exact copy, written on the blackboard.

1. “If you would know the deeds of him who chews,
Enter the house of God, and see the pews.”

2. “The man that dares traduce because he can
[illegible]y to himself, is not a man.”

3. “[illegible] passed by, I heard the complaints of the laborers who had reaped down his fields, and the cries of the poor whose covering he had taken away.”

4. “The time must come when all will have been said that can be said to exalt the character of any individual of our race.”

5. “Mysterious are his ways, whose power
Brings forth that unexpected hour,
When minds that never met before,
Shall m[illegible]d part no more.”

6. “M[illegible] within me when I think
[illegible]miracle that still goes on,
In [illegible], round me.”

7. "When we consider carefully what appeals to our minds, and exercise upon it our own reason—taking into respectful con sideration what others say upon it—and then come to a conclusion of our own, we act as intelligent beings."
8. "Before we passionately desire what another enjoys, we should examine into the happiness of its possessor."
9. "With what loud applause didst thou beat heaven with blessing Bolingbroke, before he was what thou wouldst have him be!"

PROMISCUOUS EXAMPLES.

1. "The troubled ocean feels his steps, as he strides from wave to wave."
2. "Beneath the spear of Cathmar rose that voice which awakes the bards."
3. "As they sat down, one said to his friend on his right, 'We shall soon see who is who.'"
4. "He sunk to sleep,
With all the nameless shapes that haunt the deep."
5. "Go to the mat *where squalid Want reclines*,"
6. "Go to the shade obscure *where Merit pines*,"
7. "Abide with him *whom Penury's charms control*,
And bind the rising yearnings of his soul."
8. "Survey his sleepless couch, and standing there,
Tell the poor pallid wretch *that life is fair*."
9. "It must be sweet in childhood to give back
The spirit to its Maker, ere the heart
Has grown familiar with the ways of sin."
10. "Wheresoe'er our best affections dwell,
And strike a healthful root, is happiness."
11. "A *man* of refinement never *has recourse* to proverbs and vulgar aphorisms."
12. "Across the ocean *came* a pilgrim *bark*."
13. The *bark* of the trunk of the white oak *is* frequently *variegated* with large spots.
14 The *wood* of the young stocks *is* very *elastic*, and is *susceptible* of minute divisions.
15. The *flowers put forth* in the month of Ma[illegible]
16. "*Night*, sable goddess, from her ebon thron[illegible]
In rayless majesty, now *stretches* forth
Her leaden *sceptor* o'er a slumbering world."

17. "Vulgarism in language is a distinguishing characteristic of bad company and a bad education."
18. "The *wood* of the silver fir is not much used as timber."
19. "The hemlock spruce is not much esteemed for timber."
20. "Milton's learning has all the effect of intuition."
21. "His imagination has the force of nature."
22. "Heaven, from all creatures, hides the book of fate."
23. "And *as Jesus passed by*, he saw a man *who was blind*."
24. "If a noble squire had conducted himself well, during the period of his service, the honor of knighthood was generally conferred upon him at the age of twenty."
25. "Another bright day's sunset bathes the hills
That gird Samaria."
26. "One glance of wonder, as we pass, deserve
The books of Time."
27. "A fretful temper will divide
The choicest knot that may be tied,
By ceaseless, sharp corrosion.
28. A temper, passionate and fierce,
May suddenly your joys disperse
At one immense explosion."
29. "But no mere human work or character is perfect."
30. "The profoundest depths of man's intellect can be fathomed."
31. "In the loftiest flights of his imagination, he can be followed."
32. "None of his richest mines, are inexhaustible."
33. "Then began he to upbraid the cities wherein most of his mighty works were done, because they repented not."
34. "That secrets are a sacred trust,
That friends should be sincere and just,
That constancy befits them—
Are observations on the case,
That savor much of commonplace,
35. And all the world admits them."
36 "The dilatory caution of Pope enabled him to condense his sentiments, to multiply his images, and to accumulate all that study might produce, or chance supply."
37 "Dryd[illegible]rpasses expectation—
38 B[illegible]s below it."
39 [illegible]ead with frequent astonishment—
40. [illegible], with perpetual delight."

REM.—For the encouragement of Pupils who may not be able properly to analyze the more difficult of the preceding Sentences, the following Exercises are simplified:—

1. The Principal Elements of the Principal Sentences are printed in SMALL CAPITALS;

2. The Principal Elements of the Auxiliary Sentences are printed in *Italic Letters;*

3. The letters in the margin refer to the appropriate DIAGRAMS on page 45;

4. The *forms* and the *offices* of the Phrases are indicated by appropriate references.

THE AMERICAN FLAG.—*J. R. Drake.*

B. When *Freedom*, from her mountain height,*b
Unfurled her *standard* to the air,*b
1. I. SHE TORE the azure ROBE of night,*a
And SET the STARS of glory*a there;
2. I. SHE MINGLED with the gorgeous dyes*b
The milky BALDRIC of the skies,*a
And STRIPED its pure celestial WHITE
With streakings*b of the morning light,*a
Then, from his mansion,*b in the sun,*b
3. I. SHE CALLED her EAGLE-BEARER down,
And GAVE into his mighty hand*b
The SYMBOL of her chosen land.*a

Majestic monarch of the cloud,*a
B. *Who rear'st* aloft thy regal *form*,
To hear the tempest-trumpings loud,†b
And see the lightning lances†b driven,†b
A. When *strike* the *warriors* of the storm,*a
A. And *rolls* the *thunder-drum* of heaven,*a
A. Child of the Sun,*a to thee*b 'TIS GIVEN,
To guard the banner†c of the free,*a
To hover†c in the sulphur smoke,*b
To ward away the battle-stroke,†c
And bid its blendings†c shine afar†b,
Like rainbows*b on the cloud*b of war,*a
The harbinger of victory.*a

5. A. Flag of the brave,*a thy FOLDS SHALL FLY,
The sign of hope and triumph,*a high.
A. When *speaks* the signal *trumpet-tone*,
A. And the long *line comes* gleaming on
B. (Ere yet the *life-blood*, warm and wet,
Has dimmed the glist'ning *bayonet*),
6. M.* Each soldier's EYE SHALL brightly TURN
A. To where thy *meteor-glories burn*,*b
A. And, as his springing *steps advance*,
CATCH WAR and VENGEANCE from the glance;*b
B. And, when the *cannon-mouthings* loud
Heave, in wild wreaths,*b the *battle-shroud*,
C. And gory *sabres rise* and *fall*,
Like shoots*b of flame*a on midnight's pall!*b
7. A. There SHALL thy VICTOR-GLANCES GLOW;
8. A. And cowering FOES SHALL SHRINK beneath
A. Each gallant arm*b *that strikes* below
That lovely messenger*b of death.*a

Flag of the seas,*a on ocean's wave,*b
9. A. Thy STARS SHALL GLITTER o'er the brave;*b
A. When *death*, careering on the gale,*b
Sweeps darkly round the bellied sail,*b
A. And frightened *waves rush* wildly back,
Before the broadside's reeling rack,*b
10. C. The dying WANDERER of the sea*a
SHALL LOOK at once*b to heaven and thee,*b
And SMILE to see thy splendors†b fly†b
In triumph*b o'er his closing eye.*b

Flag of the free heart's only home,*a
By angel-hands*b to valor*b given,
11. B. Thy STARS HAVE LIT the welkin DOME,
12. A. And all thy HUES WERE BORN in heaven:*b
13. B. For ever*b FLOAT that standard SHEET!
14. A. Where BREATHES the FOE *but falls* before us.*b
With Freedom's soil beneath our feet,*b
And Freedom's banner streaming o'er us!*b

---

* Prepositional Phrase. † Infinitive Phrase.
a Adjective Phrase. *b* Adverbial Phrase. *c* Independent Phrase.

PART II.

ETYMOLOGY.

REMARK 1.—In PART I. we have considered by analysis,

1. The *Structure* of Sentences and of Phrases.
2. The *Elements* which compose a Sentence or a Phrase.
3. The *Classification* of Sentences and of Phrases.
4. The *Analysis* of Sentences—*Proximate* and *Ultimate*.

REM. 2.—In our progress through PART I. we have seen,

1. That the *Proximate Analysis* of a Sentence consists in resolving it into its *immediate Constituent Elements*.
2. That the *Ultimate Analysis* of a Sentence consists in reducing its Proximate Elements to the WORDS which compose them.

REM. 3.—We have next to consider the history of WORDS—considered as ultimate Elements of Sentences—including

1. Their *Formation*.
2. Their *Functions*.
3. Their *Classifications*.
4. Their *Modifications*.

PRIN.—The Science of Language embraces,

1. ORTHOGRAPHY—which treats of the *Structure* and *Form* of Words.
2. ETYMOLOGY—which treats of the *Classification* and *Modification* of Words.
3. SYNTAX—which treats of the *Relation* and mutual *Dependence* of Words.
4. PROSODY—which treats of the *Arrangement* and *Utterance* of Words.

REM.—A true system of Analysis requires that the *Functions* of Words be discussed previous to the consideration of their Elements. Hence we have placed ORTHOGRAPHY in the Appendix to this Work.

CLASSIFICATION AND MODIFICATION OF WORDS.

PRIN.—*Words* are distinguished by their *Forms* and by their *Uses.*

I. THE FORMS OF WORDS.

PRIN.—By their *forms,* Words are distinguished as
Radical or *Derivative,*
Simple or *Compound.*

DEF. 52.—A *Radical Word* is a word that does not derive its original from another word in the same language.

EXAMPLES.—Sun—cloud—rose—friend—chief—swift—just—sell.

DEF. 53.—A *Derivative Word* is a word derived from a Radical by prefixing or adding one or more letters to it.

EXAMPLES.—Sunny—swiftly—cloudy—sinful—selling—unconscious—roseate—friendly—justify—chieftain.

OBS.—A Word that is Radical in the English language, may be a Derivative in the language from which it comes.

EXAMPLES.—Conscience—optics—algebra—philosophy—signify.

DEF. 54.—A *Simple Word* is a word that is used separately from another word.

EXAMPLES.—Have—brightly—freedom—parlor—music—study—times—patience—loved—cottage—peace—cold.

DEF. 55.—A *Compound Word* is a word that is made of two or more words combined.

EXAMPLES.—Star-light—household-words—rose-bud—steam-engine—pencil-case—never the-less—moon-beam—rail-road.

OBS.—The parts of a Compound Word are printed as one word without space between them, or they are joined by a short horizontal line (-) called a hyphen.

EXAMPLES (*without the hyphen.*)—Overlay—underwrite—withstand—sometimes—nevertheless.

" (*with the hyphen*)—Hour-glass—warm-hearted—praise-worthy.

PRIN.—The *Parts* of a Compound Word are the BASIS and the ADJUNCT.

DEF. 56.—The *Basis* of a Compound Word, is the Principal Element in the word.

EXAMPLES.— Race-*horse* — horse-*race* — hour-*glass* — *father*-in-law — *sergeant*-at-arms—*aid*-de-camp.

DEF. 57.—The Adjunct of a Compound Word is the Part that *limits* or modifies the Basis.

EXAMPLES.— *Race*-horse — *Horse*-race — *Hour*-glass — father-*in-law* — jack-*o'-lantern* — aid-*de-camp*.

OBS.—The Adjunct of a Word may be one *Word* or a *Phrase*.

EXAMPLES.—*One Word.*—*Man*-stealer—*race*-horse—*book*-maker.
A Phrase.—Father-*in-law*—aid-*de-camp*—will-*o'-the-wisp*.

REM.—*Derivative* and *Compound Words* have this distinction, viz.: *Compound Words* consist of *two or more complete Words;* whereas, *Derivative Words* consist of *one Word* with *Letters* or *Particles* prefixed or attached. These *Particles* are called PREFIXES and SUFFIXES.

DEF. 58.—A *Prefix* is one or more Letters placed before a Radical to form a Derivative Word.

EXAMPLES.— *Re*form — *de*grade — *over*look — *under*take — *in*volve — *ab*solve—*e*lect—*per*fect.

DEF. 59.—A *Suffix* is one or more letters added to a Word to make it Derivative.

EXAMPLES.—Form*ing*—grad*ed*—home*ly*—good*ness*.

REM.—Words may have more than one Prefix or Suffix. Hence,

PRIN.—Prefixes and Suffixes are distinguished as *Simple* or *Compound*.

EXAMPLES OF SIMPLE.

Prefixes.		*Suffixes.*	
*Ab*solve,	*Com*pose,	Form*ing*,	Tak*en*,
*Dis*solve,	*De*pose,	Form*ation*,	Verb*ose*,
*Re*solve,	*Re*pose,	Danger*ous*,	Rude*ly*,
*De*form,	*Be*take,	Coin*age*,	Hope*ful*,
*In*form,	*Over*take,	Good*ness*,	Consul*ar*,
*Uni*form,	*Under*take,	Bigot*ry*,	Lamb*kin*.

COMPOUND

Prefixes.	*Suffixes.*
Re con struct,	Lone *li ness*
Mis con ceive,	Might i ly,
In co herent,	Fear less ness,
Un pre tending,	Right ful ly
Ir re vocable,	Form at ion,
Im per forated.	Modi fi cation.

Prefixes and Suffixes.

Reducing,	*Abnegation,*
Dissolved,	*Confinement,*
Conformable,	Substantial,
Reconciliation,	Unconditionally,
Transubstantiation,	Disseminating,
Indissoluble.	Conformability.

PRIN.—The *Radicals* of Derivative Words are SEPARABLE OR INSEPARABLE.

DEF. 60.—A *Separable Radical* constitutes a perfect Word, without its Prefixes or Suffixes.

EXAMPLES.

Words	Radical	Words	Radical
Reform, Deform, Inform, Conform,	*Form.*	Adjoin, Conjoin, Enjoin, Unjoin,	*Join.*

DEF. 61.—An *Inseparable Radical* is not used as a distinct word in the language without the aid of its Prefixes or Suffixes.

EXAMPLES.

Words	Radical	Words	Radical
Collect, Delectable, Election, Recollecting,	*lect.*	Advert, Convertable, Diverting, Inversion, Undiverted,	*vert.*

NOTE.—For an extended list of Prefixes and Suffixes, see "*Derivation of Words*" in the APPENDIX.

II. The Uses of Words.

Prin.—By their *uses*, Words are distinguished as

1. *Nouns*, 2. *Pronouns*, 3. *Verbs*,	Principal Elements in Sentences.
4. *Adjectives*, 5. *Adverbs*,	Adjunct Elements.
6. *Prepositions*, 7. *Conjunctions*, 8. *Exclamations*, 9. *Words of Euphony*,	Attendant Elements.

Def. 62.—A *Noun* is a Word used as the *Name* of a being, a place, or a thing.

Examples.—"The *King* of *Shadows* loves a shining *mark*."

Obs. 1.—Nouns are names of

1. Material things, as—*Man—book—house—apples*.
2. Ideas or things not material, as—*Mind—hope—desire—aversion—remorse—joy*.

Obs.—Let the Pupil be careful here to distinguish a *name* from the *thing* named; and remember that the *name* is the *Noun*. Thus, a *house* is a *thing*—the *name* of that thing is a *Noun*.

CLASSIFICATION OF NOUNS.

Remark.—Some Nouns are appropriated to individual persons or places, or to things personified; others are general in their application, being used to designate classes or sorts. Hence,

Prin.—Nouns are distinguished as

Proper and *Common*.

Def. 63.—A *Proper Noun* is a name appropriated to an individual person or place, or to a thing personified.

Examples.—*William—Boston—Hudson—Oregon*.

"And old *Experience* learns too late
That all is vanity below."

DEF. 64.—A *Common Noun* is a name used to designate one or more of a *class* or *sort* of beings or things.

EXAMPLES.—Man—book—conscience—feeling—landscape.
"Now fades the glimmering *landscape* on the *sight.*"

OBS. 1.—A Common Noun is a name by which the individuality of a being or thing is designated; but, in addition to this Office, some Nouns are the names of *qualities.*

DEF. 65.—An *Abstract Noun* is the name of a *quality* of a thing, and not of the Substance.

EXAMPLES.—Goodness—meekness—impracticability.
"These all, in sweet *confusion*, sought the shade."

DEF. 66.—A *Collective Noun* is a Noun appropriated to many individuals in one term.

EXAMPLES.—Committee—assembly—army—tribe—clan—multitude.
"The village master taught his little *school.*"

DEF. 67.—A *Verbal Noun* is a Noun derived from a Verb; being in *form*, a Participle—in *office*, a Substantive.

EXAMPLES.—Beginning—gatherings—spelling—joining.
"In the *beginning*, God created the heaven and the earth."

OBS. 1.—The Classification of Nouns as *Common* and *Proper*, is one rather of curiosity than of practical utility in the Science of Language.

OBS. 2.—A Word is known to be a Noun,
1st. By its being a *Name.*
2d. By its performing a *Substantive office.*

OBS. 3.—A *Substantive* may be,
1. The *Subject* of a Sentence.
2. The *Object* of a Sentence or of a Phrase.
3. A Name or an Equivalent, *independent* in construction.

But,

OBS. 4.—A *Substantive office* may be performed by *Words*, by *Phrases*, and by *Sentences.*

EXAMPLES.

1. By *Words*, NOUNS.—*Paul* the *Apostle* wrote an *Epistle* to *Timothy*.
PRONOUNS.—Was *it you that* introduced *me* to *him?*
2. By *Phrases*.—"*Taking a madman's sword*, to prevent *his doing mischief*, can not be regarded as *robbing him*."
3. By *Sentences*.—"*That all men are created equal*, is a self-evident truth."
"But Brutus says, *he was ambitious*."
"There is no question as to *which must yield*."

Hence,

OBS. 5.—A *Noun* is generally *Substantive*. But a Word commonly used as a Noun may become,

1. An Adjective; as, An *iron* fence—*gold* leaf.
2. An Adverb; as, Go *home* and come *back*.
3. A Verb; as, "But if you *mouth* it."

Obs. 6.—A Substantive office is sometimes performed by words commonly used,

1. As *Adjectives*—"The *good* alone are great."
"Nor grudge I thee the *much* the Grecians give,
Nor, murm'ring, take the *little* I receive."—*Dryden*.
2. As *Adverbs*—
"'Tis Heaven itself that points out an *hereafter*."—*Addison*.
3. As *Conjunctions*—
"Your *if* is the only peace-maker; much virtue is in *if*."
Shakspeare.
4. As an *Exclamation*—
"With *hark* and *whoop* and wild *halloo*."—*Scott*.

MODIFICATION OF NOUNS.

REM.—Some Nouns and Pronouns, by their form, by their position in a Sentence, or by their obvious uses, indicate—

1. The *sex*—as male or female, or neither.
2. The *speaker*, the being addressed, or the being or thing spoken of.
3. The *number* of beings or things—as one or more.
4. The *condition*, with regard to other Words in the Sentence; as,
   (1.) The *Subject* of a Sentence.
   (2.) The *Object* of a Sentence or Phrase.
   (3.) *Independent* in construction. Hence,

PRIN.—Nouns are modified by *Gender*, *Person*, *Number* and *Case*.

GENDER.

DEF. 68.—Gender is the modification of such Nouns and Pronouns as, by their form, distinguish the sex.

DEF. 69.—Nouns and Pronouns that indicate *Males* are of the *Masculine Gender*.

EXAMPLES.—Man—lion—ox—David—John.

DEF. 70.—Nouns and Pronouns indicating *Females* are of the *Feminine Gender*.

EXAMPLES.—Woman—lioness—cow—Dollie—Jane.

DEF. 71.—Nouns and Pronouns that do not indicate the sex, are said to be of the *Neuter Gender*.

EXAMPLES.—Book—pen—table—star—planet.

OBS. 1.—Strict propriety will allow the names of *animals only* to be modified by Gender.

OBS. 2.—Young animals and infants are not always distinguished by Gender; as, "Mary's kitten is very playful—*it* is quite a pet with the whole family."

"Calm as an infant as *it* sweetly sleeps."

OBS. 3.—Things personified are often represented by Pronouns of the Masculine or the Feminine Gender.

EXAMPLES.—1. "Then Fancy *her* magical pinions spread wide."
2. "Time slept on flowers, and lent *his* glass to Hope."
3. "For the Angel of Death spread *his* wings on the blast,
And breathed in the face of the foe as *he* pass'd."

OBS. 4.—Many Nouns which denote the office or condition of persons, and some others, are not distinguished by Gender.

EXAMPLES.—Parent—cousin—friend—neighbor—teacher.

OBS. 5.—Whenever Words are used which include both Males and Females, without having a direct reference to the sex, the Word appropriated to males is commonly employed.

EXAMPLES.—1. "The proper study of *mankind* is *man*."
2. "There is no flesh in *man's* obdurate heart—
It does not feel for *man*."

But to this rule there are exceptions; as, geese, ducks.

PRIN.—The Gender of Nouns is determined,

1. By the termination; as,

Masc.	*Fem.*	*Masc.*	*Fem.*
Actor,	Actress.	Patron,	Patroness.
Administrator,	Administratrix.	Prince,	Princess.
Author,	Authoress.	Protector,	Protectress.
Governor,	Governess.	Shepherd,	Shepherdess.
Heir,	Heiress.	Songster,	Songstress.
Host,	Hostess.	Tiger,	Tigress.
Hero,	Heroine.	Tutor,	Tutoress.
Jew,	Jewess.	Tailor,	Tailoress.
Lion,	Lioness.	Widower,	Widow.

2. By different Words; as,

Masc.	*Fem.*	*Masc.*	*Fem.*
Bachelor,	Maid.	Husband,	Wife.
Beau,	Belle.	King,	Queen.
Boy,	Girl.	Lad,	Lass.
Brother,	Sister.	Lord,	Lady.
Drake,	Duck.	Man,	Woman.
Father,	Mother.	Master,	Mistress.
Friar,	Nun.	Nephew,	Niece.

3. By prefixing or affixing other Words; as,

Masc.	*Fem.*
Man-servant,	Maid-servant.
He-goat,	She-goat.
Cock-sparrow,	Hen-sparrow.
Landlord,	Landlady.
Gentleman.	Gentlewoman.

NOTE.—In the English language, less importance is attached to the Gender of Nouns than in the Latin, Greek, and other languages—the relation of Words in Sentences depending more upon *position* and less upon the terminations. Hence, in parsing Nouns and Pronouns, the Gender need not be mentioned, unless they are obviously Masculine or Feminine.

PERSON.

REM.—All Nouns are the Names of

1. The person speaking.
2. The persons or things addressed. Or,
3. The persons or things spoken of. Hence,

PRIN.—Nouns and Pronouns are of the

First Person, Second Person, or *Third Person.*

DEF. 72.—The name of the *speaker* or writer is of the *First Person.*

EXAMPLES.—"*I, John,* saw these things." "*We Athenians* are in fault."

DEF. 73.—The name of a pers[illegible]r thing addressed is of the *Second Person.*

EXAMPLE.— "*Father,* thy hand
Hath reared these venerable columns; *thou*
Didst weave this verdant roof."

DEF. 74.—The name of the person or thing spoken of is of the *Third Person.*

EXAMPLES.—"The *hero* hath departed." "*Honor* guides his *footsteps.*"

NUMBER.

REM.—Nouns by their form denote individuality or plurality. Hence,

PRIN.—Nouns are distinguished as

Singular and *Plural.*

DEF. 75.—Nouns denoting but one are of the

Singular Number.

EXAMPLES.—Man—boy—pen—book—mouse—ox.

DEF. 76.—Nouns denoting more than one are of the

Plural Number.

EXAMPLES.—Men—boys—pens—books—mice—oxen.

OBS. 1.—The *Number* of a Noun is usually determined by its *form.* The Plural of most Nouns differs from the Singular by having an ad-d[illegible]onal *s.*

EXAMPLES.

Singular.—Act,	Egg,	Book,	Mastiff,	Pen,	Chair.
Plural.—Acts,	Eggs,	Books,	Mastiffs,	Pens,	Chairs.

OBS. 2.—But a Noun whose Singular form ends in *s*, *ss*, *sh*, *x*, *ch* (soft), and some Nouns in *o* and *y*, form the Plural by the addition of *es*.

EXAMPLES.

Singular.—Gas,	Lynx,	Church,	Lash,	Glass,	Hero.
Plural.—Gases,	Lynxes,	Churches,	Lashes,	Glasses,	Heroes.

OBS. 3.—*Y* final, after a Consonant, is changed into *ie* (the original orthography), and *s* is added.

EXAMPLES.

Singular.—Lady,	Folly,	Quality,	City.
Old form.—Ladie,	Follie,	Qualitie,	Citie.
Plural.—Ladies,	Follies,	Qualities,	Cities.

Exception.—But Proper Nouns in *y* commonly form the Plurals by adding *s* to the *y*; as, the two *Livys*—the *Tullys*.

OBS. 4.—In the following Nouns, *f* final is changed into *v*, and the usual termination for the Plural is added:

Sing.	*Plural.*	*Sing.*	*Plural.*
Beef,	Beeves.	Self,	Selves.
Calf,	Calves.	Shelf,	Shelves.
Elf,	Elves.	Sheaf,	Sheaves.
Half	Halves.	Thief,	Thieves.
Leaf,	Leaves.	Wolf,	Wolves.
Loaf,	Loaves.		

Other Nouns in *f* form their Plurals regularly.

OBS. 5.—But most Nouns ending in *fe* are changed into *ves*.

EXAMPLES.

Singular.—Knife,	Life,	Wife,
Plural.—Knives,	Lives,	Wives.

OBS. 6.—Many Nouns form their Plurals irregularly.

EXAMPLES.

Singular.—Man,	Child,	Foot,	Ox,	Mouse.
Plural.—Men,	Children,	Feet,	Oxen,	Mice.

OBS. 7.—In most *Compound* Words, the *basis* only is varied to form the Plural, *if its Adjunct Word precedes*, or its *Adjunct Phrase follows*.

EXAMPLES.

Singular.—Fellow-servant,	Ink-stand,	Race-horse,	Camp-meeting.
Plural.—Fellow-servants,	Ink-stands,	Race-horses,	Camp-meetings.

Singular.—Father-in-law,	Aid-de-Camp.
Plural.—Fathers-in-law,	Aides-de-Camp.

OBS. 8.—But, *if the Adjunct Word follows the basis*, the Plural termination is commonly attached to the *Adjunct*.

EXAMPLES.

Singular.—Arm-full,	Camera-Obscura,	Ignis-fatuus.
Plural.—Arm-fulls,	Camera-Obscuras,	Ignis-fatuuses.

OBS. 9.—In forming the Plural of Nouns *having titles prefixed* or *annexed*, custom is not uniform.

There seems to be a propriety in regarding *a name and its title* as a Compound Noun; as, *Jonathan Edwards*, *John Smith*, *Miss Bowen*.

If, then, it is decided which part of the Compound Word—the *Name* or the *Title*—is to be regarded as the basis, and which the Adjunct, the Plural termination should be attached as directed in Obs. 7 and 8, above. Thus, Miss Bowen and her sister, two ladies unmarried, are Misses. "I called to see the *Misses Bowen*."

"We purchase goods of the *Messrs.* Barber." Here the *titles* constitute the *bases*, the *names*, the Adjuncts.

Again: Patterson the father and Patterson the son are two *Pattersons*. They are both doctors. If we speak of them as *men*, we make the *Name* the basis and the Title as Adjunct; thus, "I visited the two Doctor Pattersons." But if we speak of them as *Doctors*, we make the *Title* the basis, and pluralize it: thus, "We employed Doctors J. & A. Patterson."

OBS. 10.—Some Nouns have no Plurals.

EXAMPLES.—Wheat—silver—gold—iron—gratitude.

OBS. 11.—Some Nouns have no Singular.

EXAMPLES.—Tongs—embers—vespers—literati—scissors.

OBS. 12.—Some Nouns have the same Form in both Numbers.

EXAMPLES.

Singular.—Apparatus,	News,	Wages,	Sheep,	Vermin.
Plural.—Apparatus,	News,	Wages,	Sheep,	Vermin.

OBS. 13.—Some Nouns, having a Singular form, are used in a Plural sense.

EXAMPLES.—Horse—foot—cavalry—cannon—sail. One thousand *horse* and two thousand *foot*—five hundred *cavalry*—fifty cannon—twenty *sail* of the line—and, for supplies, five hundred *head* of cattle.

OBS. 14.—Some Nouns, having no Plural form to indicate Number, receive a Plural Termination to indicate different Species.

EXAMPLES.—Wines.—"Most wines contain over twenty per cent. of alcohol." Tea.—"The teas of the Nankin Company are all good."

OBS. 15.—Many Latin, Greek, and Hebrew Nouns used in English composition, retain their original Plurals. Commonly the terminations *um*, *us*, and *on*, of the Singular, are changed into *a*, for the Plural; *x* into *ces*, and *is* into *es*.

EXAMPLES.

Singular.—Datum,	Genus,	Criterion,	Index,	Axis,
Plural.—Data,	Genera,	Criteria,	Indices,	Axes.

NOTE.—For other examples of Number, see Appendix, Note C.

EXERCISES IN GENDER, PERSON, AND NUMBER.

☞ Let the Class give, 1st, the Gender—2d, the Person—3d, the Number of each of the following Names—always giving a reason for the modification, by repeating the Definitions.

William,	Boy,	Town,	Army,
Ganges,	Girl,	County,	Data,
Andes,	Aunt,	Troy,	Index,
Cuba,	Cousin,	City,	Question.

☞ Let Sentences be made, in which the following Words shall be in the Second Person.

MODEL.

"Father, thy hand hath reared this venerable column."

Father,	Stars,	Thou,	Heralds,
Mother,	Hills,	You,	Messengers,
Sun,	Rivers,	Ye,	Walls,
Earth,	Woods,	Men,	Floods.

☞ Let other Sentences be made, having the same Words in the Third Person, after the following

MODEL.

"My *Father* made them all."

☞ Let the following Singular Nouns be changed to their Plurals, and placed in Sentences, always giving the Rule for the change of Number.

Boy,	Motto,	Fox,	Ox,	Son-in-law,
Father,	Hero,	Staff,	Pea,	Spoon-full,
Man,	Knife,	Goose,	Basis,	Cousin-german,
Child,	Hoof,	Mouse,	Stratum,	Knight-errant.

MODEL.

"The *boys* have accomplished their tasks."

☞ Let the Gender and Number of the following Nouns be changed and placed in Sentences.

Man,	Bachelor,	Brother,	Poetess,
Boys,	Lioness,	Sons,	Prince,
Uncles,	Geese,	Sister,	Tutor,
Cousin,	Cow,	Maid,	Widower.

MODELS.

"Two *women* shall be grinding at the mill."

"And the *widows* of Asher are loud in their wail."

CASE.

REM.—All Nouns and Pronouns are used,

1. As the Subject of a Sentence.
2. As a Definitive of some other Noun.
3. As the Object of an action or relation, or
4. Independent of other Words in the Sentence.

REM. 2.—These different conditions of Nouns suggest their modifications in regard to Case; for *Case*, in Grammar, means *condition*. Hence,

PRIN.—Nouns are distinguished as being in the

Nominative Case,	*Objective Case,*
Possessive Case,	*Independent Case.*

OBS.—In the Latin, Greek, German, and many other languages, the Cases of Nouns are determined *by their terminations*. But, as English Nouns have no inflections, *except to form Adjuncts*, the Cases are determined *only by the offices* of Nouns in Sentences. Hence,

DEF. 77.—A Noun or a Pronoun which is the subject of a Sentence, is in the *Nominative Case.*

EXAMPLES.—*Animals* run—*John* saws wood—*Resources* are developed.
"The *King* of Shadows loves a shining mark."

OBS. 1.—The Subject of a Sentence may be a Noun, Pronoun, Phrase, or Sentence.

EXAMPLES.

1. *A Noun.*—*Virtue* secures happiness.
2. *A Pronoun.*—"*He* plants his footsteps in the sea."
3. *A Phrase.*—"*To be able to read well,* is a valuable accomplishment."
4. *A Sentence.*—*That good men sometimes commit faults,* can not be denied.

OBS. 2.—In Example (1), "*Virtue*" is the Subject of the Sentence; hence it is in the "*condition*" *of the Nominative.*

DEF. 78.—A Noun or a Pronoun varied in its orthography, so that it may indicate a relation of possession, is in the *Possessive Case.*

OBS. 1.—The Possessive is formed by adding an apostrophe and *s* to the Nominative.

EXAMPLES.

Nominative.—Man,	Boy,	World,	George.
Possessive.—Man's,	Boy's,	World's,	George's.

"I would not yield to be your house's guest."—*Shakspeare.*

OBS. 2.—In a few Words, ending in the Singular, with the sound of *s* or of *c* soft, the additional *s* is omitted for euphony.

EXAMPLES.—"For conscience' sake."—"Festus came into Felix' room."

OBS. 3.—Most Plural Nouns ending in s, add the apostrophe only.

EXAMPLES.

Nominative.—Horses,	Eagles,	Foxes.
Possessive.—Horses',	Eagles',	Foxes'.

"Then shall *man's* pride and dullness comprehend
His *action's, passion's, being's,* use and end."—*Pope.*

OBS. 4.—The term *Possessive Case* is applied to Nouns and Pronouns, to indicate a peculiar variation of Words in respect of *form;* and, because this form *commonly* indicates a relation of possession, it is termed *Possessive Case* But,

OBS. 5.—The Possessive Case does not always indicate "possession or ownership."

Children's shoes.—Here the word "children's" does not imply ownership. It simply specifies "shoes" as to size.

Small shoes.—Here "small" specifies "shoes" in a similar manner. "Small" and "children's" performing similar offices, are similar in their etymology. "Small" is an Adjective—"Children's" is an Adjective.

OBS. 6.—A System of Grammar, having its foundation in the doctrine that Words and other Elements of Sentences are to be classified *according to their offices*—and that is the proper criterion—must class Possessive Nouns and Pronouns as *Adjectives.*

Note the *Exceptions* to this Proposition, Obs. 9, below.

OBS. 7.—Words commonly used as Nouns and Pronouns become Adjectives *whenever their principal office is to limit or describe beings or things;* and they may have the *form* of the *Nominative*, the *Possessive*, or the *Objective Case.*

EXAMPLES.

Nominative Form.—A *gold* pen—a *he* goat.

Possessive Form.—*Wisdom's* ways—*thine* enemy—*my* self.

Objective Form—A *gold* pen—*silver* steel—*them* selves.

OBS. 8.—When such Words are not used as Adjuncts, they are *Substantives*, and are found to be in some case *other than the Possessive*, although they retain the Possessive form. [See Obs. and Examples below, p. 86.]

DEF. 79.—A Noun or a Pronoun which is the Object of a Sentence or a Phrase, is in the *Objective Case.*

EXAMPLES.

1. John saws *wood.*
2. Science promotes *happiness.*
3. "The King of Shadows loves a shining *mark.*"
4. "In the *beginning* God created the *heaven* and the *earth.*"
5. "Scaling yonder *peak*, I saw an *eagle* wheeling near its *brow.*"

DEF. 80.—A Noun or a Pronoun not dependent on any other Word in construction, is in the *Independent Case.*

OBS. 1.—The Independent Case includes

1. The names of persons addressed.

EXAMPLES.—O Liberty!—"Friends, Romans, countrymen."

2.—Names used to specify or define other names previously mentioned.

EXAMPLES.

Paul the *Apostle* wrote to Timothy.

Here, "Paul" is the subject of "wrote;" hence in the Nominative Case (See Def. 78). "Apostle" designates which "Paul" is intended; hence in the Independent Case.

Webster, the *Statesman*, has been mistaken by some foreign authors, for Webster, the *Lexicographer*.

Here, the Words "*Statesman*" and "*Lexicographer*" are used to *limit*, *define*, and *describe* the two "Websters." Hence,

3.—Words thus used are to be regarded as *Logical Adjuncts* (See Part I., p. 29, Obs. 3.)

4.—Nouns used to introduce Independent Phrases.

EXAMPLE.—The *hour* having arrived, we commenced the exercises.

5.—Nouns and Pronouns used in predication with Verbs.

EXAMPLES.—"God is *love*."—"It is *I*."—"The wages of sin is death."

6.—Nouns and Pronouns used for euphony, titles of books, cards, signs, &c.

EXAMPLES.—1. "The moon *herself* is lost in heaven."
2. "Webster's *Dictionary*."
3. "*J. Barber, Son, and Company*."

OBS. 7.—In the English language, Nouns are not varied in form to distinguish the Cases, except for the Possessive. The Case is always determined by its *office*.

(1.) If it is the *Subject* of a Sentence, it is, *therefore*, in the *Nominative Case*.

(2.) If it is the *Object* of a Sentence or the Object of a Phrase, it is, *therefore*, in the *Objective Case*.

(3.) If it performs neither of these offices, and has not a Possessive form, it is not joined to any word going before in construction, and is, *therefore*, in the *Independent Case*.

(4.) If it has a Possessive form, or any other form, and limits or describes a being or a thing, it performs the office of an Adjunct, and is, *therefore*, an *Adjective*.

OBS. 8.—Nouns and Pronouns in the *Nominative* and the *Objective* Cases are used Substantively. In the *Independent* Case they are used *Substantively*, or as *Logical Adjuncts*. (See Obs. 2 & 3, above.) In the *Possessive* Case they are commonly used as *Grammatical Adjuncts*.

OBS. 9.—EXCEPTION.—Nouns and Pronouns of the Possessive form are sometimes used *Substantively;* but, when thus used, they are in the *Nominative,* in the *Objective,* or in the *Independent* Case.

EXAMPLES.

Nominative.—My book is new; *John's* is old.
Mine is little used; *yours* is soiled.

"Mine" is the Subject of the Sentence; hence in the *Nominative Case.*

Objective.—John is a friend of *mine.*

"Mine" is the Object of the Preposition "*of*"; hence in the *Objective Case.*

NOTE.—It is a mistaken notion of certain grammarians, that "mine," in the above example, is equivalent to "my friend," and must therefore be "in the Possessive Case, and governed by friend understood."

John is a friend of *mine;* i. e., he is friendly to me.

John is my enemy; but he is a friend of "*my friend.*"

Is "mine" equivalent to "my friend"? How the notion vanishes before the test.

Independent.—The book is *mine;* it was *yours.*

"Mine" is used *in Predicate* with "is"; hence in the *Independent Case.*

QUESTIONS FOR REVIEW.

PAGE

69.—What are the principal subjects discussed in Part I?.See Rem. 1.
What is *Proximate Analysis* of Sentences?..........See Rem. 2.
What is *Ultimate Analysis?*...................... " "
What is the province of Part II.? ....See Rem. 3.
The Science of Language embraces *what divisions?*

70.—In how many ways are Words *distinguished?*........See Prin.
By their *forms,* how are Words distinguished?...... "
What is a *Radical Word?* ....See Def. 52.
What is a *Derivative Word?* ....See Def. 53.
What is a *Simple Word?* ....See Def. 54.
What is a *Compound Word?* ....See Def. 55.

71.—The *Elements* of a Compound Word are called what?.See Prin.
What is the *Basis* of a Compound Word? ....See Def. 56.
What is an *Adjunct* of a Compound Word? ....See Def. 57.
What is a *Prefix?*—What is a *Suffix?*.............See Def. 58–9

72.—What is a *Separable Radical?* ....See Def. 60.
What is an Inseparable Radical? ....See Def. 61.

PAGE

73.—By their *uses*, how are Words distinguished? .... See Prin.
What is a *Noun?* .... See Def. 62.
What are their *Classes?* .... See Prin.
What is a *Proper Noun?* Give Examples. .... See Def. 63.
74.—What is a *Common Noun?* Give Examples. .... See Def. 64.
What is an *Abstract Noun?* Give Examples. .... See Def. 65.
What is a *Collective Noun?* Give Examples. .... See Def. 66.
What is a *Verbal Noun?* Give Examples. .... See Def. 67.
What are the several *offices* of Nouns? .... See Obs. 3.
75.—What other Words perform Substantive offices?
Give Examples. .... See Obs. 6.
76.—How are Nouns *modified?* .... See Prin.
What Nouns and Pronouns are of the *Masculine Gender?* . See Def. 69.
What of the *Feminine Gender?*—of the Neuter Gender? See Def. 70–1
Are *all* Nouns modified by Gender? .... See Obs. 1–4
77.—How are the distinctions of Gender indicated? ...... See Prin.
78.—What occasions the modifications of *Person?* .... See Rem.
What Nouns and Pronouns are of the *First Person?* .. See Def. 72.
What of the *Second Person?* Give Examples. ...... See Def. 73.
What of the *Third Person?* Give Examples. .... See Def. 74.
What are the Modifications of *Number?* .... See Prin.
What Nouns are of the *Singular Number?* Give Exs. . See Def. 75.
What Nouns are of the *Plural Number?* Give Exs. . See Def. 76.
How are Numbers *indicated?* .... See Obs. 1.
79.—What Nouns add *es* to form the Plural? .... See Obs. 2.
80.—How are the Plurals of *Compound* Nouns formed? .. See Obs. 7, 8, 9.
81.—What is said of the Plural forms of *Foreign Nouns?* . See Obs. 15.
Repeat the Exercises in Gender, Person, and Number,
after the *Models* given.
82.—What does the term *Case* indicate? .... See Rem. 2.
How many Cases in English Grammar? .... See Prin.
83.—When is a Noun or a Pronoun in the *Nominative Case?* . See Def.
When " " " " " *Possessive Case?* .. See Def.
How is the Possessive Case formed? .... See Obs. 1, 2, 3
84.—The term Possessive Case indicates what? .... See Obs. 4, 5.
What *office* is commonly performed by the Possessive
Form of Words? .... See Obs. 6.
When do Words, commonly used as Nouns and Pro-
nouns, *become Adjuncts?* .... See Obs. 7
When is a Noun or a Pronoun in the *Objective Case?* .. See Def.

PAGE
84.—When is a Noun or a Pronoun in the *Independent Case?* See Def. 79
85.—What is said of the variations of Nouns to denote Cases. . See Obs. 7.
86.—When are Nouns of the *Possessive form* used *Substantively?* See Obs. 9

PRONOUNS.

REM.—To avoid an unpleasant repetition of the same Word in a Sentence, a class of Words is introduced as *Substitutes for Names.* Hence,

DEF. 81.—A *Pronoun* is a Word used instead of a Noun.

OBS. 1.—As Pronouns are of general application, the Noun for which any given Pronoun is substituted is commonly determined by the context—and, because it generally precedes the Pronoun, it is called its *Antecedent.*

OBS. 2.—The Antecedent of a Pronoun may be a Word, a Phrase, or a Sentence.

EXAMPLES.

1. *A Word.*—"*James* has injured HIMSELF; HE has studied too much."
2. *A Phrase.*—"*William's abandoning a good situation* in hopes of a better, was never approved by me. IT has been the prime cause of all his troubles."
3. *A Sentence.*—"I am glad *that Charles has secured a liberal education* IT is what few poor boys have the perseverance to accomplish."

CLASSIFICATION OF PRONOUNS.

REM.—Some Pronouns, by their forms, denote their modification of Gender, Person, Number, and Case.

Others *relate* directly to the Nouns for which they are used.

Others, in addition to their ordinary office, are used in *asking questions.*

Others describe the Names for which they are *substituted.* Hence,

PRIN.—Pronouns are distinguished as

Personal,	*Interrogative,* and
Relative,	*Adjective.*

PERSONAL PRONOUN.

DEF. 82.—A *Personal Pronoun* is a Pronoun whose *form* determines its Person and Number.

OBS.—The Personal Pronouns are *Simple* or *Compound*.

LIST.

Simple.—I, thou, you, he, she, it.
Compound.—Myself, thyself, yourself, himself, herself, itself.

MODIFICATION.

REM.—Whenever one Word is used in the place of another, it is properly subjected to the same laws as the other: this is true of Pronouns. Hence,

PRIN.—Pronouns have the same modifications of Gender, Person, Number, and Case, as Nouns.

REM.—To denote these several modifications, some Pronouns are varied in form. This variation of form is called Declension.

DECLENSION OF PRONOUNS.

1. Simple Personal Pronouns.

	Nominative.	*Possessive.*	*Objective.*	*Independent.*
FIRST PERSON.				
Singular.	I,	my,	me,	I or me.*
Plural.	We,	our,	us,	we or us.
SECOND PERSON.				
Singular.	You,	your,	you,	you.
Plural.	You,	your,	you,	you.
SECOND PERSON.—*Solemn Style.*				
Singular.	Thou,	thy	thee,	thou or thee.
Plural.	Ye,	your,	you,	ye or you.
THIRD PERSON.—*Masculine.*				
Singular.	He,	his,	him,	he or him.
Plural.	They	their	them,	they or them.
THIRD PERSON—*Feminine.*				
Singular.	She,	her,	her,	she or her.
Plural.	They,	their,	them,	they or them.
THIRD PERSON.—*Neuter.*				
Singular.	It,	its,	it,	it.
Plural.	They,	their,	them,	they or them.

* Pronouns in the Independent Case commonly take the form of the Nominative, as, "O happy *they!*"—"Ah, luckless *he!*"—"It is *I!*" But they sometimes take the form of the Objective, as, "*Him* excepted."—"I found it to be *him.*"—"Ah *me!*"

OBS. 1.—From the above Paradigm, notice,

1. That Pronouns of the *Third Person Singular only* are varied to denote the *sex.*

2. That the Pronoun *you* is not varied to denote the *Number.* This is a modern innovation; but the idiom is too well established to yield to criticism or protest.

3. That the principal variations are made to distinguish the *Cases.*

4. That, to distinguish the PERSONS, *different words* are employed.

OBS. 2.—*Mine, thine, his, hers, ours, yours,* and *theirs,* are commonly used "*to specify or otherwise describe* Nouns and Pronouns"; and when thus used, they are therefore *Adjectives.* They are placed here to denote their *origin,* and to accommodate such teachers as, by force of habit, are inclined to call them Pronouns in all conditions. (See Possessive Specifying Adjectives, p. 98.)

OBS. 3.—*Mine, thine, his, hers, ours, yours,* and *theirs,* are sometimes used Substantively, i. e., as the Subjects or the Objects of a Sentence—the Objects of Phrases, or as Independent Substantives; and when thus used, they are therefore *Substantives.* (See "Adjective Pronouns.")

EXAMPLES.

Subject of a Sentence.—"My sword and *yours* are kin."—*Shakspeare.*

Object of a Sentence.—"You seek your interests; we follow ours."

Object of a Phrase.—"Therefore leave your forest of beasts for ours of brutes, called men."—*Wesley to Pope.*

"John is a friend of *mine.*"

Independent.—"*Thine* is the kingdom."

"Theirs had been the vigor of their youth."

OBS. 4.—The Pronoun *it* is often used indefinitely, and may have an Antecedent of the First, the Second, or the Third Person, of the Singular or the Plural number; and sometimes it has no antecedent.

EXAMPLES.—"*It* is *I.*"—*It* was *me.* "Was *it thou?*"—Is *it* you.
It was *John.*—Was *it* the *boys?*
It snows.—It blows.—It seems.

OBS. 5.—That for which a Pronoun is used may also be a Phrase or a Sentence.

EXAMPLES.

A Phrase.—1. "IT is good *to be zealously affected in a good thing.*"

A Sentence.—2. "IT remains *that we speak of its moral effects.*"

RELATIVE PRONOUNS.

DEF. 83.—A *Relative Pronoun* is a Pronoun used to introduce a Sentence which qualifies its own antecedent.

EXAMPLES.—1. The youth *who was speaking*, was applauded.
2. We saw the man *whom you described*.
3. "Mount the horse *which I have chosen for thee*."
4. There is something in their hearts *which passes speech*.

OBS. 1.—In Example (1), "who" relates to "youth," and introduces the Auxiliary Sentence ("who was speaking,") whose office it is to describe "youth."

The word "who" not only introduces the Adjunct Sentence, but is also an Element in that Sentence—a Principal Element—the Subject.

In Example (2), "whom you described," is an Auxiliary Sentence, used to describe or point out a particular "man"; "*whom*" introduces that Adjective Sentence, is the *object* of "described," and relates to "man."

LIST.

The Words used as Relative Pronouns are, *who*, *which*, *that*, and *what*.

OBS. 2.—The Words *as* and *than* are sometimes, by ellipsis, used as Relative Pronouns.

EXAMPLES.—1. "Such *as I have* give I unto thee.
2. "We have more *than heart could wish*."

But, generally, on supplying the ellipsis, we may make those words supply the offices of Prepositions or of Conjunctions. Thus,

1. "I give unto thee such [things] as [those which] I have."
2. "We have more [things] than [those things which] heart could wish."

OBS. 3.—*Who* is varied in Declension to indicate the *Cases* only.

Which, *that*, and *what*, are not declined. But the word *whose* is also used as the Possessive of *which*.

Nom.	*Pos.*	*Obj.*	*Indep.*
Who,	Whose,*	Whom,	Who or whom,
Which,	Whose,	Which,	Which,
That,		That,	That,
What,		What,	What.

* *Whose* is always a definitive, attached to Nouns, and may relate to persons or to things; as, "*Whose* I am, and whom I serve."—"*Whose* body Nature is, and God the soul."

OBS. 4.—*Who* is applied to man, or to beings supposed to posses intelligence.

EXAMPLES.—He *who* studies will excel those *who* do not. "He *whom* sea-severed realms obey."

OBS. 5.—*Which* and *what* are applied to brute animals and to things.

EXAMPLES.—The books *which* I lost. The pen *which* I use, is good. We value most *what* costs us most.

OBS. 6.—*That* is applied to man or to things.

EXAMPLES.—Them *that* honor me, I will honor.

"Where is the patience now,
That you so oft have boasted to retain."—*Lear.*

OBS. 7.—*What,* when used as a Relative, is always compound; and is equivalent to *that which,* or the *things which.*

The two Elements of this Word never belong to the same Sentence; one part introduces a Sentence which qualifies the antecedent part of the same word.

"Our proper bliss depends on what we blame."

In this example, "what" is a Compound Relative, equivalent to the two words, *that which.* *That,* the Antecedent part, is the object of "on;" "*which,*" the Relative part, is the object of "blame." The Auxiliary sentence, "we blame which," is used to qualify "that." [See page 00, Diagram 00.]

OBS. 8.—The Compounds, *whoever, whosoever, whichever, whichsoever, whatever,* and *whatsoever,* are construed similarly to *what.*

INTERROGATIVE PRONOUNS.

DEF. 84.—An *Interrogative Pronoun* is a Pronoun used to ask a question.

EXAMPLES.—"*Who* will show us any good?"
"*Which* do you prefer?"
"*What* will satisfy him?"

LIST.

OBS. 1.—The Interrogative Pronouns are,

Who,........applied to man.
Which, } ....applied to man or to things.
What, }

OBS. 2.—A Sentence is made *Interrogative*,

1. By a transposition of the Principal Elements,—the Predicate being placed before its Subject.

EXAMPLES.—*Will* you go?
"*Did* Claudius waylay Milo?"

2. By the use of an Interrogative Pronoun.

EXAMPLES.—"*What* will a man give in exchange for his soul?"
"*Who* will show us any good?"

OBS. 3.—The Antecedent—technically so called—of an Interrogative Pronoun, is the Word which answers the question.

EXAMPLES.—*Who* gave the valedictory? *William.*
Whom shall we obey? Your *parents.*

OBS. 4.—*Which* and *what* are often used as *Interrogative Adjectives.*

EXAMPLES.—*Which* book is yours? "*What* evil hath he done?"

OBS. 5.—A Word which asks a question is to be construed as is the Word which answers it.

EXAMPLES.—*Who* has the book? *John* [has the book.]
Whose book is it? [It is] *William's* [book.]

"*Who*" is the Subject of the Sentence given; hence in the Nominative Case.

"*John*" is the Subject of a similar Sentence; hence in the Nominative Case.

"*William's*" describes "book"; hence an *Adjunct* of "book."

"*Whose*" has the same construction; hence an Adjunct of "book."

ADJECTIVE PRONOUNS.

DEF. 85.—An *Adjective Pronoun* is a Definitive Word, used to supply the place of the Word which it limits.

EXAMPLE.—"*Some* [ ] said one thing, and *some*, *another*" [ ].

OBS. 1.—In this Example, "some" defines *people* (understood), and is, therefore, used Adjectively. It is substituted for the Word "people," constituting the Subject of the Sentence; hence it is used Substantively. But the Substantive office being the principal office, the Word is properly called a Pronoun. Its secondary office being Adjective, it is properly called an *Adjective Pronoun.*

OBS. 2.—An Adjective Pronoun always performs, at the same time, two distinct offices—an *Adjective* office and a *Substantive* office; and it may have, at the same time, an *Adjective* and an *Adverbial* Adjunct.

EXAMPLE.—"*The professedly* good are not always really so."

"Good" describes people (understood), thus performing an Adjective office.

"Good" is the Subject of the Sentence; hence a Substantive.

As a *Substantive*, "good" is limited by the Adjective "*the*."

As an *Adjective*, "good" is modified by the Adverb, "*professedly*."

OBS. 3.—Words thus used are, by some grammarians, called "Pronominal Adjectives." We prefer the term, "Adjective Pronoun," because the *Principal* office is *Substantive*—the Adjective office being *secondary* in the structure of Sentences and Phrases.

OBS. 4.—The following Words are often thus used:—

All,	Former,	Neither,	Such,
Both,	Last,	None,	That,
Each,	Latter,	One,	These,
Either,	Least,	Other,	Those,.
Few,	Less,	Several,	This.

Most specifying and all qualifying Adjectives may be thus used.

EXAMPLES.—"The *good* alone are *great*." "The *poor* respect the *rich*." "One step from the *sublime* to the *ridiculous*."

OBS. 5.—Mine, thine, his, hers, ours, yours, and theirs, are used—in common with other Definitives—substantively, *i. e.*, as the Representatives of Nouns, which it is their primary office to specify. They are then properly called Adjective Pronouns

EXAMPLES.—"He is a friend of mine." "Thine is the kingdom." "Theirs had been the vigor of his youth."

PROMISCUOUS EXAMPLES OF ADJECTIVE PRONOUNS.

1. "Brutus and Aruns killed *each other*."
2. "Thou shalt be *all* in *all*, and I in thee."—*Milton*.
3. "They sat down in ranks, by *hundreds* and by *fifties*."
4. "Teach me to feel another's woe, to hide the fault I see;
   The mercy I to *others* show, that mercy show to me."—*Pope*.
5. "Who are the *called*, according to his purpose."

RECAPITULATION.

- WORDS are distinguished by their
  - Forms
    - Radical,
      - Separable,
      - Inseparable.
    - Derivative,
      - Prefix,
      - Root,
      - Suffix.
    - Simple,
    - Compound,
      - Basis.
      - Adjunct.
  - and
  - Uses.
    - Noun,
    - Pronoun,
    - Adjective,
    - Verb,
    - Adverb,
    - Preposition,
    - Conjunction,
    - Exclamation,

- NOUNS are
  - Proper
  - or
  - Common.
    - Substantive,
    - Abstract,
    - Collective,
    - Verbal.

- PRONOUNS are
  - Personal,
  - Relative,
  - Interrogative,
  - Adjective.

MODIFICATION OF NOUNS AND PRONOUNS.

- NOUNS and PRONOUNS are modified by
  - Gender,
    - Masculine,
    - Feminine,
    - Neuter.
  - Person,
    - First,
    - Second,
    - Third.
  - Number
    - Singular,
    - Plural.
  - Case,
    - Nominative,
    - Possessive,
    - Objective,
    - Independent.

QUESTIONS FOR REVIEW.

PAGE

88.—What is a *Pronoun?* .... See Def.
Why are Pronouns *used?* .... See Rem.
What is an *Antecedent* of a Pronoun? .... See Obs. 1
Antecedents may *consist* of what? .... See Obs. 2
Why are Pronouns *classified?* .... See Rem.
How are Pronouns *classified?* .... See Prin.
What is a *Personal Pronoun?* .... See Def.

89.—How are Personal Pronouns *distinguished?* .... See Obs.
How are Pronouns *modified?* .... See Prin.
Decline the Personal Pronoun.

90.—What Pronouns are varied in form to denote *Gender?* . See Obs. 1.
For what are the principal variations made? .... See "
How do we distinguish the *Persons* of Pronouns? ... See "
Why are Possessive Specifying Adjectives placed with Pronouns? .... See Obs. 2.
When are *mine, thine, his, hers, ours, yours,* and *theirs* used as *Substantives?* and why? .... See Obs. 3.
Make Sentences having each of these Words as *Subjects*—as *Objects*—as *Objects of Phrases*—in *Predicate* with a Verb.
What may be some of the different Antecedents of it? . See Obs. 4.

91.—What is a *Relative Pronoun?* .... See Def.
Give the List of Relative Pronouns.
What is said of the words *as* and *than?* .... See Obs. 2.
Which of the Relative Pronouns are varied in form? . See Obs. 3.

92.—What are the peculiar uses of *who, which,* and *that?* . See Obs. 4, 5, 6.
What is there peculiar in the use of the Word *what?* . See Obs. 7.
What other Double Relatives have we? .... See Obs. 8.
What is an *Interrogative Pronoun?* .... See Def.
Give the List of Interrogative Pronouns .... See Obs. 1.

93.—Sentences are made Interrogative—*how?* .... See Obs. 2.
What is the *Antecedent* of an Interrogative Pronoun? . See Obs. 3.
An Interrogative Pronoun is to be construed—*how?*—See Obs. 5.
What is an *Adjective Pronoun?* .... See Def.

94.—What *distinct offices* are performed by Adjective Pronouns? . See Obs. 2.
Why is the term Adjective Pronoun given to this class of Words? .... See Obs. 3.
Give the List of Words most frequently used as Adjective Pronouns .... See Obs. 4.

ADJECTIVES.

REM.—As things possess individuality, and have points of difference from each other, so we have Words which point out and describe those things, and mark their differences from other things. Hence,

DEF. 86.—An *Adjective* is a Word used to qualify or otherwise describe a Noun or a Pronoun.

EXAMPLES.—Good—amiable—the—our—earnest—falling—young—conscientious—correct—famous.

A good boy.	*Falling* leaves.
An amiable young lady.	*Conscientious* Christian.
Our national resources.	*Correct* expression.
An earnest culture.	*Famous* orators.
A loving sister.	*Injured* fruit.

CLASSIFICATION.

REM.—Adjectives are used—

1. To express a quality—as, *good* boy—*red* rose—*sweet* apple.
2. To specify or limit—as, *the* book—*thy* pen—*three* boys.
3. To express, incidentally, a condition, state, or act—as, *loving*—*wheeling*—*injured*. Hence,

PRIN.—Adjectives are distinguished as

Qualifying Adjectives,
Specifying Adjectives, and
Verbal Adjectives.

DEF. 87.—A *Qualifying Adjective* is a Word used to describe a Substantive by expressing a quality.

EXAMPLES.—Good—sweet—cold—honorable—amiable—virtuous.

An *honorable* man.	Some *good* fruit.
An *amiable* disposition.	Three *sweet* oranges.
A *virtuous* woman.	Much *cold* water.

DEF. 88.—A *Specifying Adjective* is a Word used to define or limit the application of a Substantive without denoting a quality.

EXAMPLES.—A—an—the—this—that—some—three—my.

A man of letters.	*That* mountain in the distance.
An educated man.	*Some* good fruit.
The question at issue.	*Three* sweet oranges.
This road.	*My* enemy.

OBS. 1.—Adjectives derived from Proper Nouns are called *Proper Adjectives*.

EXAMPLES.—Arabian—Grecian—Turkish—French.

OBS. 2.—*Which*, *what*, and sometimes *whose*, when used as Adjectives, are called *Interrogative Adjectives when they indicate a question*.

EXAMPLES.—1. *Which* side will you take?
2. *What* evil hath he done?
3. *Whose* book is that?

REM.—Adjectives may specify—
1. By simply pointing out things—by limiting or designating.
2. By denoting relation of ownership, adaptation, or origin.
3. By denoting number, definite or indefinite. Hence,

PRIN.—Specifying Adjectives are distinguished as *Pure*, *Numeral*, and *Possessive*.

DEF. 89.—A *Pure Adjective* is a Word used only to point out or designate things.

EXAMPLES.—The—that—those—such—next—same—other.

Thou art *the* man.	The *next* class.
That question is settled.	The *same* lesson.
Those books are received.	*Other* cares intrude.
"*Such* shames are common."	*Any* man may learn wisdom.

DEF. 90.—A *Possessive Adjective* is a Word that describes a being or thing by indicating a relation of ownership, origin, fitness, &c.

EXAMPLES.—My—our—their—whose—children's—John's—Teacher's.

My father—*my* neighbor.	*Children's* shoes.
Our enemies.	*John's* horse.
Their losses are severe.	*Teacher's* absence.

"O *my* offense is rank: it smells to heaven;
It hath the primal, eldest curse upon it,
A *brother's* murder."

"He heard the *king's* command, and saw that *writing's* truth

NOTE.—A Possessive Adjective is generally derived from a substantive, by changing the Nominative into the Possessive form.

NUMERAL ADJECTIVES.

DEF. 91.—A *Numeral Adjective* is a Word used to denote *Number.*

EXAMPLES.—One—ten—first—second—fourfold—few—many.

OBS. 1.—Numeral Adjectives may be,

Cardinal.—One—two—three—four.
Ordinal.—First—second—third—fourth.
Multiplicative.—Single—double—quadruple.
Indefinite.—Few—many—some (denoting number).

OBS. 2.—*A* and *an*, when they denote number, are to be classed as Numeral Adjectives.

EXAMPLES.—"Not *a* drum was heard, nor a funeral note."
"Not *an* instance is on record."

VERBAL ADJECTIVES.

DEF. 92.—A *Verbal Adjective* is a Word used to describe a Noun or a Pronoun, by expressing, incidentally, a condition, state, or act.

OBS.—This class of Adjectives consists of Participles, used primarily to describe Nouns and Pronouns.

EXAMPLES.

A *running* brook.	I saw a boy *running* to school.
A *standing* pond.	Another *standing* by the way.
Disputed territory.	It is a truth *undisputed*.
Undoubted fact.	It is a fact *undoubted*.

"*Scaling* yonder peak,
I saw an eagle *wheeling* near its brow."

In this example the Sentence is, "*I saw eagle:*" and "scaling yonder peak," is a Phrase used to describe "I." "Wheeling near its brow," describes "eagle." *Scaling* and *wheeling* are Participles used to describe a Noun and a Pronoun—hence they are, in their office, Adjectives. (See Def. 86.) They describe by expressing (not in the character of Predicates, but), "incidentally, a condition, state, or act," of "I" and "eagle"—hence they are Verbal Adjectives.

Rem. 1.—To render the classification more simple, I have preferred to class all Participles used *chiefly* to describe Nouns and Pronouns, as *Adjectives*—and, because they are derived from Verbs and retain more or less of the properties of the Verbs from which they are derived, I use the term *Verbal Adjectives*.

But Teachers who are unwilling to do more than simply to call them Participles, will not find it difficult to adapt their views to the *plan* of this work; the Pupil being taught that—

"*Participles, like Adjectives, belong to Nouns and Pronouns.*"

And, in the use of Diagrams—

"*Participles* used to limit Substantives, *occupy the same position as Adjectives*."

Rem. 2.—Participles used as Adjectives, commonly retain their verbal character, and like their Verbs, may have Objects after them. Hence,

Prin.—Verbal Adjectives are distinguished as *Transitive* and *Intransitive*.

EXAMPLES.

Intransitive.—"He possessed a *well-balanced* mind."
"Truth, *crushed* to earth, will rise again."
Transitive.—"*Scaling* yonder *peak*, I saw an eagle."
"We saw the children *picking berries*."

MODIFICATION OF ADJECTIVES.

REM.—Most Qualifying Adjectives express, by variations in form, different degrees of quality. Hence,

PRIN.—Some Adjectives are varied in form to denote *Comparison.*

There may be four degrees of Comparison.

1. *Diminutive,*....bluish,........saltish.
2. *Positive,* ......blue, ...salt.
3. *Comparative,*...bluer,.........salter.
4. *Superlative,* ...bluest, ...saltest.

DEF. 93.—The *Diminutive Degree* denotes an amount of the quality less than the Positive.

It is commonly formed by adding *ish* to the form of the Positive.

DEF. 94.—The *Positive Degree* expresses quality in its simplest form, without a comparison.

EXAMPLES.—Large—pure—rich—good—glimmering.
"Now fades the *glimmering* landscape on the sight."

DEF. 95.—The *Comparative Degree* expresses an increase or a decrease of the Positive.

It is commonly formed by adding *er*, or the Words *more* or *less*, to the form of the Positive.

EXAMPLES.—Larger—purer—richer—*more* common—*less* objectionable.
"*Richer* by far is the heart's adoration."

DEF. 96.—The *Superlative Degree* expresses the highest increase of the quality of the Adjective.

It is commonly formed by adding *est*, or the Words *most* or *least*, to the form of the Positive.

EXAMPLES.—Larg*est*—pur*est*—*most* ungrateful—upper*most*.
"The purest treasure mortal times afford
Is—spotless reputation."

OBS. 1.—By the use of other Words, the degrees of Comparison may be rendered indefinitely numerous.

EXAMPLES.—Cautious—*somewhat* cautious—*very* cautious—*unusually* cautious—*remarkably* cautious—*exceedingly* cautious—*too little* cautious—*uncautious*—*quite uncautious*.

OBS. 2.—Comparison descending, is expressed by prefixing the Words *less* and *least* to the Adjective.

EXAMPLES.—Wise, *less* wise, *least* wise—ambitious, *less* ambitious, *least* ambitious.

OBS. 3.—Most Adjectives of two or more syllables, are compared by prefixing the words *more* and *most*, or *less* and *least*, to the Positive.

EXAMPLES.

Positive.	*Comparative.*	*Superlative.*
Careful,	*more* careful,	*most* careful.
Careful,	*less* careful,	*least* careful.

OBS. 4.—Some Adjectives may be compared by either method specified above.

EXAMPLES.

Positive.	*Comparative.*	*Superlative.*
Remote,	remot*er*,	remot*est*.
Remote,	*more* remote,	*most* remote.

IRREGULAR COMPARISON.

PRIN.—Some Adjectives are irregular in comparison.

EXAMPLES.

Positive.	*Comparative.*	*Superlative.*
Good,	better,	best.
Bad,	worse,	worst.
Little,	less,	least.
Many,	more,	most.
Much,	more,	most.
Far,	farther, further,	farthest, furthermost.
Old,	older, elder.	oldest, eldest.

OBS. 5.—Some Adjectives want the Positive.

EXAMPLES.—After, aftermost—nether, nethermost.

"He was in the *after* part of the ship."

OBS. 6.—Some Adjectives want the Comparative.

EXAMPLES.—Top—topmost.

"He stood upon the *topmost* round."

OBS. 7.—Some Adjectives can not be compared—the qualities they indicate not being susceptible of increase or diminution.

EXAMPLES.—Round—square—triangular—infinite.

RECAPITULATION.

ADJECTIVES are distinguished as	Qualifying, ...	Superlative, Comparative, Positive, Diminutive.
	Specifying, ...	Pure, Numeral, Possessive.
	Verbal, ...	Transitive, Intransitive.

EXERCISES.

☞ Let the Pupil determine which of the following Adjectives are Qualifying, which are Specifying, and which are Verbal. Of the Qualifying Adjectives, which can be compared, and how compared—of the Specifying Adjectives, which are Pure, which Numeral, which Possessive—of the Verbal, which are Transitive, which are Intransitive.

Able,	False,	That,	Forgotten,
Bold,	Good,	Three,	Standing,
Capable,	Honest,	Tenth,	Loving,
Doubtful,	Infinite,	Twice,	Admonished,
Eager,	Just,	Several,	Unknown.

☞ Let the Pupil point out the Adjectives, Nouns, and Pronouns, in the following Sentences, and name their classes and modifications. Let him be careful to give a reason for the classification and modification of each, by repeating the appropriate definitions and observations.

1. *Good* scholars secure *the highest* approbation of *their* teacher.
2. *Some* men do not give *their* children *a proper* education.
3. A trifling accident often produces great results.
4. An ignorant rich man is less esteemed than a wise poor man.
5. The richest treasure mortal times afford, is, spotless reputation.
6. "These dim vaults,
These winding aisles, of human pomp or pride,
7. Report not. No fantastic carvings show
The boast of our vain race, to change the form
8. Of thy fair works. Thou art in the soft winds
That run along the summits of these trees
9. In music: thou art in the cooler breath,
That, from the inmost darkness of the place,
10. Comes, scarcely felt: the barky trunks, the ground,
The fresh, moist ground, are all instinct with thee."

FIRST MODEL.

These...describes "vaults;" hence an Adjective—for "a Word used to qualify or otherwise describe a Noun or Pronoun, is an Adjective."

" Specifies; hence Specifying—for "an Adjective used only to specify is a Specifying Adjective."

Dim....qualifies "vaults;" hence an Adjective—for "a Word used to qualify or otherwise describe a Noun or Pronoun, is an Adjective."

" Expresses a quality; hence Qualifying—for "a Word used to describe a Noun by expressing a quality, is a Qualifying Adjective."

Vaults ..is a Name; hence a Noun—for "the Name of a being, place, or thing, is a Noun."

" Name of a sort or class; hence common—for "a Name used to designate a class or sort of beings, places, or things; is a Common Noun."

" Spoken of; hence, Third Person—for "the Name of a person or thing spoken of, is of the Third Person."

" Denotes more than one; hence Plural Number—for "Nouns denoting more than one, are of the Plural Number."

" Subject of the Sentence; hence Nominative Case—for the subject of a Sentence is in the Nominative Case."

Winding..describes "aisles;" hence an Adjective—for "a Word used to qualify or otherwise describe a Noun or Pronoun, is an Adjective."
Describes, by expressing a condition; hence Verbal—for "a Word used to describe a Noun by expressing incidentally a condition, state, or act, is a Verbal Adjective."

Human..describes "pomp" or "pride;" hence an Adjective—for "a Word used to qualify or otherwise describe a Noun or Pronoun, is an Adjective."
Expresses a quality; hence Qualifying—for "a Word used to describe a Noun by expressing a quality, is a Qualifying Adjective."

[It is profitable to repeat the Definitions until they become familiar: after that they may be omitted—the parts of speech and the classes and modifications of the several Words being simply named, as in the following exercise.]

SECOND MODEL.

"No fantastic carvings show
The boast of our vain race, to change the form
Of thy fair works."

			Class.	*Person.*	*[illegible]r.*	*Case.*
No	is an	Adjective	Specifying,	——	[illegible]	limits "carvings."
Fantastic	"	Adjective	Qualifying,	——	——	qualifies "carvings."
Carvings	"	Noun	Common,	Third,	Plu.	Nom. to "show."
The	"	Adjective	Specifying,	——	——	limits "boast."
Boast	"	Noun	Common,	Third,	Sing.	Obj. of "show."

☞ The Teacher will abridge or extend these Exercises at pleasure. Then let four Sentences be made, each containing the Word *good*, so that, in the first, it will qualify the Subject—in the second, the Object—in the third, the Object of a Phrase attached to the Subject—in the fourth, the Object of a Phrase attached to the Object.

In like manner use the Words *amiable—honest—industrious—wise—this—some—loving—loved.* Thus,

1. That *amiable* young lady was at the lecture.
2. We saw the *amiable* gentleman.
3. The benefits of an *amiable* disposition are numerous.
4. She possesses the advantages of an *amiable* temper

ADJECTIVE PHRASES AND SENTENCES.

REM.—Things may be described not only by *Words* but also by *Phrases* and by *Sentences.*

EXAMPLES.

Adjective Phrases.—1. "The TIME *of my departure* is at hand."
2. "Night is the TIME *for rest.*"
3. "Turn, gentle HERMIT *of the vale.*"

Adjective Sentences.—1. "HE *that getteth wisdom* loveth his own soul."
2. Mount the HORSE *which I have chosen for thee.*
3. "THOU, *whose spell can raise the dead,*
Bid the prophet's form appear."

QUESTIONS FOR REVIEW.

PAGE

97.—What is an *Adjective?* .... See Def. 86.
Why are Adjectives used? .... See Rem. 1.
For what various purposes are Adjectives *used?* .... See Rem. 2.
How are Adjectives *distinguished?* .... See Prin.
What is a *Qualifying* Adjective? .... See Def. 87.
98.—What is a *Specifying* Adjective? .... See Def. 88.
What is [illegible]*ner* Adjective? .... See Obs. 1.
What is an *In*[illegible]*tive* Adjective? .... See Obs.
How are Specify[illegible]ectives *distinguished?* ...... See Prin.
What is a *Pure* Specifying Adjective? .... See Def. 89.
What is a *Possessive* Specifying Adjective? .... See Def. 90
99.—*How* are Possessive Adjectives *formed?* .... See Note.
What is a *Numeral* Adjective? .... See Def. 91.
What is a *Verbal* Adjective? .... See Def. 92.
100.—*How* are Verbal Adjectives *distinguished?* .... See Prin.
101.—*How* are Adjectives modified? .... See Prin.
How many Degrees of Comparison may some Adjectives have? .... See Prin.
When is an Adjective of the *Diminutive* form? ..... See Def. 93.
When " " *Positive* " ..... See Def. 94.
When " " *Superlative* " ..... See Def. 96
102.—What is said of Comparison *descending?* .... See Obs. 2.
When do we *prefix* a Word to denote comparison? . See Obs. 3.
What Adjectives are compared *irregularly?* .... See Prin.
103.—Are *all* Adjectives compared? .... See Obs. 7

VERBS.

REM.—As all things in the universe *live*, *move*, or *have a being*, we necessarily have a class of Words used to express the *act*, *being*, or *state* of those things. Hence,

DEF. 97.—A *Verb* is a Word used to express the act, being, or state of a person or thing.

CLASSIFICATION.

REM.—The act expressed by some Verbs *passes over* to an Object. Hence,

PRIN.—Verbs are distinguished as
Transitive or *Intransitive*.

DEF. 98.—A *Transitive Verb* is a Verb that expresses an action which terminates on an Object.

EXAMPLES.—John *saws wood*—God *created heaven and earth*.

DEF. 99.—An *Intransitive Verb* is a Verb that expresses the being or state of its Subject, or an action which does not terminate on an Object.

EXAMPLES.—Animals *run*—I *sit*—John *is* sleepy.

OBS. 1.—Some Verbs are used transitively or intransitively.

EXAMPLES.—"Cold *blows* the wind."
"The wind *blows* the dust."
"It has *swept* through the earth."
"Jane has *swept* the floor."
"God *moves* in a mysterious way."
"Such influences do not *move* me."

DEF. 100.—The Verbs *be*, *become*, and other Intransitive Verbs, whose subjects are not represented as performing a physical act, are called *Neuter Verbs*.

EXAMPLES.—He *is*—God *exists*—we *become* wise—they *die*.

LIST.

OBS.—The Verbs commonly called Neuter are—*appertain*—*be*—*become*—*belong*—*exist*—*lie*—*rest*—*seem*—*sleep*.

MODIFICATION OF VERBS.

REM.—Verbs that denote action have two methods of representing the action.

1st—As done *by* its Subject—as, *Jane loves* Lucy.

2d—As done *to* its Subject—as, *Lucy is loved by* Jane.

Hence,

PRIN.—Transitive Verbs have two *Voices*—*Active* and *Passive*.

DEF. 101.—The *Active Voice* represents the Subject as performing an action.

EXAMPLE.—Columbus *discovered* America.

DEF. 102.—The *Passive Voice* represents the Subject as being acted upon.

EXAMPLE.—America *was discovered* by Columbus.

OBS. 1.—The same fact may commonly be expressed by either the Active or the Passive form.

EXAMPLES.—William *assists* Charles. } The same fact stated.
Charles *is assisted* by William. }

"William," the Subject of the Active Verb, becomes the Object of "by," when the Verb becomes Passive; and "Charles," the Object of the Active Verb, becomes the Subject of the Passive.

OBS. 2.—In the English language, the formation of the Passive Voice is less simple than in many other languages. Thus, the corresponding assertions,

IN LATIN—*Doceo*, in the Active Voice, has *Doceor* in the Passive.
IN ENGLISH—*I teach*, " " " *I am taught* " "

Hence, the English Verb does not form its Passive Voice by an "inflection of the form of the Active," but by combining the Verb *be*, in its various modifications, with a Participle of the given Verb.

EXAMPLES.

Active.—To see,	I love,	They applaud,	Man worships
Passive.—To *be* seen,	I *am* loved,	They *are* applauded,	God *is* worshipped.

OBS. 3.—Most Transitive Verbs may take the Passive form.

OBS. 4.—A Verb taking the Passive form becomes grammatically intransitive. The action is directed to no object. The Subject receives the action.

OBS. 5.—But few Intransitive Verbs take the Passive form.

EXAMPLES.

We *laughed* at his clownish performances.—(Active Intrans.)
His clownish performance *was laughed at.*—(Passive.)

MODE.

REM.—In addition to their primary signification, Verbs perform a secondary office—*i. e.*, they indicate some attendant or qualifying circumstances. This is indicated by the variations of the form of the Verb, or by prefixing Auxiliary Words.

1. A Verb may simply express a fact.
2. It may express a fact as *possible, probable, obligatory,* &c.
3. It may express a fact *conditionally.*
4. It may express a *command* or request.
5. It may express the *name* of an act, or a fact unlimited by a subject. Hence,

PRIN.—Verbs have five modes of expressing their signification—

Indicative, | *Subjunctive,*
Potential, | *Imperative,* and
Infinitive.

DEF. 103.—A Verb used simply to indicate or assert a fact or to ask a question, is in the

Indicative Mode.

EXAMPLES.—"God *created* the heaven and the earth."
"*Is* he not honest?" "Whence *come* wars?"

DEF. 104.—A Verb indicating *probability power*, *will*, or *obligation*, of its subject, is in the

Potential Mode.

OBS.—Words which may be regarded as signs of the Potential Mode, are, *may—might—can—could—must—shall—should—will—would*, either alone, or followed by the Word *have*.

EXAMPLES.—I *may go*—you *might have gone*—John *should study*—Mary *can learn*—It *could not be done*—John *shall study*.

DEF. 105.—A Verb expressing a fact conditionally (hypothetically) is in the

Subjunctive Mode.

EXAMPLES.—"If he *repent*, forgive him."

OBS.—*If*, *though*, *unless*, and other Conjunctions, are commonly used with the Subjunctive Mode. But they are not to be regarded as the signs of this Mode, for they are also used with the Indicative and the Potential.

EXAMPLES.—If the boat *goes* to-day, I shall go in it.
I *would* stay if I *could* conveniently.

The condition expressed by "if the boat goes," is assumed as a fact—hence, "goes" is in the Indicative Mode.

NOTE.—The Subjunctive Mode is limited to Auxiliary (Adverbial) Sentences.

DEF. 106.—A Verb used to command or intreat is in the *Imperative Mode.*

EXAMPLES.—1. "If he repent, *forgive* him."
2. "*Come* to the bridal chamber, Death!"

OBS.—As we can command only a person or thing addressed, the subject of an Imperative Verb must be of the Second Person; and, as a person addressed is supposed to be present to the speaker, the name of the subject is usually understood.

EXAMPLES.—*Cry* aloud—*Spare* not.

But it is often expressed.

"Go *ye* into all the world."

DEF. 107.—A Verb used without limitation by a Subject, is in the

Infinitive Mode.

OBS. 1.—The Preposition *to*, is usually placed before the Infinitive Verb.

EXAMPLES.—"*To* enjoy is *to* obey."
"I came not here *to* talk."

OBS. 2.—But that Word is sometimes suppressed.

EXAMPLES.—"Let me hear thy voice, awake, and bid her
Give me new and glorious hopes."

OBS. 3.—As a Verb in the Infinitive has no grammatical Subject, it cannot be a Predicate. It is used, in combination with its Preposition,

1. Substantively; as—*To do good* is the duty of all.
2. Adjectively; as—The way *to do good*.
3. Adverbially; as—I ought *to do good*.

PARTICIPLES.

REM.—In the three Sentences,

1. Birds *sing*,
2. Birds are *singing*,
3. *Singing* birds delight us,

the Word "*sing*" (in Example 1) is a Verb—used to assert an act of "birds."

In Example (2) "singing" is derived from the same Verb; and *with the aid of the Auxiliary Verb* "are," it makes the same assertion.

In Example (3), "*singing*" does not *assert*, but it *assumes* the same act.

The same signification remains in the three Words, while they perform different grammatical offices. Hence,

DEF. 108.—A *Participle* is a word derived from a Verb, retaining the signification of its Verb, while it also performs the office of some other "part of speech."

OBS. 1.—Participles are Derivative Words, formed from their Radicals—commonly by the addition of *ing* or *ed*.

EXAMPLES.—Be,....being. Love,....loving,....loved.
Have,..having. Walk,...walking,...walked.

REM.—A Participle is used with or without an Auxiliary prefixed Hence,

PRIN —Participles are *Simple* or *Compound.*

DEF. 109.—A *Simple Participle* is a single Word derived from its Verb.

EXAMPLES.—Loving, loved—having, had—being, been.

DEF. 110.—A *Compound Participle* consists of a simple Participle, with the Auxiliary Participles "having" or "being," or "having been."

EXAMPLES.

Simple,	1. Loving,	Fearing.
	2. Loved,	Feared.
Compound,	3. Being loved,	Being feared.
	4. Having loved,	Having feared.
	5. Having been loved,	Having been feared.
	6. Having been loving,	Having been fearing.

REM.—In giving names to the different Participles, grammarians are not agreed. By different authors the Simple Participles are distinguished as *Present* and *Past,*
" Active and Passive,
" Imperfect and Perfect,
" First and Second, and by other terms.

REM.—While none of the above names can be regarded as wholly free from imperfections, those first mentioned are perhaps less objectionable than others. Hence,

PRIN.—The *Simple Participles* are distinguished as

1. *Present,* or *First;* and,
2. *Past,* or *Second.*

DEF. 111.—The *Present Participle* is the Participle formed by adding *ing* to the root of the Verb, and commonly indicates a present act, being, or state.

EXAMPLES.—Being—having—loving—walking—doing—fearing.

OBS. 1.—When the Participle is used with a Verb, the *time* is indicated by the *Verb*, and may be Present, Past, or Future.

EXAMPLES.—*Present.*—I am writing letters.
Past.—I was writing letters.
Future.—I shall be writing letters.

DEF. 112.—A *Past Participle* is the Participle that is regularly formed by adding *ed* to the root of its Verb.

EXAMPLES.—Lov*ed*—fear*ed*—hat*ed*—respect*ed*.

OBS. 1.—The Past Participles of Irregular Verbs are variously formed (See list.)

OBS. 2.—The Past Participle may be used with a Verb indicating time, *Present*, *Past*, or *Future*.

EXAMPLES.—*Present.*—I am loved,........William is seen.
Past.—I was loved,........William was seen.
Future.—I shall be loved, ...William will be seen.

OBS. 3.—The Present Participle is commonly *Active* in signification.

EXAMPLES.—1. A *falling* leaf.
2. A *fading* flower.
3. "*Scaling* yonder peak,
I saw an eagle, *wheeling* near its brow."

OBS. 4.—The Past Participle is commonly *Passive* in signification.

EXAMPLES.—1. *Injured* reputation.
2. *Lost* opportunity.
3. "Truth *crushed* to earth, will rise again."

OBS. 5.—The Past Participle, preceded by the Auxiliary *having* is used actively.

EXAMPLES.—1. Having loved.
2. Having lost a day.
3. "The hour *having arrived*, we commenced the exercises."
4. *Having seen* the elephant, the rustic was satisfied.

OBS. 6.—Preceded by the Auxiliary *being*, or *having been*, the Past Participle is used Passively..

EXAMPLES.—1. Being loved.
2. Having been censured for idleness, John resolved to be diligent.

OBS. 7.—A Compound Participle may be *Present* or *Prior Present*—*Active* or *Passive*.

EXAMPLES.—*Present*.—Being loved, ...Being seen.
Prior Present.—Having loved, ...Having seen.
Active. { Having loved, ...Having seen.
Having been walking,....Having been seeing.
Passive. { Being loved,... ....Being seen,
Having been loved,......Having been seen.

OBS. 8—Participles have no distinct Etymological character. They find a place in all the "parts of speech," being used as

1. *Nouns*,
2. *Adjectives*,
3. *Adverbs*,
4. *Prepositions*,
5. *Conjunctions*,
6. *Exclamations*.
7. In *Predicate* with Auxiliary Verbs.
8. To introduce a *Participial Phrase*.

EXAMPLES.

1. *Noun*. ....(*a*). *Singing* is a pleasing exercise.
(*b*). William maintains a fair *standing* in society.
(*c*). "In the *beginning*, God created the heaven."
2. *Adjective*........(*d*). A *running* BROOK—a *standing* TREE.
(*e*). Behold the GOOSE *standing* on one foot.
3. *Adverb*. ....(*f*). "'Tis strange; 'tis *passing* STRANGE."
(*g*). The task was *exceedingly* DIFFICULT.
4. *Preposition*. .....(*h*). "I speak *concerning* Christ and the Church."
(*i*). "Nothing was said *touching* that question."
5. *Conjunction*. .....(*k*). "*Seeing* we can not agree, the discussion may be dropped."
6. *Exclamation*. ....(*l*). *Shocking! Astonishing!*
7. *In Predicate*. ....(*m*). "Birds are *singing*—bees are *humming*."
8. *Leader of Phrase*. (*n*). *Wounding* the feelings of others.
(*o*). "Avoid *wounding the feelings of others*."
(*p*). A habit of *moving quickly*, is another way of *gaining time*.

OBS. 9.—Participles, like the Verbs from which they are derived, ar *Transitive* or *Intransitive*.

OBS. 10.—A Participle used as a Preposition, *must* be Transitive.

EXAMPLES.—I speak *concerning Christ* and the *Church*.

OBS. 11.—A Participle used as a Noun, as an Adjective, or in Predicate, or as the Leader of a Participial Phrase, *may* be Intransitive.

EXAMPLES.

1. *Noun*......"*Scolding* has long been considered ungenteel."
2. *Adjective*..."The curfew tolls the knell of *parting* day."
3. *Predicate*...Spring-time of year is coming.

OBS. 12.—A Participle used as a Conjunction or as an Adverb must be Intransitive.

EXAMPLES.—"Wherefore is there a price in the hands of a fool to get wisdom, *seeing* he hath no heart to it."
"A virtuous household, but *exceeding* poor."

TENSE.

REM.—Generally the form of the Verb denotes not only the *manner*, but also the *time*, of the action or event expressed by it. Hence the distinction of Tense.

DEF. 113.—Tense is a modification of Verbs, denoting a distinction of *time*.

REM.—Time is *Present*, *Past*, or *Future*: of each of these periods we have two varieties, represented by different forms. Hence,

PRIN.—Most Verbs have six Tenses—

Prior Past and *Past*,
Prior Present and *Present*,
Prior Future and *Future*.

DEF. 114.—The *Prior Past Tense* denotes time past at some other past time mentioned, or implied.

EXAMPLE.—I *had* already *expressed* my opinion.

OBS.—*Had* is usually the sign of this Tense.

DEF. 115.—The *Past Tense* denotes time fully past.

EXAMPLES.—I *wrote* you a letter—We *walked* to Troy.
I *saw* an eagle—David loved Jonathan.

OBS.—In Regular Verbs, the *sign* of this Tense is *d* or *ed* added to the root of the Verb.

In Irregular Verbs, a distinct form is used. [See List.]

DEF. 116.—The *Prior Present Tense* denotes time past, but in a period reaching to the present.

EXAMPLES.—I *have completed* my task.—John *has returned*.
Mary *has been prospered*.—Thou *hast destroyed* thyself.

OBS. 3.—*Have*, *hast*, and *has*, are the *signs* of this Tense.

DEF. 117.—The *Present Tense* denotes time present.

EXAMPLES.—Eliza *studies*.—Ellen is *reading*.
Do you *hear* the bell?—Emily *may write* that Diagram.

OBS. 1.—This is the simplest form of the Verb;—the sign *do* is used to denote intensity, and in asking questions.

OBS. 2.—Present Tense may be—

1. *Definite*—as, I am writing—William studies.
2. *Indefinite*—as, Virtue is commendable.

DEF. 118.—The *Prior Future Tense* denotes time past, as compared with some future time specified.

EXAMPLE.—We *shall have finished* this recitation before the next class will come.

OBS.—*Shall have* and *will have* are the signs of this Tense.

DEF. 119.—The *Future Tense* denotes future time, as compared with the present.

EXAMPLE.—James *will return* to-morrow—I *shall see* him.

OBS.—*Shall*, in the First Person, and *will*, in the Second and Third, are the signs of this Tense.

REM.—Distinctions of time are not indicated with precision by the form of the Verb. This must be done by the use of Adjuncts.

In the Potential Mode, the Tenses are quite Indefinite—one form being often used for another.

The same remarks will apply to Participles—to the Infinitive, the Subjunctive, and sometimes the Indicative.

RECAPITULATION.

- VERB.
  - Transitive,
    - Active,
    - Passive,
  - Intransitive,
    - Active,
    - Neuter,
  - *Indicative,*
    - Prior Past,
    - Past,
    - Prior Present,
    - Present,
    - Prior Future,
    - Future.
  - *Potential,*
    - Prior Past,
    - Past,
    - Prior Present,
    - Present.
  - *Subjunctive,*
    - Past,
    - Present.
  - *Imperative,*
    - Present.
  - *Infinitive,*
    - Past,
    - Present.
  - *Participle,*
    - Past,
    - Present,
    - Compound.

EXERCISES.

☞ Let each Verb and Participle in the following Exercises be pointed out, and its Class and Modification given.

1. I wrote.
2. Thou art reading.
3. James may recite.
4. Mary can study.
5. Joining the multitude.
6. Accustomed to study.
7. Willing to be taught.
8. Having seen the teacher.
9. Retire.
10. Let us alone.
11. Permit me to pass.
12. Let me go.
13. It is pleasant to ride in a sail-boat.
14. We are all fond of singing.
15. Some are accustomed to sing by rote.
16. The young ladies ought to have attended the lecture.
17. By teaching others we improve ourselves.
18. Being accustomed to study, we can learn that lesson easily.
19. Having been censured for idleness, John has resolved to be diligent.
20. By endeavoring to please all, we fail to please any.

21. "To be or not to be—that is the question"
22. "Spirit! I feel that thou
Wilt soon depart!
23. This body is too weak longer to hold
The immortal part.
24. The ties of earth are loosening,
25. They soon will break;
26. And thou, even as a joyous bird,
Thy flight wilt take
To the eternal world."
27. Go forth when midnight winds are high,
And ask them whence they come;
28. Who sent them raging through the sky,
29. And where is their far home!
30. "Mark the sable woods,
That shade sublime yon mountain's nodding brow
31. With what religious awe the solemn scene
Commands your steps.
32. As if the reverend form
Of Minos or of Numa should forsake
The Elysian seats, and down the embowering glade
Move to your pausing eye."
33. "In the pleased infant see its power expand,
When first the coral fills his little hand;
34. Throned in his mother's lap, it dries each tear,
As her sweet legend falls upon his ear;
35. Next it assails him in his top's strange hum,
Breathes in his whistle, echoes in his drum;
36. Each gilded toy that doting love bestows,
He longs to break, and every spring expose."
37. "Could I forget
What I have been, I might the better bear
What I am destined to.
38. I am not the first
That has been wretched; but to think how much
I have been happier."
39. "Truth crushed to earth will rise again,
40. The eternal years of God are hers:
41. But Error, wounded, writhes in pain,
And dies amid her worshipers."

MODEL.

Crushed ....is [a *Participle*, from the Verb *crush*;] used here to describe a condition of "Truth;" hence, a Verbal Adjective.
Will rise ....asserts an act of "Truth;" hence, a Verb.
" has no object; hence, Intransitive.
" simply declares; hence, Indicative Mode.
" denotes time future; hence, Future Tense.
Are.........asserts being of "years;" hence, a Verb.
Are ....has no object; hence, Intransitive.
" simply declares; hence, Indicative Mode.
" denotes time present; hence, Present Tense.
Wounded ...is [a *Participle*, from the Verb *wound*;] used here to describe a condition of "Error;" hence, a Verbal Adjective.
Writhes.....asserts an act of "Error;" hence, a Verb.
" has no object; hence, Intransitive.
" simply declares; hence, Indicative Mode.
" denotes time present; hence, Present Tense.

"The surging billows and the gamboling storms
Come crouching to his feet."

Surging.....is [a *Participle*, from the Verb *surge*.]
" used here to describe "billows;" hence, a Verbal Adjective.
Gamboling..is [a *Participle*, from the Verb *gambol*.]
" used here to describe "storms;" hence, a Verbal Adjective.
Come.......asserts an act of "billows" and "storms;" hence, a Verb.
" has no object; hence, Intransitive.
" simply declares; hence, Indicative Mode.
" denotes time present; hence, Present Time.
Crouching...is [a *Participle*, from the Verb *crouch*.]
" used here to modify the act expressed by "come;"
" (it declares the *manner of coming*;) hence, an Adverb.

"In the beginning God created the heaven and the earth."

Beginning...is [a *Participle*, from the Verb *begin*.]
" used here as the *name* of an event; hence, a Verbal Noun.
Created.....asserts an act of "God;" hence, a Verb.
" act passes to objects (heaven and earth).
" simply declares; hence, Indicative Mode.
" denotes a particular time past; hence, Past Tense.

CONJUGATION OF VERBS

REMARK 1.—We have seen that most verbs are varied in form to denote different *modes* and *times* of action or being.

They are also varied to correspond with their subjects in *Person* and *Number*

The regular arrangement of the various forms of a Verb is called its *Conjugation*.

REM. 2.—Verbs are varied by inflection of their Radicals, or by the use of different Radicals. Hence,

PRIN.—Verbs are distinguished as
Regular and *Irregular*.

REGULAR VERBS.

DEF. 120.—A *Regular Verb* is a Verb whose Past Tense is formed by the addition of *d* or *ed* to the Radical.

EXAMPLES.—*Present Tense.*—I love, act, save, fear.
Past Tense.—I lov*ed*, act*ed*, sav*ed*, fear*ed*.

OBS. 1.—Some Verbs, for euphony, drop the final letter of the Radical.

EXAMPLES.—Love, lov*ed*—Save, sav*ed*—Recite, recit*ed*.

OBS. 2.—Some Verbs, for euphony, double a final letter of the Radical.

EXAMPLES.—Tan, tan*ned*—Transmit, transmit*ted*.

IRREGULAR VERBS.

DEF. 121.—An *Irregular Verb* is a Verb whose Past Tense is not made by the addition of *d* or *ed* to the Radical.

EXAMPLES.—*Present Tense.*—I am, see, do, hide, lay,
Past Tense.—I was, saw, did, hid, laid.

REM.—Some Irregular Verbs are not used in all the Modes and Tenses. Hence,

DEF. 122.—A *Defective Verb* is a Verb that is not used in all the Modes and Tenses.

LIST.

Present.—Can,	may,	must,	ought,		shall,	will.
Past.—Could,	might.	——	ought,	quoth,	should,	would.

REM.—We have seen (see Part I., p. 25)—

1. That the *Predicate* of a Sentence must have at least one *Verb.*
2. That it may have other Words.
3. That in Predicates formed of more than one Word, the last Word constitutes the *Principal Part* of the Predicate, *i. e.,* makes the *Principal Assertion.*
4. That the Principal Part of a Predicate may be—
   A *Verb.*—I *love*—I do *see.*
   A *Participle.*—I am *loved*—I have *seen.*
   An *Adjective.*—John is *weary*—Velvet feels *smooth.*
   A *Noun.*—We are *friends*—He is a *scholar.*
   A *Pronoun.*—It is *I*—*Thine* is the kingdom.
5. That the Words prefixed to the Principal Part are *Auxiliaries,* and may be *Verbs* only, or Verbs and Participles. Hence,

DEF. 123.—An *Auxiliary Verb* is a Verb that is prefixed to another Verb or to a Participle, to distinguish the *Voice, Mode,* or *Tense* of the Principal Verb.

LIST.

Always Auxiliaries.

Present.—Can,	may,	must,	shall.
Past.—Could,	might,	——	should.

Sometimes Principal Verbs

Present.—Am,	be,	do,	have,	will.
Past.——	was,	did,	had,	would.

OBS.—These Words, when used as *Auxiliaries,* perform peculiar offices; thus,

Be, with its various modifications, is used before a Past Participle to indicate the *Passive Voice.*

Can, may, must, shall (used to command), and *will* (signifying volition), indicate the Present Tense of the *Potential Mode.*

Could, might, should, and *would,* are the signs of the *Past Tense Potential.*

Do	is used in the	*Present Tense,*	Indicative-intensive form
Did	" "	*Past Tense,*	" " "
Had	" "	*Prior Past Tense,*	" " "
Have	" "	*Prior Present Tense, Indicative*	"
May have	" "	*Prior Present Tense, Potential*	"
Might have	" "	*Prior Past Tense,*	" "
Shall	" "	*Future, Indicative (First Person).*	
Will	" "	*Future, Indicative (Second or Third Person)*	

NOTE.—The Future and Prior Future Tenses are placed in the Indicative Mode in conformity to the general custom of grammarians. A strict regard to uniformity and consistency would place them with their kindred forms in the Potential Mode. For,

The "*Indicative Mode* is that form of the Verb used to *indicate* or *assert* an act, being, or state." Now a thing *future* may be predicted, but cannot be declared or asserted. We may declare a *purpose* or make a *prediction.* So may we declare the *possibility* of an act, or the *obligation* to perform an act. But these are done by a modification of the Predicate, called *Potential Mode.*

In the Sentence "I shall go," we have asserted a prediction of an act.
" " "I may go," we have asserted a probability of an act.
" " "I can go," we have asserted a possibility of an act.

"I should go," asserts obligation to perform an act.
"I might go," asserts liberty to perform an act.
"I could go," asserts power to perform an act.

Neither of the above assertions declares the performance of an act. They assert "*probability, power, will,* or *obligation,*" but no actual event.

The Potential *Present* and *Past* alike assert a *present* probability, prediction, possibility, &c., of a *future* act or event.

"I shall go if I choose,"
"I may go if I will,"
"I can go if I will,"
"I should go if I were invited,"
"I might go if I were invited,"
"I could go if I were invited,"
} all refer to a future act.

EXERCISES.

(1.)

SUBJECT.	PREDICATE.			
	Auxiliaries.			*Principal.*
1	2	3	4	5
			am	
		have	been	
			was	
		had	been	
	shall		be	
I	shall	have	been	singing.
	may		be	
	may	have	been	
	might		be	
	might	have	been	

(2.)

			is	
		has	been	
			was	
		had	been	
	will		be	
John	will	have	been	loved.
	may		be	
	may	have	been	
	might		be	
	might	have	been	

☞ Let the Pupil substitute for the Word "John" the following Subjects, and notice what changes in the various Auxiliary Verbs must consequently be made. Thus,

I	requires	(am—have—shall—shall have).
Thou	"	(art—hast—hadst—wilt—mayest—mightst.)
They	"	(are—have.)
People	"	(are—have).
He	"	[*no change.*]

Hence,

OBS.—The practical object of the following Paradigms is to teach the Pupil what are the various changes in the form of the Predicate to correspond to the Subject, and to indicate the various Modes, Tenses, Persons, and Numbers.

Paradigm of the Irregular Verb "Be."

PRINCIPAL PARTS.

Am, was, being, been.

INDICATIVE MODE.

PRESENT TENSE.

	Singular Number.	*Plural Number.*
First Person....	I am,	We are,
Second "	Thou art, You are,	Ye are, You are,
Third "	He is.	They are.

PRIOR PRESENT TENSE.

1.	I have been,	We have been,
2.	Thou hast been, You have been,	Ye have been, You have been,
3.	He has been.	They have been.

PAST TENSE.

1.	I was,	We were,
2.	Thou wast, You was,	Ye were, You were,
3.	He was.	They were.

PRIOR PAST TENSE.

1.	I had been,	We had been,
2.	Thou hadst been, You had been,	Ye had been, You had been,
3.	He had been.	They had been.

FUTURE TENSE.

1.	I shall be,	We shall be,
2.	Thou wilt be, You will be,	Ye will be, You will be,
3.	He will be.	They will be.

PRIOR FUTURE TENSE.

1.	I shall have been,	We shall have been,
2.	Thou wilt have been, You will have been,	Ye will have been, You will have been,
3.	He will have been.	They will have been

POTENTIAL MODE.

PRESENT TENSE.

	Singular.	*Plural.*
1.	I may be,	We may be,
2.	Thou mayst be, You may be,	Ye may be, You may be,
3.	He may be.	They may be.

PRIOR PRESENT TENSE.

	Singular.	*Plural.*
1.	I may have been,	We may have been,
2.	Thou mayst have been,	Ye may have been,
	You may have been,	You may have been,
3.	He may have been.	They may have been.

PAST TENSE.

1.	I might be,	We might be,
2.	Thou mightst be,	Ye might be,
	You might be,	You might be,
3.	He might be.	They might be.

PRIOR PAST TENSE.

1.	I might have been,	We might have been,
2.	Thou mightst have been,	Ye might have been,
	You might have been,	You might have been,
3.	He might have been.	They might have been.

SUBJUNCTIVE MODE.

PRESENT TENSE.

1.	If I be,	If we be,
2.	If thou be,	If ye be,
	If you be,	If you be,
3.	If he be.	If they be.

PAST TENSE.

1.	If I were,	If we were,
2.	If thou wert,	If ye were,
	If you were,	If you were;
3.	If he were.	If they were.

IMPERATIVE MODE.

PRESENT TENSE.

2.	Be thou, *or*	Be ye, *or* Do ye be.
	Do thou be.	Be you, *or* Do you be.

INFINITIVE MODE.

PRESENT TENSE,............To be.
PRIOR PRESENT TENSE,......To have been.

PARTICIPLES.

PRESENT,.................*Being.*
PAST,....................*Been.*
COMPOUND,.................*Having* been.

FORMULÆ OF REGULAR VERBS.

Transitive Verb—"RECITE."

ACTIVE VOICE.

The Principal Parts of this Verb are—

PRESENT TENSE, ...	Recite.
PAST TENSE, ...	Recit*ed*.
PRESENT PARTICIPLE, ...	Recit*ing*.
PAST PARTICIPLE, ...	Recit*ed*.

INDICATIVE MODE.

PRESENT TENSE, ... Recite.

	Simple Form.	*Progressive Form*
	Singular.	
1.	I recite,	I *am* recit*ing*,
2.	Thou recit*est*, / You recite,	Thou *art* recit*ing*, / You *are* recit*ing*,
3.	He recite*s*.	He *is* recit*ing*.
	Plural.	
1.	We recite,	We *are* recit*ing*,
2.	Ye recite, / You recite,	Ye *are* recit*ing*, / You *are* recit*ing*,
3.	They recite.	They *are* recit*ing*.

PRIOR PRESENT TENSE.

	Singular.	
1.	I *have* recit*ed*,	I *have been* recit*ing*,
2.	Thou *hast* recit*ed*, / You *have* recit*ed*,	Thou *hast been* recit*ing*, / You *have been* recit*ing*,
3.	He *has* recit*ed*.	He *has been* recit*ing*.
	Plural.	
1.	We *have* recit*ed*,	We *have been* recit*ing*,
2.	Ye *have* recit*ed*, / You *have* recit*ed*,	Ye *have been* recit*ing*, / You *have been* recit*ing*,
3.	They *have* recit*ed*.	They *have been* recit*ing*.

PAST TENSE.

Singular.

1.	I recit*ed*,	I *was* recit*ing*,
2.	Thou recit*edst*,	Thou *wast* recit*ing*,
	You recit*ed*,	You *was* recit*ing*,
3.	He recit*ed*.	He was recit*ing*.

Plural.

1.	We recit*ed*,	We *were* recit*ing*,
2.	Ye recit*ed*,	Ye *were* recit*ing*,
	You recit*ed*,	You *were* recit*ing*,
3.	They recit*ed*.	They *were* recit*ing*.

PRIOR PAST TENSE.

Singular.

1.	I *had* recited,	I *had been* recit*ing*,
2.	Thou *hadst* recited,	Thou *hadst been* recit*ing*
	You *had* recited,	You *had been* recit*ing*,
3.	He *had* recited.	He *had been* recit*ing*.

Plural.

1.	We *had* recited,	We *had been* recit*ing*,
2.	Ye *had* recited,	Ye *had been* recit*ing*,
	You *had* recited,	You *had been* recit*ing*,
3.	They *had* recited.	They *had been* recit*ing*.

FUTURE TENSE.

Singular.

1.	I *shall* recite,	I *shall be* recit*ing*,
2.	Thou *wilt* recite,	Thou *wilt be* recit*ing*
	You *will* recite,	You *will be* recit*ing*,
3.	He *will* recite.	He *will be* recit*ing*.

Plural.

1.	We *shall* recite,	We *shall be* recit*ing*,
2.	Ye *will* recite,	Ye *will be* recit*ing*,
	You *will* recite,	You *will be* recit*ing*,
3.	They *will* recite.	They *will be* recit*ing*.

PRIOR FUTURE TENSE.

Singular.

1.	I *shall have* recited,	I *shall have been* recit*ing*,
2.	Thou *wilt have* recited,	Thou *wilt have been* recit*ing*,
	You *will have* recited,	You *will have been* recit*ing*,
3.	He *will have* recited.	He *will have been* recit*ing*.

Plural.

1.	We *shall have* recited,	We *shall have been* recit*ing*,
2.	Ye *will have* recited,	Ye *will have been* recit*ing*,
	You *will have* recited,	You *will have been* recit*ing*,
3.	They *will have* recited.	They *will have been* recit*ing*.

POTENTIAL MODE.

PRESENT TENSE.

Singular.

1.	I *may* recite,	I *may be* reciting,
2.	Thou *mayst* recite,	Thou *mayst be* reciting
	You *may* recite,	You *may be* reciting,
3.	He *may* recite.	He *may be* reciting.

Plural.

1.	We *may* recite,	We *may be* reciting,
2.	Ye *may* recite,	Ye *may be* reciting,
	You *may* recite,	You *may be* reciting,
3.	They *may* recite.	They *may be* reciting.

PRIOR PRESENT TENSE.

Singular.

1.	I *may have* recited,	I *may have been* reciting,
2.	Thou *mayst have* recited,	Thou *mayst have been* reciting
	You *may have* recited,	You *may have been* reciting,
3.	He *may have* recited.	He *may have been* reciting.

Plural.

1.	We *may have* recited,	We *may have been* reciting,
2.	Ye *may have* recited,	Ye *may have been* reciting,
	You *may have* recited,	You *may have been* reciting,
3.	They *may have* recited.	They *may have been* reciting.

PAST TENSE.

Singular.

1.	I *might* recite,	I *might be* reciting,
2.	Thou *mightst* recite,	Thou *mightst be* reciting
	You *might* recite,	You *might be* reciting,
3.	He *might* recite.	He *might be* reciting.

Plural.

1.	We *might* recite,	We *might be* reciting,
2.	Ye *might* recite,	Ye *might be* reciting,
	You *might* recite,	You *might be* reciting,
3.	They *might* recite.	They *might be* reciting.

PRIOR PAST TENSE.

Singular.

1	I *might have* recited,	I *might have been* reciting,
2.	Thou *mightst have* recited,	Thou *mightst have been* reciting
	You *might have* recited,	You *might have been* reciting
3.	He *might have* recited.	He *might have been* reciting.

Plural.

1.	We *might have* recited,	We *might have been* reciting,
2.	Ye *might have* recited,	Ye *might have been* reciting,
	You *might have* recited,	You *might have been* reciting,
3.	They *might have* recited.	They *might have been* reciting.

SUBJUNCTIVE MODE.

PRESENT TENSE.

Singular.

1.	If I recite,	If I *be* recit*ing*,
2.	If thou recite,	If thou *be* recit*ing*,
	If you recite,	If you *be* recit*ing*,
3.	If he recite.	If he *be* recit*ing*.

Plural.

1.	If we recite,	If we *be* recit*ing*,
2.	If ye recite,	If ye *be* recit*ing*,
	If you recite,	If you *be* recit*ing*,
3.	If they recite.	If they be recit*ing*.

PAST TENSE.

Singular.

1.	Though I recit*ed*,	Though I *were* reciting,
2.	Though thou recit*ed*,	Though thou *wert* recit*ing*
	Though you recit*ed*,	Though you *were* reciting,
3.	Though he recit*ed*.	Though he *were* recit*ing*.

Plural.

1.	Though we recit*ed*,	Though we *were* recit*ing*,
2.	Though ye recit*ed*,	Though ye *were* reciting,
	Though you recit*ed*,	Though you *were* recit*ing*,
3.	Though they recit*ed*.	Though they *were* recit*ing*.

IMPERATIVE MODE.

PRESENT TENSE.

Singular.

2.	Recite thou, *or*	*Be* thou recit*ing*, *or*
	Do thou recite.	*Do* thou be recit*ing*

Plural.

2.	Recite ye or you, *or*	*Be* ye recit*ing*, or
	Do ye or you recite.	*Do* ye *be* recit*ing*.

INFINITIVE MODE.

PRESENT.

To recite. | To *be* recit*ing*.

PRIOR PRESENT.

To *have* recit*ed*. | To *have been* recit*ing*.

PARTICIPLES.

PRESENT.

Recit*ing*.

PRIOR PRESENT.

Having recit*ed*. | *Having been* recit*ing*.

Paradigm of the Verb "Love."

ACTIVE VOICE. PASSIVE VOICE.

INDICATIVE MODE.

PRESENT TENSE.

Singular

1.	I love,	I am loved,
2.	Thou lovest,	Thou art loved,
	You love,	You are loved,
3.	He loves.	He is loved.

Plural.

1.	We love,	We are loved,
2.	Ye love,	Ye are loved,
	You love,	You are loved,
3.	They love.	They are loved.

PRIOR PRESENT TENSE.

Singular.

1.	I have loved,	I have been loved,
2.	Thou hast loved,	Thou hast been loved,
	You have loved,	You have been loved,
3.	He has loved.	He has been loved.

Plural.

1.	We have loved,	We have been loved,
2.	Ye have loved,	Ye have been loved,
	You have loved,	You have been loved,
3.	They have loved.	They have been loved.

PAST TENSE.

Singular.

1.	I loved,	I was loved,
2.	Thou lovedst,	Thou wast loved,
	You loved,	You was loved,
3.	He loved.	He was loved.

Plural.

1.	We loved,	We were loved,
2.	Ye loved,	Ye were loved,
	You loved,	You were loved,
3.	They loved.	They were loved.

PRIOR PAST TENSE.

Singular.

1.	I had loved,	I had been loved,
2.	Thou hadst loved,	Thou hadst been loved,
	You had loved,	You had been loved,
3	He had loved.	He had been loved.

Plural.

1.	We had loved,	We had been loved,
2.	Ye had loved,	Ye had been loved,
	You had loved,	You had been loved,
3.	They had loved.	They had been loved.

FUTURE TENSE.

Singular.

1.	I shall love,	I shall be loved,
2.	Thou wilt love,	Thou wilt be loved,
	You will love,	You will be loved,
3.	He will love.	He will be loved.

Plural.

1.	We shall love,	We shall be loved,
2.	Ye will love,	Ye will be loved,
	You will love,	You will be loved,
3.	They will love.	They will be loved.

PRIOR FUTURE TENSE.

Singular.

1.	I shall have loved,	I shall have been loved,
2.	Thou wilt have loved,	Thou wilt have been loved,
	You will have loved,	You will have been loved,
3.	He will have loved.	He will have been loved.

Plural.

1.	We shall have loved,	We shall have been loved,
2.	Ye will have loved,	Ye will have been loved,
	You will have loved,	You will have been loved,
3.	They will have loved.	They will have been loved.

POTENTIAL MODE.

PRESENT TENSE.

Singular.

1.	I may love,	I may be loved,
2.	Thou mayst love,	Thou mayst be loved,
	You may love,	You may be loved,
3.	He may love.	He may be loved.

Plural.

1.	We may love,	We may be loved,
2.	Ye may love,	Ye may be loved,
	You may love,	You may be loved,
3.	They may love.	They may be loved.

PRIOR PRESENT TENSE.

Singular.

1.	I may have loved,	I may have been loved,
2.	Thou mayst have loved,	Thou mayst have been loved,
	You may have loved,	You may have been loved.
3.	He may have loved.	He may have been loved.

Plural.

1.	We may have loved,	We may have been loved,
2.	Ye may have loved,	Ye may have been loved,
	You may have loved,	You may have been loved,
3.	They may have loved.	They may have been loved.

PAST TENSE.

Singular.

1.	I might love,	I might be loved,
2.	Thou mightst love,	Thou mightst be loved,
	You might love,	You might be loved,
3.	He might love.	He might be loved.

Plural.

1.	We might love,	We might be loved,
2.	Ye might love,	Ye might be loved,
	You might love,	You might be loved,
3.	They might love.	They might be loved.

PRIOR PAST TENSE.

Singular.

1.	I might have loved,	I might have been loved,
2.	Thou mightst have loved,	Thou mightst have been loved,
	You might have loved,	You might have been loved,
3.	He might have loved.	He might have been loved.

Plural.

1.	We might have loved,	We might have been loved,
2.	Ye might have loved,	Ye might have been loved,
	You might have loved,	You might have been loved,
3.	They might have loved.	They might have been loved.

SUBJUNCTIVE MODE.

PRESENT TENSE.

Singular.

1.	If I love,	If I be loved,
2.	If thou love,	If thou be loved,
	If you love,	If you be loved,
3.	If he love.	If he be loved.

Plural.

1. If we love, — If we be loved,
2. { If ye love, / If you love, — { If ye be loved, / If you be loved,
3. If they love. — If they be loved.

PAST TENSE.

Singular.

1. If I loved, — If I were loved,
2. { If thou loved, / If you loved, — { If thou wert loved, / If you were loved,
3. If he loved. — If he were loved.

Plural.

1. If we loved, — If we were loved,
2. { If ye loved, / If you loved, — { If ye were loved, / If you were loved,
3. If they loved. — If they were loved.

IMPERATIVE MODE.

PRESENT TENSE.

Singular.

2. { Love thou, *or* / Do thou love. — { Be loved, *or* / Do thou be loved.

Plural.

2. { Love ye, *or* / Do ye love. — 2. { Be ye loved, *or* / Do ye be loved.

INFINITIVE MODE.

PRESENT TENSE.

To love. — To be loved.

PRIOR PRESENT TENSE.

To have loved. — To have been loved.

PARTICIPLES.

PRESENT.

Loving. — { Loved, *or* / Being loved.

PRIOR PRESENT.

Having loved. — Having been loved.

Synopsis of the Verb "STUDY."

Active Voice.

INDICATIVE MODE.

First Person.

	DECLARATIVE FORM.	DECLARATIVE FORM.—*Negative.*
PRESENT,	I study,	I study *not*, or I do not study.
PRIOR PRESENT,	I have studied,	I have *not* studied.
PAST,	I studied,	I studied *not*, or I did not study
PRIOR PAST,	I had studied,	I had *not* studied.
FUTURE,	I shall study,	I shall *not* study.
PRIOR FUTURE,	I shall have studied,	I shall *not* have studied.

POTENTIAL MODE.

PRESENT,	I may study,	I may *not* study.
PRIOR PRESENT,	I may have studied,	I may *not* have studied.
PAST,	I might study,	I might *not* study.
PRIOR PAST,	I might have studied,	I might *not* have studied.

SUBJUNCTIVE MODE.

PRESENT,	If I study,	If I study *not*.
PAST,	If I studied,	If I studied *not*.

IMPERATIVE MODE.

Second Person.

PRESENT,	Study, or	Study *not*, or
"	Do thou study,	Do *not* study.

INFINITIVE MODE.

PRESENT	To study,	*Not* to study.
PRIOR PRESENT,	To have studied,	*Not* to have studied.

PARTICIPLES.

SIMPLE,	Studying,	*Not* studying, or studying *not*.
COMPOUND,	Having studied,	*Not* having studied.

Synopsis of the Verb "TURN."

Active Voice.

INDICATIVE MODE.

DECLARATIVE FORM.	INTERROGATIVE FORM.*
I turn,	Do I turn?
I have turned,	Have I turned?
I turned,	Did I turn?
I had turned,	Had I turned?
I shall turn,	Shall I turn?
I shall have turned,	Shall I have turned?

POTENTIAL MODE.

I may turn,	May I turn?
I may have turned,	May I have turned?
I might turn,	Might I turn?
I might have turned,	Might I have turned?

Synopsis of the Verb "SELL."

Passive Voice.

INDICATIVE MODE.

Third Person.

	INTERROGATIVE FORM.	INTERROGATIVE FORM.—*Negative.*
PRESENT,	Is it sold?	Is it not sold?
PRIOR PRESENT,	Has it been sold?	Has it not been sold?
PAST,	Was it sold?	Was it not sold?
PRIOR PAST,	Had it been sold?	Had it not been sold?
FUTURE,	Will it be sold?	Will it not be sold?
PRIOR FUTURE,	Will it have been sold?	Will it not have been sold?

POTENTIAL MODE.

Third Person.

May it be sold?	May it not be sold?
May it have been sold?	May it not have been sold?
Might it be sold?	Might it not be sold?
Might it have been sold?	Might it not have been sold?

* The SUBJUNCTIVE, IMPERATIVE, and INFINITIVE MODES are not used in Interrogative Sentences.

Paradigm of the Irregular Verb "SEE."

DECLARATIVE FORM. INTERROGATIVE FORM.

INDICATIVE MODE.

PRESENT TENSE.

Singular.

	Declarative Form	Interrogative Form
1.	I see,	See I?
2.	Thou seest,	Seest thou?
	You see,	See you?
3.	He sees,	Sees he?

Plural.

	Declarative Form	Interrogative Form
1.	We see,	See we?
2.	Ye see,	See ye?
	You see,	See you?
3.	They see,	See they?

OBS.—The above is the *Simple form*, which, in Interrogative Sentences, is not much used, the *Intensive* form being commonly employed. Thus,

PRESENT TENSE.

Singular.

	Declarative Form	Interrogative Form
1.	I do see,	Do I see?
2.	Thou dost see,	Dost thou see?
	You do see,	Do you see?
3.	He does see,	Does he see?

Plural.

	Declarative Form	Interrogative Form
1.	We do see,	Do we see?
2.	Ye do see,	Do ye see?
	You do see,	Do you see?
3.	They do see,	Do they see?

PRIOR PRESENT TENSE.

Singular.

	Declarative Form	Interrogative Form
1.	I have seen,	Have I seen?
2.	Thou hast seen,	Hast thou seen?
	You have seen,	Have you seen?
3.	He has seen,	Has he seen?

Plural.

	Declarative Form	Interrogative Form
1.	We have seen,	Have we seen?
2.	Ye have seen,	Have ye seen?
	You have seen,	Have you seen?
3.	They have seen,	Have they seen?

PAST TENSE.—*Simple Form.*

Singular

1.	I saw,	Saw I?
2.	Thou sawest,	Sawest thou?
	You saw,	Saw you?
3	He saw,	Saw he?

Plural.

1.	We saw,	Saw we?
2.	Ye saw,	Saw ye?
	You saw,	Saw you?
3.	They saw,	Saw they?

PAST TENSE.—*Intensive Form.*

Singular.

1.	I did see,	Did I see?
2.	Thou didst see,	Didst thou see?
	You did see,	Did you see?
3.	He did see,	Did he see?

Plural.

1.	We did see,	Did we see?
2.	Ye did see,	Did ye see?
	You did see,	Did you see?
3.	They did see,	Did they see?

PRIOR PAST TENSE.

Singular.

1.	I had seen,	Had I seen?
2.	Thou hadst seen,	Hadst thou seen?
	You had seen,	Had you seen?
3.	He had seen,	Had he seen?

Plural.

1.	We had seen,	Had we seen?
2.	Ye had seen,	Had ye seen?
	You had seen,	Had you seen?
3.	They had seen,	Had they seen?

POTENTIAL MODE.

PRESENT TENSE.

Singular.

1.	I can see,	Can I see?
2.	Thou canst see,	Canst thou see
	You can see,	Can you see?
3.	He can see,	Can he see?

Plural.

1.	We can see,	Can we see?
2.	Ye can see,	Can ye see?
	You can see,	Can you see?
3.	They can see,	Can they see?

PRIOR PRESENT TENSE.

Singular.

1.	I can have seen,	Can we have seen?
2.	Thou canst have seen,	Canst thou have seen?
	You can have seen,	Can you have seen?
3.	He can have seen,	Can he have seen?

Plural.

1.	We can have seen,	Can we have seen?
2.	Ye can have seen,	Can ye have seen?
	You can have seen,	Can you have seen?
3.	They can have seen,	Can they have seen?

PAST TENSE.

Singular.

1.	I could see,	Could I see?
2.	Thou couldst see,	Couldst thou see?
	You could see,	Could you see?
3.	He could see,	Could he see?

Plural.

1.	We could see,	Could we see?
2.	Ye could see.	Could ye see?
	You could see,	Could you see?
3.	They could see,	Could they see?

PRIOR PAST TENSE.

Singular.

1.	I could have seen,	Could I have seen?
2.	Thou couldst have seen,	Couldst thou have seen?
	You could have seen,	Could you have seen?
3.	He could have seen,	Could he have seen?

Plural.

1.	We could have seen,	Could we have seen?
2.	Ye could have seen,	Could ye have seen?
	You could have seen,	Could you have seen?
3.	They could have seen,	Could they have seen?

QUESTIONS FOR REVIEW.

PAGE.

107.—What is a *Verb?* .... See Def. 97.
How are Verbs *distinguished?* .... See Prin.
What is a *Transitive* Verb? .... See Def. 98.
What is an *Intransitive* Verb? .... See Def. 99.
What is a *Neuter* Verb? .... See Def. 100.
108.—What are the sub-classes of Transitive Verbs? .... See Prin.
When are Verbs in the *Active Voice?* .... See Def. 101
When are Verbs in the *Passive Voice?* .... See Def. 102.
How is the Passive Voice formed? .... See Obs. 2.
109.—What gives occasion for distinctions of *Mode?* .... See Rem.
Name the different Modes .... See Prin.
When are Verbs in the *Indicative Mode?* .... See Def. 103.
110.—When is a Verb in the *Potential Mode?* .... See Def. 104.
When is a Verb in the *Subjunctive Mode?* .... See Def. 105.
When is a Verb in the *Imperative Mode?* .... See Def. 106.
111.—When is a Verb in the *Infinitive Mode?* .... See Def. 107.
What is a Participle? .... See Def. 108.
112.—What are the principal distinctions of Participles? .. See Prin.
What is a *Simple Participle?* .... See Def. 109
What is a *Compound Participle?* .... See Def. 110
How are the Simple Participles distinguished? .... See Prin.
What is the *Present Participle?* .... See Def. 111
113.—What is the *Past Participle?* .... See Def. 112.
114.—What various offices do Participles perform? .... See Obs. 8.
115.—What is *Tense?*—What *Names* are given to the Tenses? .. See Prin.
Define the *Prior Past Tense,* and give Examples .... See Def. 114.
Define the *Past Tense,* " " .... See Def. 115.
116.—Define the *Prior Present Tense,* " " .... See Def. 116
Define the *Present Tense,* " " .... See Def. 117.
Define the *Prior Future Tense,* " " .... See Def. 118
Define the *Future Tense,* " " .... See Def. 119.
Give the various Tenses in the different Modes .. See Recapitulation.
120.—What does the term *Conjugation* indicate? .... See Rem.
How are Verbs distinguished, in *Inflections?* .... See Prin.
What is a *Regular Verb?* .... See Def. 120.
What is an *Irregular Verb?* .... See Def. 121.
121.—What is a *Defective Verb?* .... See Def. 122.
What is an *Auxiliary Verb?* .... See Def. 123.
Give the various offices of the Auxiliary Verbs .... See Obs. 1.

EXERCISES.

(I.)

Let the Pupils give the Class, Voice, Mode, Tense, Person, and Number of the following Verbs—and complete the Sentences.

1. Am writing a letter.
2. Are reading poetry.
3. Didst see the eclipse.
4. Had known duty.
5. May feel the worm.
6. Ought to study.
7. Couldst have favored him.
8. Thou love me.
9. Couldst love to study.
10. Has walked to Boston.
11. Hast wandered from home.
12. Shall learn wisdom.
13. Will improve in writing.
14. Could recite lessons.
15. Canst be false to any man.
16. Wish to see home.
17. Wilt have returned my books.
18. Shall have returned from Europe.

(II.)

Repeat the First Person singular of each Mode and Tense of the following Verbs:—

Am,	Eat,	Neglect,	Receive,
Arise,	Fly,	Need,	Reject,
Begin,	Go,	Owe,	Select,
Blow,	Hold,	Ought,	Squander,
Come,	Know,	Practice,	Yoke,
Cut,	Lay,	Purchase,	Touch,
Do,	Lie,	Quiet,	Use,
Drink,	Make,	Qualify,	Wish.

Repeat the Third Person Plural of the same.

(III.)

Let the appropriate Auxiliary Verbs be inserted in the blank spaces indicated.

1. "Now the shades of night —— gone."
2. "The bell's deep tones —— swelling."
3. "The palace —— wrapped in flames."
4. "How —— my heart encrusted with the world!"
5. "Every thing in the life of such persons —— misplaced."
6. "Science —— raise thee to eminence."
7. "But I alone —— guide thee to felicity."

8. "Ten years I —— allot to the attainment of knowledge."
9. "A chieftain's vengeance thou —— feel."
10. "The injuries of Fortune —— not affect the mind."

(IV.)

Let two Auxiliary Verbs be inserted in the following Sentences.

1. John —— not —— gone to the river.
2. We —— —— finished our task at five.
3. The earth —— —— dissolved like snow.
4. How —— we —— reconciled?
5. Who —— —— thought it?
6. You —— —— fatigued.
7. He —— not —— frightened.
8. You —— —— brought my letters.
9. The boy —— —— been injured by it.
10. No doctor —— —— made that man well.

IRREGULAR VERBS.

REM.—The following are the IRREGULAR and the REDUNDANT VERBS of the English language.

Present.	*Past.*	*Present Participle.*	*Past Participle.*
Abide,	abode,	abiding,	abode or abided.*
Am or be,	was,	being,	been.
Arise,	arose,	arising,	arisen.
Awake,	awoke or awaked,	awaking,	awoke or awaked.
Bear,	bore or bare,	bearing,	born.
Bear, *to sustain,*	bore or bare,	bearing,	borne.
Beat,	beat,	beating,	beaten or beat.
Begin,	began or begun,	beginning,	begun.
Behold,	beheld,	beholding,	beheld.
Belay,	belayed or belaid,	belaying,	belayed or belaid.
Bend,	bent or bended,	bending,	bent or bended.
Bereave	bereft or bereaved,	bereaving,	bereft or bereaved.
Beset,	beset,	besetting,	beset.
Beseech,	besought or beseeched,*	beseeching,	besought or beseeched.*
Bet,	bet or betted,	betting,	betted or bet.

Present.	*Past.*	*Present Participle.*	*Past Participle.*
Betide,	betid or betided,	betiding,	betided or betid.
Bid,	bade or bid,	bidding,	bidden or bid.
Bind,	bound,	binding,	bound.
Bite,	bit,	biting,	bitten or bit.
Bleed,	bled,	bleeding,	bled.
Blend,	blended or blent,	blending,	blended or blent.
Bless,	blessed or blest,	blessing,	blessed or blest.
Blow,	blew or blowed,	blowing,	blowed or blown.
Break,	broke,	breaking,	broken.
Breed,	bred,	breeding,	breed.
Bring,	brought,	bringing,	brought.
Build,	built or builded,*	building,	built or builded.*
Burn,	burned or burnt,	burning,	burned or burnt.
Burst,	burst or bursted,*	bursting,	burst or bursted.*
Buy,	bought,	buying,	bought.
Cast,	cast,	casting,	cast.
Catch,	caught or catched,*	catching,	caught or catched
Chide,	chid,	chiding,	chidden or chid.
Choose,	chose,	choosing,	chosen.
Cleave,	clove or cleft,	cleaving,	cloven or cleft.
Cleave,	cleaved or clave,	cleaving,	cleaved.
Cling,	clung,	clinging,	clung.
Clothe,	clothed or clad,	clothing,	clothed or clad.
Come,	came,	coming,	come.
Cost,	cost.	costing,	cost.
Creep,	crept or creeped,*	creeping,	crept or creeped.*
Crow,	crowed or crew,	crowing,	crowed.
Curse,	cursed or curst,	cursing,	cursed or curst.
Cut,	cut,	cutting,	cut.
Dare,	dared or durst,	daring,	dared or durst.
Deal,	dealt or dealed,*	dealing,	dealt or dealed.*
Dig,	dug or digged,*	digging,	dug or digged.*
Dive,	dived or dove,	diving,	dived or diven.
Do,	did,	doing,	done.
Draw,	drew,	drawing,	drawn.
Dream,	dreamed or dreamt,	dreaming,	dreamed or dreamt.
Dress,	dressed or drest,	dressing,	dressed or drest.
Drink,	drank,	drinking,	drunk or drank.
Drive,	drove,	driving,	driven.

Present.	*Past.*	*Present Participle.*	*Past Participle.*
Dwell,	dwelt or dwelled,*	dwelling,	dwelt or dwelled.*
Eat,	ate or eat,	eating,	eaten or eat.
Fall,	fell,	falling,	fallen.
Feed,	fed,	feeding,	fed.
Feel,	felt,	feeling,	felt.
Fight,	fought,	fighting,	fought.
Find,	found,	finding,	found.
Flee,	fled,	fleeing,	fled.
Fling,	flung,	flinging,	flung.
Fly,	flew,	flying,	flown.
Forbear,	forbore,	forbearing,	forborne.
Forget,	forgot or forgat,	forgetting,	forgotten.
Forsake,	forsook,	forsaking,	forsaken.
Freeze,	froze or freezed,*	freezing,	frozen or freezed.*
Geld,	gelded or gelt,*	gelding,	gelded or gelt.*
Get,	got or gat,*	getting,	got or gotten.*
Gild,	gilded or gilt,	gilding,	gilded or gilt.
Gird,	girded or girt,	girding,	girded or girt.
Give,	gave,	giving,	given.
Go,	went,	going,	gone.
Grave,	graved,	graving,	graved or graven.
Grind,	ground,	grinding,	ground.
Grow,	grew,	growing,	grown.
Hang,	hung or hanged,	hanging,	hung or hanged.
Have,	had,	having,	had.
Hear,	heard,	hearing,	heard.
Heave,	heaved or hove,	heaving,	heaved or hoven.
Hew,	hewed,	hewing,	hewed or hewn.
Hide,	hid,	hiding,	hidden or hid.
Hit,	hit,	hitting,	hit.
Hold,	held,	holding,	held or holden.*
Hurt,	hurt,	hurting,	hurt.
Keep,	kept,	keeping,	kept.
Kneel,	kneeled or knelt,	kneeling,	kneeled or knelt.
Knit,	knit or knitted,	knitting,	knit or knitted.
Know,	knew,	knowing,	known.
Lade,	laded,	lading,	laded or laden.
Lay,	laid or layed,*	laying,	laid or layed.*
Lead,	led.	leading,	led.

Present.	*Past.*	*Present Participle.*	*Past Participle.*
Lean,	leaned or leant,	leaning,	leaned or lent.
Leap,	leaped or leapt,	leaping,	leaped or leapt.
Learn,	learned or learnt,	learning,	learned or learnt.
Leave,	left,	leaving,	left.
Lend,	lent,	lending,	lent.
Let,	let,	letting,	let.
Lie,	lay,	lying,	lain.
Light,	lighted or lit,	lighting,	lighted or lit.
Loose,	lost,	loosing,	lost.
Make,	made,	making,	made.
Mean,	meant or meaned,*	meaning,	meant or meaned*
Meet,	met,	meeting,	met.
Mow,	mowed,	mowing,	mowed or mown.
Mulct,	mulcted or mulct,*	mulcting,	mulcted or mulct*
Outdo,	outdid,	outdoing,	outdone.
Pass,	passed or past,	passing,	passed or past.
Pay,	paid or payed,*	paying,	paid or payed.*
Pen,	penned or pent,	penning,	penned or pent.
Plead,	pleaded or pled,	pleading,	pleading or pled.
Prove,	proved,	proving,	proved or proven.
Put,	put,	putting,	put.
Quit,	quitted or quit,	quitting,	quitted or quit.
Rap,	rapped or rapt,	rapping,	rapped or rapt.
Read,	read,	reading,	read.
Rend,	rent,	rending,	rent.
Rid,	rid,	ridding,	rid.
Ride,	rode,	riding,	rode or ridden.
Ring,	rung or rang,	ringing,	rung.
Rise,	rose,	rising,	risen.
Rive,	rived,	riving,	riven or rived.
Roast,	roasted or roast,	roasting,	roasted or roast.
Rot,	rotted,	rotting,	rotten or rotted.
Run,	ran or run,	running,	run.
Saw,	sawed,	sawing,	sawn or sawed
Say,	said,	saying,	said.
See,	saw,	seeing,	seen.
Seek,	sought,	seeking,	sought.
Sell,	sold,	selling,	sold.
Send,	sent,	sending,	sent.

Present	*Past.*	*Present Participle.*	*Past Participle.*
Set,	set,	setting,	set.
Shake,	shook or shaked,*	shaking,	shaken or shaked.*
Shape,	shaped,	shaping,	shaped or shapen.
Shave,	shaved,	shaving,	shaved or shaven.
Shear,	sheared,	shearing,	sheared or shorn.
Shed,	shed,	shedding,	shed.
Shine,	shined or shone,	shining,	shined or shone.
Show,	showed,	showing,	showed or shown.
Shoe,	shod,	shoeing,	shod.
Shoot,	shot,	shooting,	shot.
Shred,	shred,	shredding,	shred.
Shrink,	shrunk,	shrinking,	shrunk.
Shut,	shut,	shutting,	shut.
Sing,	sung or sang,	singing,	sung.
Sink,	sunk or sank,*	sinking,	sunk.
Sit,	sat,	sitting,	sat.
Slay,	slew,	slaying,	slain.
Sleep,	slept,	sleeping,	slept.
Slide,	slid,	sliding,	slidden or slid.
Sling,	slung,	slinging,	slung.
Slink,	slunk,	slinking,	slunk.
Slit,	slitted or slit,	slitting,	slitted or slit.
Smell,	smelled or smelt,	smelling,	smelled or smelt.
Smite,	smote,	smiting,	smitten or smit.
Sow,	sowed,	sowing,	sowed or sown.
Speak,	spoke or spake,	speaking,	spoken.
Speed,	sped,	speeding,	sped.
Spell,	spelled or spelt,	spelling,	spelled or spelt.
Spend,	spent,	spending,	spent.
Spill,	spilled or spilt,	spilling,	spilled or spilt.
Spin,	spun,	spinning,	spun.
Spit,	spit or spat,*	spitting,	spit.
Split,	split,	splitting,	split.
Spoil,	spoiled or spoilt,	spoiling,	spoiled or spoilt.
Spread,	spread,	spreading,	spread.
Spring	sprung or sprang,	springing,	sprung.
Stand,	stood,	standing,	stood.
Stave,	stove or staved,	staving,	stove or staved.
Stay,	staid or stayed,*	staying,	staid or stayed.*

7

Present.	*Past.*	*Present Participle.*	*Past Participle.*
Steal,	stole,	stealing,	stolen.
Stick,	stuck,	sticking,	stuck.
Sting,	stung,	stinging,	stung.
Stink,	stunk or stank,*	stinking,	stunk.
Stride,	strode or strid,	striding,	stridden
Strike,	struck,	striking,	struck or stricken.
String,	strung or stringed,	stringing	strung or stringed
Strive,	strove,	striving,	striven.
Strow,	strowed,	strowing,	strowed or strown
Swear,	swore,	swearing,	sworn.
Sweat,	sweated or sweat,	sweating,	sweated or sweat
Sweep,	swept,	sweeping,	swept.
Swell,	swelled,	swelling,	swelled or swollen.
Swim,	swam,	swimming,	swam.
Swing,	swung,	swinging,	swung.
Take,	took,	taking,	taken.
Teach,	taught,	teaching,	taught.
Tear,	tore,	tearing,	torn.
Tell,	told,	telling,	told.
Think,	thought,	thinking,	thought.
Thrive,	thrived or throve,	thriving,	thrived or thriven
Throw,	threw or throwed,	throwing,	thrown or throwed
Thrust,	thrust,	thrusting,	thrust.
Tread,	trod,	treading,	trodden or trod.
Wake,	waked or woke,	waking,	waked or woke.
Wax,	waxed,	waxing,	waxed or waxen.
Wear,	wore,	wearing,	worn.
Weave,	wove,	weaving,	woven or wove.
Wed,	wedded or wed,	wedding,	wedded or wed.
Weep,	wept,	weeping,	wept.
Wet,	wet or wetted,	wetting,	wet or wetted.
Whet,	whetted or whet,	whetting,	whetted or whet.
Win,	won,	winning,	won.
Wind,	wound or winded,*	winding,	wound or winded.
Work,	worked or wrought,	working,	worked or wrought
Wring	wrung or wringed,	wringing,	wringed or wrung.
Write,	wrote,	writing,	written or writ.

OBS. 1.—Words in the above list, marked with a star (*), are not much used by modern writers.

OBS. 2.—A Verb often has a Preposition or other prefix placed before it; the conjugation, however, remains the same.

EXAMPLES.

Take,................took,.......... ...taken.
*Mis*take,.............*mis*took,...........*mis*taken.
*Over*take,............*over*took,...........*over*taken.
*Misunder*stand,.......*misunder*stood,......*misunder*stood.

REM.—The class should repeat this list *in concert*—prefixing to each Verb one of the Personal Pronouns. For the Third Person a Noun may be used—thus:

I write,......I wrote,......I have written,......having written
You tread,...you trod,.....you have trod, ...having trod.
He sweeps,...he swept, ...he has swept, ...having swept.
John does, ...John did, ...John has done, ...having done.
Men sit, ...men sat, ...men have sat, ...having sat.
Some hear,...some heard, ..some have heard, ...having heard.
They see, ...they saw, ...they are seen,.......being seen.

To the Transitive Verbs, Objects may be attached—thus:

We saw wood,.....we sawed wood,....we have sawn wood.
Birds build nests,...birds built nests, ...birds have built nests.
John writes letters,.John wrote letters,..John will write letters.
Thou seest me,.....thou sawest me, ...thou wilt see me.

Other variations in these concert exercises may be profitable—such as placing the words *now, to-day*, &c., after the Present—*yesterday*, &c., after the Past Tense—and *heretofore, recently*, &c., after the Prior Present—thus:

I begin to-day,........I began yesterday,...I have begun recently.
The wind blows now,.the wind blew then,.the wind has blown often.
The bell rings often,..the bell rang lately, .the bell will ring to-morrow
William writes now, .William wrote then,.William will write often.

UNIPERSONAL VERBS.

DEF. 124.—A Verb used only as the Predicate of the Indefinite Pronoun "*it*," is called a *Unipersonal Verb.*

EXAMPLES.—It snows—It rains—It seems—It becomes—It behoves—It seems—It is evident.

Methinks is an anomalous form of the Verb *think*.

EXERCISES IN REVIEW.

REM.—Let the pupil give the *Voice, Mode, Tense, Person,* and *Number* of the Verbs in the following Sentences.

1. People *applaud* benefactors.
2. *Do* they *esteem* vagabonds?
3. William *has visited* Europe.
4. *Have* we *exercised* discretion?
5. Columbus *discovered* America.
6. *Did* Washington *secure* renown?
7. Ye had accomplished purposes.
8. I *shall understand* you.
9. *Will* Warner *study* Greek?
10. Thou *wilt* not *comprehend* it.
11. Ye *will have accomplished* much
12. We *may receive* instruction.
13. *Canst* thou *guide* Arcturus?
14. *Shall* William *accompany* us?
15. I *will study* Greek.
16. They *are* not *appreciated*.
17. *Could* it not *be accomplished?*
18. Mary *might have been misinformed*.
19. Wisdom *should be honored*.
20. Thou *canst* not *have been understood*.
21. Sevastopol *could* not *have been taken*.
22. Meteors *might have been seen*.
23. What *should have been done?*
24. Who *can be trusted?*
25. *Have* you *been reading* poetry?
26. Cora *will be writing* letters.
27. Stephen *could* not *have been giving* attention.
28. *Might* Clara *have been admitted?*
29. Boys *had been reciting* lessons.
30. We *will* not *be enslaved*.
31. Pupils *might* not *have been giving* attention.
32. Caroline *will have visited* Syria.
33. *Accompany* Henry.
34. *Cheer* him.
35. *Be* honored.

ADVERBS.

REM.—As actions are modified by circumstances, and as qualities vary in degree, so words expressing actions, and words denoting qualities, are modified by other words, denoting *time, place, degree, manner, cause, &c.* Hence,

DEF. 125.—*An Adverb* is a Word used to modify the signification of a Verb, an Adjective, or another Modifier.

OBS. 1.—Adverbial Words are of great utility in rendering the language *concise* and *spirited.* They are commonly substituted for Phrases.

EXAMPLES.

"Brilliantly," ...for...."With a brilliant appearance.'
"Solemnly,".....for...."In a solemn manner."
"Vainly,".......for...."In a vain attempt."
"Here," ....for...."In this place."
"Now," ....for.. ."At this time."

1. "*Brilliantly* the glassy waters mirror back his smiles."
2. "*Solemnly* he took the earthly state."
3. "*Vainly* we offer each ample oblation."
4. "*Here* sleeps he *now.*"
5. "The waves are white *below.*"
   The waves are white *below him.*
6. "Heat *me* these irons hot."
   Heat *for me* these irons hot.
7. "Willie has come *home*—early."
   Willie has come *to his home—at an early hour.*

REM.—"Below"—"me"—"home,"—and "early," are *substituted* for Adverbial Phrases.—[See Part I., page 23.]

OBS. 2.—Words are also substituted for Adverbial Sentences.

EXAMPLES.—"While *there* we visited the prison;" for, while *we were at Auburn*, we visited the prison.
"*Then, when I am thy captive*, talk of chains."

OBS. 3.—An Adverb often modifies a Phrase.

EXAMPLES.—1. We went *almost* TO BOSTON.
2. Wilkes sailed *quite* AROUND THE WORLD.
3. Engraved *expressly* FOR THE LADIES' GARLAND.

OBS. 4.—Adverbs may consist of Words, Phrases, and Sentences.

1. *A Word.*—The *very* best men *sometimes* commit faults.
2. *A Phrase.*—"*In the beginning,* God created the heaven and the earth."
3. *A Sentence.*—"They kneeled *before they fought.*"

OBS. 5.—The Words which Adverbs properly modify are sometimes understood.

EXAMPLE.—Thou canst but add one bitter wo
To those [ ] *already there.*

OBS. 6.—Adverbs sometimes take the place of Verbs, which they modify.

EXAMPLES.—"*Off, off,* I bid you." "*To arms!*"
"*Back* to thy punishment, false fugitive!"

OBS. 7.—Adverbs sometimes take the place of Nouns, and hence become *Pro*nouns.

EXAMPLES.—1. "Till *then*"—for, till that time.
2. "From *there*"—for, from that place.
3. "And I have made a pilgrimage *from far.*"—*Hosmer.*
4. "Oh, let the ungentle spirit learn from *hence*
A small unkindness is a great offense."

OBS. 8.—Participles become Adverbs when they indicate the manner of an action, or modify a quality.

EXAMPLES.—1. "The surging billows and the gamboling storms
Come, *crouching,* to his feet."
2. "Now it mounts the wave,
And rises, *threatening,* to the frowning sky."
3. "'Tis strange, 'tis *passing* strange."
4. "A virtuous household, but *exceeding* poor."

OBS. 9.—A few words, commonly used as Prepositions, are sometimes used Adverbially.

EXAMPLES.—1. "Thou didst look *down* upon the naked earth."
2. "And may at last my weary age
3. Find *out* the peaceful hermitage."—*Milton.*

CLASSIFICATION OF ADVERBS.

REM.—The classes of Adverbs are very numerous. The following are the most important:

I. OF THE FORMS OF ADVERBS.

OBS. 1.—Some Words are used almost exclusively as Adverbs; such are *Primitive Words.*

EXAMPLES.—Ever—here—now—not—then—there.

OBS. 2.—But most Words used as Adverbs are *Derivative Words*—their Radicals being commonly used as *Nouns* or as *Adjectives.*

EXAMPLES

1. *From Nouns.*—*Al*ways—night*ly*—hour*ly*—*a*loft—*a*shore.
2. *From Adjectives.*— Brilliant*ly*—right*ly*—soft*ly*—virtuous*ly*.

OBS. 3.—Many Words, commonly used as Nouns, Adjectives, Prepositions, &c. become Adverbs *by representation* or *substitution.*

EXAMPLES.—1. "William rises *early*"—*at an early hour.*
2. "You have come too *late*"—*at too late a day.*
3. "Warner will come *home*"—*to his home.*
4. "He will return *to-morrow*"—*on the morrow.*
5. "The captain had gone *below*"—*below deck.*
6. "Is the agent *within?*"—*within the house.*

[See page 23, Obs. 2.]

II. OF THE FUNCTIONS OF ADVERBS.

PRIN.—Adverbs are commonly divided into two primary classes:—

1. Adverbs of *Manner,* and
2. Adverbs of *Circumstance.*

DEF. 126.—*Adverbs of Manner* are those which answer to the question *How?*

OBS. 1.—Adverbs of *Manner* are such as indicate—

1. *Affirmation.*—Aye—certainly—doubtless—surely—verily, &c.
2. *Doubt.*—Perchance—perhaps—possibly, &c.
3. *Mode.*—Aloud—asunder—how—so—together—thus, &c.
4. *Negation.*—Nay—not.

OBS. 2.—Phrases and Sentences often indicate the *manner of an act.*

EXAMPLES.

Phrases.—1. God moves *in a mysterious way.*"

2. "Silence now
Is brooding *like a gentle spirit* o'er
The still and pulseless world."

3. "Omar had passed seventy-five years *in honor and prosperity.*"

Sentences.—4. "He died *as he lived*—a devotee of mammon."

5. "There are departed beings that I have loved *as I never again shall love* in this world."

DEF. 127.—*Adverbs of Circumstance* are such as ask or answer the questions *When? Where? How much? Why?* —indicating *Time, Place, Degree, Cause.*

I. OF TIME.

REM.—All Words used to *ask* or to *answer* the questions "*When?*" or "*How often?*" are properly called *Adverbs of Time.*

EXAMPLES.—1. *Present.*—Instantly—now—presently—yet, &c.

2. *Past.* — Already — heretofore —hitherto—lately—yesterday, &c.

3. *Future.*—Henceforth—hereafter—soon, &c.

4. *Absolute.*—Always—ever—never, &c.

5. *Repeated.*—Continually—often—rarely—sometimes, &c.

OBS. 1.—Phrases and Sentences also perform the office of *Adverbs of time.*

EXAMPLES.

Phrases.—1. "*In the beginning,* God created the heaven and the earth."

2. "The Christmas rose is in bloom during the month of January."

3. "*At midnight,* in his guarded tent,
The Turk was dreaming."

Sentences.—4. "And as Jesus passed by, he saw a man who was blind."

5. "I think of the friends who had roamed with me there
When the sky was so blue, and the flowers were so fair."

6. "Ye that keep watch in heaven, *as earth, asleep,
Unconscious lies,* effuse your mildest beams."

II. OF PLACE.

OBS. 2.—All Words used to *ask* or to *answer* the questions Where? Whither? or Whence? are classed as *Adverbs of Place.*

EXAMPLES.—1. *In a Place.*—Here—there—where? &c.
2. *To a Place.*—Hither—thither—whither? &c.
3. *From a Place.*—Hence—thence—whence? &c.

OBS. 3.—Most Adverbs of Place are in the form of *Phrases.*

EXAMPLES.—We came { in the cars, from Boston, through Springfield, to New York, viâ Norwalk.

And many in the form of *Sentences.*

EXAMPLE.—"*Where wealth and freedom reign,* contentment fails."

OBS. 4.—Words which answer to the questions, "*How much? How far? To what extent?*—are classed as *Adverbs of Degree.*

EXAMPLES.—Altogether—hardly—little—much—quite—merely—too—very, &c.

OBS. 5.—Words used to ask or to answer the questions, *Why? Wherefore?* &c., are classed as *Adverbs of Cause.*

EXAMPLES.—Accordingly—consequently—hence—therefore—wherefore, &c.
"Let others brave the flood *in quest of gain.*"

MODIFICATION.

PRIN.—Some Adverbs are modified, like Adjectives, by comparison.

EXAMPLES.

	Pos.	*Comp.*	*Superl.*
1. *By use of Suffixes*..........	Soon,....	Sooner,......	Soonest.
2. *By " Auxiliary Adverbs*...	Wisely,..	*More* wisely..	*Most* wisely

EXERCISES.

☞ Let the following Adverbs be classified and their Modification given:

How,	Already	In a moment,
Not,	Quickly	In flower,
There,	Vilely,	O'er the ruins,
Soon,	Eagerly	At pile.

☞ Let the Adverbial Words, Phrases, and Sentences, in the following Examples, be pointed out and parsed after the following

MODEL.

1. "E'en *now, where Alpine solitudes ascend,*
I sit me *down, a pensive hour to spend;*
And placed *on high, above the storm's career,*
Look *downward, where a hundred realms appear.*"

Now............Modifies "sit"—denoting *time;* hence, an Adverb.
Where Alpine solitudes ascend, . } Modifies "sit"—denoting *place;* hence, an Adverb.
Down............Modifies "sit"—denoting *place;* hence, an Adverb.
A pensive hour to spend,........ } Modifies "sit"—denoting *cause;* hence, an Adverb.
On high,..........Modifies "placed"—denoting *place;* hence, an Adverb
Above the storm's career, ... } Modifies "placed"—denoting *place;* hence, an Adverb.
Downward,.......Modifies "look"—denoting *place;* hence, an Adverb.
Where a hundred realms appear,. } Modifies "look"—denoting *place;* hence, an Adverb.

2. "Earth keeps me *here*
Awhile; yet I shall leave it, and shall rise
On fairer wings than thine, to skies more clear."

Here,.......Modifies "keeps"—denoting *place;* hence, Adverb of Place.
Awhile,.....Modifies "keeps"—denoting *time;* hence, Adverb of Time.
On wings,...Modifies "rise"—denoting *means;* hence, Adverb of Means.
("On fairer wings than thine," is the Modified Adverb.)
Than thine,..Modifies "fairer"—denoting *degree;* hence, Adverb of Degree.
To skies,....Modifies "rise"—denoting *place;* hence, Adverb of Place.
("To skies more clear," is the Modified Adverb.)
More,.......Modifies "clear"—denoting *degree;* hence, Adverb of Degree.

3. "*How much better* satisfied he is!"

How,.......Modifies "much;" hence, an Adverb.
Much.......Modifies "better;" hence, an Adverb.
Better,......Modifies "satisfied;" hence, an Adverb.

OBS. 1.—Let it be remembered that the term "Adverbs" is applied to a distinct element in the structure of Sentences—that the function of that element may be performed by a single *Word* or by a combination of Words, constituting a Phrase or a Sentence. In analyzing Sentences containing these three distinct forms of the Adverbial Element, we proceed according to the MODELS given above. But,

OBS. 2.—The *Words* composing an Adverbial Phrase or Sentence have also their distinct *individual* offices. Thus, the Adverbial Phrase "Above the storm's career," consists of a *Preposition*, (above)—an *Adjective*, (the)—an *Adjective*, (storm's)—a *Noun*, (career).

So also the Adverbial Sentence, "Where a hundred realms appear," consists of a *Conjunction*, (where)—an *Adjective*. (a)—an *Adjective*, (hundred—a *Noun*, (realms)—and a *Verb*, (appear). Hence,

OBS. 3.—In *Proximate* Analysis, it is sufficient to discuss the *Elements of Principal Sentences;* while, in *Ultimate* Analysis, each separate Word composing an Element, is to be parsed separately.

ADDITIONAL EXAMPLES.

4. "*Noiselessly* around,
From perch to perch, the solitary bird
Passes."
5. "*How* is it possible *not* to feel a profound sense of the responsibleness of this Republic to all future ages."
6. "*In a moment* he flew quickly past."
7. "For *there* the shield of the mighty is *vilely* cast *away*."
8. "Thy pencil glows in every flower;"
9. "Where Sense can reach, or Fancy rove,
From hill to field, from field to grove,
Across the wave, around the sky,
There's not a spot, nor deep, nor high,
Where the Creator has not trod,
And left the footsteps of a God."

"Eternal Hope! when yonder spheres sublime
Pealed their first notes to sound the march of Time,
10. Thy joyous youth began—but not to fade,
When all the sister planets have decayed:
When, wrapt in fire, the realms of ether glow,
And Heaven's last thunder shakes the world below,
11. Thou, undismayed, shalt o'er the ruins smile,
And light thy torch at Nature's funeral pile!"

PREPOSITIONS.

DEF. 128.—A Word used to introduce a Phrase, showing the *relation* of its Object to the Word which the Phrase qualifies, is

A Preposition.

LIST.

A, ... "Wild winds and mad waves drive the vessel *a* wreck."
About, ... "We walked *about* town."
Above, ... "There is a ferry *above* the falls."
Across, ... "*Across* the ocean came a pilgrim bark."
Aboard, ... "They came *aboard* ship."
Aboard of, ... "We succeeded in getting *aboard of* her."
After, ... "He that cometh *after* me, is preferred before me."
Against, ... "He that is not for me, is *against* me."
Along, ... "Winds that run *along* the summits of their hills."
Amid, ... "We stowed them *amid*-ships."
Amidst, ... "*Amidst* the mists, he thrusts his fists."
Among, ... "He became a great favorite *among* the boys."
Amongst, ... "We made diligent search *amongst* the rubbish."
Around, ... "The chill dews of evening were falling *around* me."
As, ... "That England can spare from her service such men *as* him."
Aslant, ... "It struck *aslant* the beam."
Astride, ... "He sat *astride* the beam."
As for, ... "*As for* me and my house."
As to, ... "*As to* that, I have nothing to say."
At, ... "He was *at* work *at* noon."
Athwart, ... "The dolphin leaped *athwart* her bows."
Before, ... "He stood *before* the people."
Behind, ... "She stood *behind* a rick of barley."
Below, ... "The captain was *below* decks."
Beneath, ... "*Beneath* the mouldering ruins."
Beside, ... "*Beside* its embers, red and clear."
Besides, ... "There was a famine in the land, *besides* the first famine."
Between......... "*Between* whom, perfect friendship has existed."
Betwixt, ... "There is no difference *betwixt* them."
Beyond, ... "*Beyond* all doubt."

But, ... "All went *but* me."
But for, ... "And *but for* these vile guns."
By, ... "To sail *by* Ephesus."—"They stood *by* the cross."
Concerning, ... "*Concerning* whom I have before written."
Despite of, ... "He will rise to fame, *despite of* all opposition."
Devoid of, ... "You live *devoid of* peace."
During, ... "This has occurred many times *during* the year."
Ere, ... "And *ere* another evening's close."
Except, ... "*Except* these bonds."
Excepting, ... "*Excepting* that bad habit, the teacher was faultless."
For, ... "*For* me your tributary stores combine."
From, ... "Playful children, just let loose *from* school."
From among, ... "*From among* thousand celestial ardors."
From between, ... "He came *from between* the lakes."
From off, ... "This lady-fly I take *from off* the grass."
In, ... "*In* the beginning."
Instead of, ... "*Instead of* the thorn shall come up the fir."
In lieu of, ... "She has that sum *in lieu of* dower."
Into, ... "*Into* these glassy eyes put light."
Like, ... "An hour *like* this may well display the emptiness of human grandeur."
Near, ... "His residence is *near* the church."
Next, ... "Plural nominatives should be placed *next* their verbs"
Nigh, ... "Come not *nigh* me."
Notwithstanding, "*Notwithstanding* this, we remain friends."
Of, ... "*Of* the arts *of* peace."
Off, ... "He fell *off* the bows."
On, ... "*On* a bed of green sea-flowers."
Opposite, ... "Our friend lives *opposite* the Exchange."
Over, ... "High *o'er* their heads the weapons swung."
Out of, ... "*Out of* the cooling brine to leap."
Past, ... "We came *past* Avon."
Per, ... "Twelve hundred dollars *per* annum."
Previous to, ... "*Previous to* this, his character has been good."
Respecting, ... "Nothing was known *respecting* him."
Round, ... "He went *round* the parish, making complaints."
Since .... "*Since* Saturday he has not been seen."
Save, ... "All, *save* this little nook of land."
Saving, ... "With habits commendable, *saving* only this—he chews tobacco."

Through,........"Dian's crest floats *through* the azure air."
Throughout,....."Nor once, *throughout* that dismal night."
Than,..........."*Than* whom none higher sat."
Till,............"He laboured hard *till* noon."
To,............."We purpose *to* go *to* Rochester to-day."
Touching,......."*Touching* these things, whereof I am accused."
Towards,........"They returned *towards* evening."
Under,.........."Then was my horse killed *under* me."
Underneath,....."And *underneath* his feet, he cast the darkness."
Unlike,........."*Unlike* all that I had ever before seen."
Until,.........."We shall not return *until* Saturday."
Unto,..........."*Unto* him who rules the invisible armies of eternity
Up,............."The whole fleet was sailing *up* the river."
Upon,..........."He stood *upon* the highest peak."
Via,............"This stage is for Buffalo, *via* Batavia."
With,..........."*With* cautious steps and slow."
Within,........."Peace be *within* these walls."
Without,........"*Without* it, what is man?"
Worth,.........."He possessed an estate, *worth* five thousand pounds."

OBS. 1.—The antecedent term of relation—the word which the Phrase, introduced by a Preposition, qualifies, may be a

Noun.—The *house* of God.
Pronoun.—*Who* of us shall go? I care not *which* of you.
Adjective.—It is *good* for nothing.
Verb.—We *love* to study, we *delight* in improvement.
Participle.—*Jumping* from a precipice.
Adverb.—He is *too* wise to err.

OBS. 2.—The antecedent term of the relation expressed by a Preposition, is sometimes understood.

EXAMPLES.—1. "O refuge
Meet for fainting pilgrims [ ] on this desert way."

NOTE.—In the above and similar examples, the ellipsis of the antecedent word need not be supplied *in parsing, unless the sense plainly requires it.* But the Phrase may be parsed as qualifying the word which its Antecedent would qualify, if expressed.

2. "*Which flung its purple o'er his path to heaven.*"

Here the Phrase "to heaven" properly modifies *leading*, or a word of similar office, *understood.* But "leading," modified by this Phrase, would qualify "path." Hence the Phrase, "to heaven"—as a *representative* of the whole Phrase "leading to heaven"—may be attached to path.

Obs. 3.—Prepositions introducing Substantive and Independent Phrases, have no Antecedents.

Examples.—1. "*As for* me and my house, we will serve the Lord."
2. "And, *on* the whole, the sight was very painful."—*Todd.*
3. "O *for* a lodge in some vast wilderness."—*Cowper.*

Obs. 4.—The Consequent term of relation may be,
A Word.—"He stood before the *people.*"
A Phrase.—"Time, spent in *receiving impertinent visits.*"
A Sentence.—"And cries of '*live for ever,*' struck the skies."

Obs. 5.—The Consequent term of relation—Object—is sometimes understood.

Examples.—"And the waves are white below [ ]."
"These crowd around [ ] to ask him of his health."

Many grammarians call these Prepositions *Adverbs*, without giving a proper explanation. They are Prepositions, having their Objects understood. But, as the Phrases of which they form parts are always used Adverbially, the Prepositions—as *representatives* of their Phrases—are Adverbs. Hence, when thus used, each Preposition performs a double office—Prepositional, as leader of the Phrase—Adverbial, as representative of the Phrase.

Obs. 6.—The Preposition is often understood—generally when its Phrase follows Verbs of *giving, selling, coming, &c.*

Examples.—1. Mary gave [ ] me a rose—Mary gave a rose *to* me.
2. I sold [ ] Mr. Shepard my wheat—sold wheat *to* Shepard.
3. William has gone *from* home to-day—he will come [ ] home to-morrow."
4. These crowd *around.* Mary gave *me* a rose.

"Me" and "around" are—in the same sense, and by the same rule—Adverbs, viz.: as *representatives* of the Adverbial Phrases to which they severally belong. As *words*, simply, "me" is a Pronoun—object of *to* understood: "around" is a Preposition—showing a relation of "crowd" and *him*, understood.

Obs. 7.—Prepositions are sometimes incorporated with their Objects

Examples.—I go a *fishing.*—He fell *a-sleep.*—Come *a-board.*

OBS. 8.—Prepositions are sometimes used in predication with Verbs.

EXAMPLES.—1. Its idle hopes are *o'er*.
2. That was not thought *of*.

OBS. 9.—A Preposition commonly indicates the office of the Phrase which it introduces.

In, *on*, *under*, *above*, &c., indicate a relation of *place*, including the idea of *rest*.

EXAMPLES.—William's hat is { *in* the hall, *on* the stool, *under* the table.

From, *to*, *into*, *through*, *out of*, &c., indicate a relation of *place*, with the idea of *motion*.

EXAMPLES.—We came { *from* New York, *to* Boston, *through* Springfield.

Of, generally indicates a relation of *possession*.

EXAMPLE.—"The lay *of the last minstrel*"—the last *minstrel's* lay.

As, *like*, *than*, &c., indicate a relation of *comparison*.

EXAMPLES.—1. "It is not fit for such *as* us
To sit with rulers of the land."—*W. Scott.*
2. "All great, learned men, *like* me,
Once learned to read their A, B, C."
3. "Thou hast been *wiser* all the while *than me*."—*Southey*

During, *till*, *since*, &c., indicate a relation of time.

EXAMPLES.—1. "We have vacation *during the whole month of July*."
2. "*Since Saturday*, we have not seen him."

But, as the kind of relation expressed by a given Preposition is not uniform, no perfect classification can be made.

☞ For other observations on Prepositions, see PART III.—*Prepositions.*

EXERCISES.

1. *Where streams of earthly joy exhaustless rise.*

Of, . . .Shows a relation of "streams" and "joy," Hence, a Preposition.

2. "*O refuge,*
Meet for fainting pilgrims."

For, . .Shows a relation of "meet" and "pilgrims." Hence, a Preposition

3. "On the plains,
And spangled fields, and in the mazy vales,
The living throngs of earth before Him fall,
With thankful hymns, receiving from His hands
Immortal life and gladness."

On, ...Shows a relation of [*existing* understood, which qualifies] "throngs" and "plains and fields." Hence, a Preposition.

In, ...Shows a relation of [*existing* understood, which qualifies] "throngs" and "vales." Hence, a Preposition.

Of, ...Shows a relation of "throngs" and "earth." Hence, a Preposition.

Before, . . .Shows a relation of "fall" and "him." Hence, a Preposition.

With, ...Shows a relation of [*worshipping*, or some equivalent word understood, which qualifies] "throngs" and "hymns." Hence, a Preposition.

☞ Let the Pupils point out the Prepositions, with their several Antecedents and Objects, in the following

ADDITIONAL EXAMPLES.

4. "The chief FAULT *of* Coleridge LIES *in* the style, which has been justly objected *to*, *on* account *of* its obscurity, general turgidness *of* diction, and a profusion *of* new-coined double epithets."

5. "Southey, among all our living poets, stands aloof, and 'alone in his glory;' for he alone of them all has adventured to illustrate, in poems of magnitude, the different characters, customs, and manners of nations.

6. To him, who, in the love of nature, holds
Communion with her visible forms, she speaks
A various language:
7. For his gayer hours
She has a voice of gladness, and a smile
And eloquence of beauty;
8. And she glides
Into his dark musings, with a mild
And gentle sympathy, that steals away
Their sharpness, ere he is aware.

CONJUNCTIONS.

Rem.—It should be remembered that Prepositions connect words *by showing a relation.*

We have another class of Words, used *simply to connect* Words and Phrases similar in construction, and to introduce Sentences. Hence,

Def. 129.—A Conjunction is a Word used to join Words or Phrases, or to introduce a Sentence.

Example.—Mary and Anna have perfect lessons *because* they study diligently.

Rem. 1.—In this example, "and" connects "Mary" and "Anna"—two words having the same construction—and "because" introduces an Auxiliary Sentence.

LIST.

The following are the principal Words which are commonly used as Conjunctions :—

After,*	Either,	Likewise,	Than,*
Again,	Else,	Moreover,	That,
Also,	Except,*	Nay,	Then,
Although,*	For,*	Neither,	Therefore,
And,	Further,	Nor,	Though,*
As,*	Furthermore,	Now,	Thus,
As well as,*	Howbeit,	Notwithstanding,*	Unless,*
Because,*	However,*	Or,	When,*
Before,*	Howsoever,*	Otherwise,	Wherefore,
Being,*	If,*	Provided,*	While,*
Besides,	Inasmuch as,*	Since,*	Whilst,*
Both,	In case,	So,	Yet.
But,	Lest,*	Still,	

Rem. 2.—A few other words are sometimes used as Conjunctions.

Rem. 3.—The words in the above List, marked thus (*), commonly introduce Auxiliary Sentences.

Obs. 1.—Conjunctions used to introduce Auxiliary Sentences, and some others, constitute also an index or type of the office of the Sentences which they introduce.

Examples.—"*If* he repent, forgive him."

"*As* you journey, sweetly sing."

In these examples, "if" renders its Sentence *conditional*:—"as" indicates that its Sentence ("you journey") modifies "sing" in respect to *time*.

NOTE.—*When*, *as*, *since*, and many other Conjunctions used to introduce Auxiliary Sentences, are called, by some grammarians, *Conjunctive Adverbs*. "And the rest will I set in order *when* I come." We are told that "when," in the above example, is an Adverb of Time, relating to the two Verbs, "will set" and "come."

We are also told (and properly) that Adverbs of *time* are those which answer to the question "*when?*"

But does "when," in the above example, "answer to the question *when?*" Certainly not. Then it cannot be an Adverb of Time. But the Auxiliary Sentence, "when I come," does answer to the question "*when*." It tells when "I will set the rest in order." Hence the *Sentence*, "when I come," is an Adverb of Time; and the Word "when"—used only to introduce that Sentence—connecting it to "will set," is a Conjunction. [See the preceding observation.]

OBS. 2.—A Word used chiefly to introduce a Sentence is therefore a Conjunction. If the Sentence introduced by it is Auxiliary Adverbial in office, it may properly be called an *Adverbial Conjunction*.

Let the Pupil remember that it is the *Sentence* that is Adverbial—*not* the *Word* used to introduce the Sentence.

OBS. 3.—The Conjunction *nor* generally performs a secondary office—that of a negative Adverb.

EXAMPLE.—"Man wants but little here below,
Nor wants that little long."

In this example "nor" introduces the Sentence, and also gives it a negative signification.

The Conjunction "*lest*" has sometimes a similar construction.

"Love not sleep, *lest* thou come to poverty."

OBS. 4.—DOUBLE CONJUNCTIONS.—Two Conjunctions are sometimes used to introduce the same Sentence.

EXAMPLES.—"It seems *as if* they were instructed by some secret instinct."

"*And yet*, fair bow, no fabling dreams."

As though, *but that*, and some other words, are often used as Double Conjunctions.

OBS. 5.—*But, when* an Auxiliary Sentence precedes a Principal Sentence, the Conjunctions introducing them are not to be regarded as double, although they may be in juxtaposition.—[See this Obs.]

OBS. 6.—In addition to those Words properly called Conjunctions, we have other words used to introduce Sentences—as a *secondary office*.

EXAMPLES.—1. "The grave, *that* never spoke before,
Hath found at length, a tongue to chide."
2. "We are watchers of a beacon,
Whose light must never die."

REM. 1.—"That never spake before," is an Auxiliary Sentence introduced by the word "*that.*"
The *principal* office of "*that*" is *Substantive*—the Subject of "spoke." Its *secondary* office is *Conjunctive*—introduces its Sentence and connects it with its Principal.

REM. 2.—In Example (2), the Word "*whose*" has a *Principal* office—Adjunct of "light"—and a *secondary* office—introduces its Sentence and connects it with its Principal.
[For other observations, the student is referred to PART III., CONJUNCTIONS.]

EXERCISES.

"*God created the heaven and the earth.*"

"And,"....Connects "heaven" and "earth." Hence, a Conjunction.

"*Temperance and frugality promote health and secure happiness.*"

"And,"....Connects "temperance" and "frugality." Hence, a Conjunction.
"And,"....Connects "promote" and "secure." Hence, a Conjunction.

"*And the eyes of the sleepers waxed deadly and chill.*"

"And,"....Introduces a Sentence. Hence, a Conjunction.
"And,"....Connects "deadly" and "chill." Hence, a Conjunction.

"*And hoary peaks that proudly prop the skies
Thy dwellings are.*"

"And,"....Introduces a Sentence. Hence, a Conjunction.
"That," ...Is the Subject of "prop." Hence, a Substantive.
It also introduces its Sentence, and connects it with "peaks."

"*My heart is awed within me when I think*
Of the great miracle that still goes on
In silence round me."

"*When*," .Introduces the Auxiliary Sentence. Hence, a Conjunction.
" Its Sentence is Adverbial in its office. Hence, an Adverbial Conjunction.
"*When*" is not an Element—*i. e.*, it bears no part in the structure of its Sentence. It is neither a Principal Part, nor an Adjunct; it *primarily* connects: *secondarily*, indicates the office of its Sentence. (See Obs. 1, above.)

"That," ..Is the Subject of "goes." Hence, a Substantive.
As a *secondary* office, "that" introduces its Sentence, and connects it with "miracle."

EXCLAMATION.

DEF. 130.—A word used to express a sudden or intense emotion, is

An Exclamation.

OBS. 1.—Exclamations may consist—

1. Of Letters—as, *O! Oh! Ah! Lo!*
2. Of Words—commonly used as Nouns, Adjectives, Verbs, and Adverbs—as, *Wo! Strange! Hark! Really! Behold. Shocking!*
3. Of Phrases—*For shame!*
4. Of Sentences—"*O, Ephraim! How can I give thee up!*"

OBS. 2.—Exclamations are followed by
Words—"O, Liberty!"—"Ah, the treasure!"
Phrases—"O, for a lodge in some vast wilderness!"
Sentences—"O, bear me to some solitary cell!"

REM.—The term *Exclamation* is preferred to *Interjection*, as being more appropriate to its office.

Exclaim—"to cry out." This we do with the use of Exclamations.

Interject—"to cast between." We very seldom *cast* these words *between* others—they are generally placed *before* other words.

WORDS OF EUPHONY.

DEF. 131.—A Word used chiefly for the sake of *sound*, or to change the *position*, *accent*, or *emphasis* of other Words in a Sentence, is

A Word of Euphony.

EXAMPLES.—1. "I think *there* is a knot of you,
Beneath that hollow tree."

"*There*" is used to allow the Predicate "*is*" to precede its Subject "*knot*."

2. "I sit *me* down, a pensive hour to spend."

"*Me*" is used to throw the accent on the word "*down*."

3. "These were thy charms, sweet village! sports like these,
With sweet succession, taught *e'en* toil to please."

"*E'en*" is used to make "toil" emphatic.

OBS. 1.—Words of Euphony are such as commonly belong to some other "part of speech." But they are properly called Words of Euphony when they do not perform their usual grammatical offices. They are, then, in their offices chiefly Rhetorical—being used,

(1.) To render other Words emphatic.

EXAMPLES.—1. "*Even* in their ashes live their wonted fires."
2. "The moon *herself* is lost in heaven."

(2.) To change the position of the parts of a Sentence.

EXAMPLES.—3. "*There* are no idlers here."
4. "Now, *then*, we are prepared to take up the main question."

(3.) To preserve the rhythm in a line of poetry.

EXAMPLES.—5. "I sit *me* down a pensive hour to spend."
6. "His teeth *they* chatter, *chatter* still."

REM. 1.—It is quite idle to call—as most grammarians do—the Word *even*, in Example (1), an Adverb, modifying "live;" for its sole office is to render the Phrase "*in their ashes*" emphatic. Such office is *Rhetorical*, not Grammatical.

REM. 2.—To call the word "*there*," in Example (3), an Adverb of Place," is manifestly absurd; since the Verb "are" is modified by the Adverb "here," and hence cannot, at the same time, be modified by a Word of directly the opposite signification.

The same remark is also applicable to the word *then*," in Example (4).

REM. 3.—The Word "*me*," in Example (5), is in *form* of a Pronoun. its *office* is to throw the accent on "down," and on the first syllable ensive." The Verb "sit," is always Intransitive; hence it cannot an object. The Word "*me*," is therefore a Rhetorical Word—a of Euphony.

OBS. 2—Words are often *transposed*, *lengthened*, *shortened*, and in other wa anged for the sake of sound. (See "Euphony," in Part III.)

WORDS VARYING IN THEIR ETYMOLOGY.

REM. 1.—Words are similar in *Orthoëpy*, when they are pronounced with the same sound of the same letter.

EXAMPLES.—*There, their—all, awl—ant, aunt.*

REM. 2.—They are similar in *Orthography* when they are formed by the same letters, similarly arranged.

EXAMPLES.—*Read, read—ex'tract, extract'—wind, wind.*

REM. 3.—They are similar in *Etymology* when they perform a similar office in the construction of a Phrase or a Sentence.

REM. 4.—But it is plain that words similar in Orthoëpy differ in their Orthography—and words of similar Orthography perform widely different offices in different connections.

☞ *It should always be remembered by the scholar that the* OFFICE *of a word—not its shape—determines its Etymology.*

OBS.—Among the Words of similar Orthography that differ in their Etymology are the following:—

A,........Adj........Webster wrote *a* Dictionary—Walker wrote another.
A,........Prep. ....Wild winds and mad waves drive the vessel *a* wreck.
Above,....Prep......He stands *above* us.
Above,....Adv. .....By the terms *above* specified.
After,.....Prep......He that cometh *after* me is preferred before me.
After,.....Conj......He came *after* you left.
After,.....Adj.......He was in the *after* part of the ship.
As,.......Prep......To redeem such a rebel *as* me.—*Wesley.*
As, ...Conj......Just *as* the twig is bent the tree's inclined.
As, ...Adv. .....Nature, *as* far as art can do it, should be imitated.
As, ...Pron......Such *as* I have give I unto thee.
Before,....Prep. ....He stood *before* the people.
Before,....Conj......They kneeled *before* they fought.
Both,.....Adj.......Situated on *both* sides of the river.
Both,.....Pron......Lepidus flatters *both*—of *both* is flattered.
Both,.....Conj......And now he is *both* loved and respected.
But,......Prep......All *but* me were rewarded.
But,......Conj. .....I go—*but* I return.
But,......Adv. .....If we go, we can *but* die.
But,......Verb......I cannot *but* rejoice at his unexpected prosperity.
Ere, ...Prep......And *ere* another evening's close.
Ere, ...Conj......And *ere* we could arrive [at] the point proposed.
For, ...Prep......They traveled *for* pleasure.
For, ...Conj......He can not be a scholar, *for* he will not study.
Like, ...Prep......Nature all blooming *like* thee.
Like, ...Adj.......*Like* causes produce *like* effects.
Like, ...Verb.....We *like* whatever gives us pleasure.
Near, ...Adj.......At the *near* approach of the star of day.
Near, ...Prep......We live *near* the springs.
Near, ...Adv. .....Books were never *near* so numerous.
Neither,...Adj.......He can debate on *neither* side of the question.
Neither,...Pron......We saw *neither* of them.
Neither,...Conj......The boy could *neither* read nor write.
Next,.....Adj.......The *next* generation.
Next,.....Prep......Adjectives should be placed *next* their substantives.

Off,	Adj.	The *off* ox should keep the furrow.
Off,	Prep.	William fell *off* the load.
Only,	Adj.	Love and love *only* is the loan for love.
Only,	Adv.	*Only* observe what a swarm is running after her
Opposite,	Adj.	On the *opposite* bank of the river.
Opposite,	Prep.	We stood *opposite* the Exchange.
Past,	Adj.	A *past* transaction.
Past,	Prep.	It was *past* mid-day
Round,	Adj.	Like the *round* ocean.
Round,	Prep.	Flung *round* the bier.
Still,	Adj.	*Still* waters reflect a milder light.
Still,	Adv.	*Still* struggling, he strives to stand.
Still,	Conj.	*Still*, the reflection has troubled me.
Since,	Prep.	*Since* yesterday, we have taken nothing.
Since,	Conj.	*Since* I cannot go, I will be contented here.
So,	Adj.	Solomon was wise—we are not *so*.
So,	Adv.	*So* calm, *so* bright.
So,	Conj.	"I'll say thee nay, *so* thou wilt woo."
Than,	Conj.	She is more nice *than* wise.
Than,	Prep.	*Than* whom none higher sat.
Than,	Pron.	We have more *than* heart can wish.
That,	Adj.	*That* book is mine.
That,	Pron. Rel.	"Him *that* cometh unto me, I will in no wise cast out."
That,	Pron. Adj.	Forgive me my foul murder? *that* cannot be.
That,	Conj.	I am glad *that* he has lived thus long.
Then,	Adv.	*Then*, when I am thy captive, talk of chains.
Then,	Conj.	*Then*, I'll look up.
Then,	Pron.	Till *then*.
Till,	Prep.	They labored hard *till* night.
Till,	Conj.	*Till* I come, give attention to reading.
Until,	Prep.	From morn, even *until* night.
Until,	Conj.	*Until* the day dawn.
What,	Adj.	At *what* hour did you arrive?
What,	Rel. Pron.	*What* Reason weaves, by Passion is undone.
What,	Inter. Pron.	*What* does it avail?
What,	Exclam.	*What!* is thy servant a dog?
Within,	Prep.	To inscribe a circle *within* a circle.
Within,	Adj.	Received on the *within* bond, five hundred dollars.

OBSERVATIONS ON SOME OF THE FOREGOING WORDS.

As. .....When this Word introduces a Sentence, it is properly called a Conjunction.

EXAMPLE.—"*As* ye journey, sweetly sing."

When it introduces a Phrase, it is a Preposition, and is then generally equivalent to the Preposition *for.*

EXAMPLES.—1. "He gave me this *as* the latest news from the army."
2. "I am always fearful, lest I should tell you that *for* news, with which you are well acquainted."
3. "*For* example."
4. "I mention these *as* a few exemplifications."
5. "And melancholy marked him *for* her own."—*Gray.*
6. "They will seek out some particular herb which they do not use *as* food."—*Taylor.*
7. "His friends were counted *as* his enemies."—*Sigourney.*
8. "All mark thee *for* a prey."—*Cowper.*

The above examples clearly indicate that *as* is sometimes a Preposition.

REM.—Many grammarians insist that *as*, in the above and similar examples, "must be a Conjunction, because, in most cases, *it connects words in opposition.*

The same is true of other Prepositions.

EXAMPLES.—1. In the *city* of *New York.*
2. "——thy shadowy hand was seen
Writing thy *name* of *Death.*"—*Pollock.*
3. I took *you* for an honest *man.*
4. "And cries of—*live forever!*—struck the skies."

We do not claim that these examples contain words precisely in apposition—*as much so*, however, as any cases claimed to be connected by *as.*

As—is often used (by ellipsis of one or more words) as a Pronoun. [See REM. on *than* below.]

BUT. ....This word, like most Conjunctions, is derived from a Saxon Verb signifying "*except*"—"set aside"—"fail," &c.—[*See Webster's Improved Grammar.*]

In the list above given, the word retains its original signification and offer

EXAMPLES.—"I can not *but* rejoice."

Equivalent.—I can not *fail—omit* to rejoice.

Here "but" is a Verb, Potential Mode—and "rejoice" Verb, Infinitive Mode, depending on "but."

BUT is also used instead of the words, *if it were not.*

EXAMPLE.—"And *but* for these vile guns, he would himself have been a soldier."

BUT sometimes supplies the places of a Relative Pronoun and a Negative Adverb.

EXAMPLE.—"I scarce can meet a monument *but* holds my younger."

Equivalent.—I scarce can meet a monument *that* holds *not* my younger.

LIKE ...When this word qualifies a word, it is an Adjective—when it represents its Noun, it is an Adjective Pronoun. But when it shows a relation of two words, it is a Preposition.

EXAMPLES.—1. "These armies once lived, and breathed, and felt *like* us."
2. "An hour *like* this, may well display the emptiness of human grandeur."
3. "Yet all great learned men, *like* me,
Once learned to read their A, B, C."

THAN....This word always expresses comparison, and comparison implies a relation. When this relation is expressed by Words, *than* is a Preposition. When it is expressed by Sentences, and when Words, Phrases, or Sentences are merely connected by it, it is a Conjunction.

The use of it as a Preposition is sanctioned by good authority, ancient and modern.

EXAMPLES.—1. "They are stronger *than* lions."
2. "Thou shalt have no other gods *than me.*"—*Com. Pr.*
3. "But in faith, she had been wiser *than me.*"—*Southey.*
4. "Their works are more perfect *than those* of men."
Taylor.

THAN is also used as a Pronoun, when it is the Subject or Object of a Verb; as—"He does no more than is done by the rabbit." "Than," in this example, is the Subject of "*is done,*"—hence, a Pronoun. But, in this and similar examples, it may become a Preposition by supplying the ellipsis; as—"He does no more than [that which] is done by the rabbit." This is probably the more correct rendering.

THAN always introduces a Word, a Phrase, or a Sentence, which constitutes a *second term of a comparison.*

EXAMPLES.—1. "She is *more* nice *than* wise."

'Than" connects words, and is therefore a Conjunction.

2. "*Than* whom none *higher* sat."

"'Than" introduces a Phrase, and is a Preposition.

3. "We have *more than* heart could wish."

Than" is the object of "could wish," and introduces the Adjective Sentence which limits "more," hence—by virtue of the ellipsis—it is a Relative Pronoun. Supply the words suppressed by ellipsis, and "than" becomes a Preposition.

OBS. 1.—Many words are used as Prepositions or Conjunctions, according as they introduce Phrases or Sentences.

EXAMPLES.—John arrived *before* me.
John arrived *before* I did.
John arrived a little earlier *than* I [than me].
John arrived a little earlier *than* I did.
John arrived as soon *as* I [as me].
John arrived as soon *as* I did.

"Before me,"...Is a Phrase, used to modify "arrived;" hence, an *Adverb.*
"Before,"......Is a Preposition.
"Before I did," .Is a Sentence, used to modify "arrived;" hence, an *Adverb.*
"Before,"......Is a Conjunction.
"Than I," .....Is a Phrase, used to modify "arrived;" hence, an *Adverb.*
"Than I did,"..Is a Sentence, used to modify "arrived;" hence, an *Adverb.*
"As I,"........Is a Phrase, used to modify "arrived;" hence, an *Adverb.*
"As I did," ....Is a Sentence, used to modify "arrived;" hence an *Adverb.*

OBS. 2.—Of the many words thus used as Prepositions and Conjunctions, custom allows two—*as* and *than*—to be followed by Pronouns in the *Nominative form.*

EXAMPLES.—1. "Thou art wiser *than* I."
2. "Thou art as tall *as* I."

OBS. 3.—But the Objective form is also used by our best writers.

EXAMPLES.—1. "It is not fit for such as *us*
To sit with rulers of the land."—*W. Scott*

2. "There are thousands in the French army who could have done as well as *him*."—*Napier.*

3. "And though by Heaven's severe decree,
She suffers hourly more than *me*."—*Swift.*

4. "Than *whom* none higher sat."—*Milton.*

THAT .. This word is primarily an *Adjective*. But it is also used as a Pronoun; and, in consequence of the obscurity of an ellipsis (which may be generally supplied), it is often used as a Conjunction.

EXAMPLE.—"He demanded *that* payment should be made."

This may be resolved into two sentences.

"Payment should be made.
He demanded *that*."

Here "That" is the object of "demanded," and is substituted for the whole of the former sentence. But as the sense is not obscured, and as a perplexing tautology is thereby obviated, I prefer to call it a Conjunction. It is commonly used to introduce an Auxiliary Sentence—and when it follows a Transitive Verb, the Auxiliary is the *logical* Object of the Phrase or Sentence.

WORTH....Worth indicates value—and value implies a relation—and relation of words is commonly expressed by a Preposition.

EXAMPLE.—"He possessed an estate worth five hundred pounds per annum."

Equivalent.—"He has an annuity *of* five hundred pounds"

This word is used also as a Noun.

EXAMPLE.—"He was a man of great *worth*."

SO ......The word *so* is commonly used as an Adverb; but it is often used as a substitute for a Word, a Phrase, or a Sentence.

EXAMPLES.—You are industrious—not *so*.
John has become a good scholar
So I predicted.

It is sometimes a Conjunction used for *if*.

EXAMPLES.—"I'll frown, and be perverse, and say thee nay,
So thou wilt woo."—*Juliet.*

Nor—composed of *not* and *other*—retains the offices of its elements.

3. "*Nor* will I at my humble lot repine."

Here "nor"—being used to modify "repine"—is an Adverb of Negation. But, because it introduces a Sentence, additional to a former Sentence, it is a Conjunction: like many other Conjunctions, it indicates the office of the Sentence which it introduces, making it negative.

OBS.—Some words perform an *individual* office, and at the same time a *representative* office.

EXAMPLES.

1. Bring *hither* that book.	Equivalent sentences, each correct.
2. Bring that book *to me*.	
3. Bring *me* that book.	

In the examples above,

"Hither,"....modifies "bring." Hence, it is an *Adverb*
"To me,"....modifies "bring." Hence, it is an *Adverb*.
[To] "*me*,"...modifies "bring." Hence, it is an *Adverb*.

"Me," in the third example, *as a representative* for the Phrase (to me) of which it is a part, is an *Adverb*. But, being used for a *Noun*, it is a Pronoun; and, as the object of the Phrase, is in the *Objective case*.

"*The captain had gone below.*"

"Below,".......shows a relation of "had gone" to *deck* understood. Hence, it is a *Preposition*.
"Below [deck]".modifies "had gone" (denoting place). Hence, it is an *Adverb*.
"Below,".......*as a representative* of its (Adverbial) Phrase, modifies "had gone" (denoting place). Hence, it is an *Adverb*.

For farther illustrations, see Obs. 5 and 6, page 159; see also page 23, Obs. 1, 2.

REM.—A careful examination of the genius of the English language will disclose the fact, that a great majority of words perform at the same time two or more distinct offices. The RULE to be observed in parsing is, that *a word should be parsed according to its* PRINCIPAL *office in the Sentence.*

PART III.

SYNTAX.

REM.—In PART II. we have given attention to the discussion of WORDS considered as Elements of Language; embracing,

1. The *Classification* of *Words*, according to their *offices*.
2. The *Modification* of such *Words* as vary their *forms* to correspond with changes in their offices.

REM. 2.—We have now to consider the *Relations* of the various Elements of Language to each other, in the construction of Sentences.

DEF. 132.—Syntax treats of the construction of Sentences by determining the relation, agreement, and arrangement of Words, and of other Elements.

GENERAL PRINCIPLES AND DEFINITIONS TO BE NOTICED IN ANALYSIS AND CONSTRUCTION.

I. SENTENCES.

I. A SENTENCE is an assemblage of Words, so arranged as to express an entire proposition.

II. A Sentence consists of { PRINCIPAL ELEMENTS and ADJUNCT ELEMENTS.

III. THE PRINCIPAL ELEMENTS of a Sentence are those Words necessary to make the unqualified assertion.

☞ Make a Sentence having *Principal Elements* only.

IV. THE ADJUNCTS of a Sentence are the Words used to modify or describe other Elements in the Sentence.

☞ Make a Sentence having *Adjuncts*.

V. THE PRINCIPAL ELEMENTS of a Sentence are, { The SUBJECT, The PREDICATE, The OBJECT.

☞ Make a Sentence, and name the *Subject*, the *Predicate*, and the *Object*.

VI. The Predicate is the Word or Words that assert something of the Subject.

VII. The Object of a Sentence is that on which the act expressed by the Predicate terminates.

VIII. The Subject of a Sentence may be
IX. The Object of a Sentence may be
{ A Word, A Phrase, or A Sentence.

☞ Make a Sentence having a *Subject Word*.
Make a Sentence having a *Subject Phrase*.
Make a Sentence having a *Subject Sentence*.

X. A Word used as the *Subject* or the *Object* of a Sentence may be { A Noun, { *Common* or *Proper*. or A Pronoun, { *Personal*, *Relative*, *Interrogative* *Adjective*.

☞ Make Sentences having for its Subject—

1. A *Common Noun*.	4. A *Relative Pronoun*.
2. A *Proper Noun*.	5. An *Interrogative Pronoun*.
3. A *Personal Pronoun*.	6. An *Adjective Pronoun*.

XI. Nouns and Pronouns are of the { *Masculine Gender*, *Feminine Gender*, or *Neuter Gender*.

XII. Nouns and Pronouns are of the { *First Person*, *Second Person*, or *Third Person*.

XIII. Nouns and Pronouns are of the { *Singular Number*, or *Plural Number*.

☞ Make Sentences having Nouns and Pronouns of the different *Genders*, *Persons*, and *Numbers*.

XIV. The Subject of a Sentence is in the *Nominative Case*.

XV. The Object of a Sentence is in the *Objective Case*.

XVI. The Grammatical Predicate of a Sentence is { A Verb, with or without { Another Verb, A Participle, An Adjective, A Noun, A Pronoun, or A Preposition.

☞ Make Sentences containing Examples of each variety of Predicate mentioned.

XVII. A VERB in Predicate may be in the
- INDICATIVE MODE,
  - Prior Past Tense,
  - Past Tense,
  - Prior Present Tense,
  - Present Tense,
  - Prior Future Tense,
  - Future Tense.
- POTENTIAL MODE,
  - Prior Past Tense,
  - Past Tense,
  - Prior Present Tense,
  - Present Tense.
- SUBJUNCTIVE MODE,
  - Past Tense,
  - Present Tense.
- IMPERATIVE MODE,
  - Present Tense.

☞ Make Sentences having Verbs in each of the Modes and Tenses mentioned.

XVIII. A VERB in Predicate must agree with its Subject in *Person* and *Number*

XIX. THE ADJUNCTS of a Sentence are PRIMARY or SECONDARY.

XX. PRIMARY ADJUNCTS are attached to the Principal Parts of a Sentence or a Phrase.

XXI. SECONDARY ADJUNCTS are attached to other Adjuncts.

XXII. ADJUNCTS may consist of WORDS, PHRASES, or SENTENCES.

☞ Make Sentences containing *Adjunct Words.*
Make Sentences containing *Adjunct Phrases.*
Make Sentences containing *Adjunct Sentences.*

XXIII. WORDS, PHRASES, and SENTENCES used as Adjuncts are
- ADJECTIVES
  - *Qualifying,*
    - Compar.
    - Superl.
    - Posit.
    - Dimin.
  - *Specifying,*
    - Pure.
    - Numer.
    - Possess.
  - *Verbal,*
    - Trans.
    - Intrans.
- or
- ADVERBS,
  - *Time,*
  - *Place,*
  - *Degree,*
  - *Manner,*
  - *Cause,*
  - *&c., &c.*

XXIV. A SENTENCE may be { INTRANSITIVE OR TRANSITIVE, SIMPLE OR COMPOUND, PRINCIPAL OR AUXILIARY

XXV. AN INTRANSITIVE SENTENCE has no *Object.*

☞ Make an *Intransitive Sentence.*

XXVI. A TRANSITIVE SENTENCE has an *Object.*

☞ Make a *Transitive Sentence.*

XXVII. A SIMPLE SENTENCE has all its Principal Parts single.

☞ Make a *Simple Sentence.*

XXVIII. A COMPOUND SENTENCE has some of its Principal Parts compound.

☞ Make a *Compound Sentence.*

XXIX. A PRINCIPAL SENTENCE asserts a Principal Proposition.

XXX. AN AUXILIARY SENTENCE asserts a Dependent Proposition.

☞ Make a *Complex Sentence*, and distinguish the *Principal Sentence* from the *Auxiliary Sentence.*

XXXI. CONJUNCTIONS introduce Sentences and connect Words and Phrases.

XXXII. A PREPOSITION shows a relation of its object to the word which its Phrase qualifies.

XXXIII. AN EXCLAMATION has no dependent construction.

XXXIV. A WORD OF EUPHONY is, in its office, chiefly *Rhetorical.*

II. PHRASES.

XXXV. A PHRASE is a combination of Words not constituting an entire proposition, but performing a distinct office in the structure of a Sentence or of another Phrase.

XXXVI. A PHRASE consists of { PRINCIPAL PARTS and ADJUNCTS.

XXXVII. THE PRINCIPAL ELEMENTS of a Phrase are those words necessary to its structure.

☞ Make a Phrase having *Principal Elements* only.

XXXVIII. THE ADJUNCTS of a Phrase are words used to modify or describe other words.

☞ Make a Phrase having *Adjuncts.*

XXXIX. THE PRINCIPAL ELEMENTS of a Phrase are { The LEADER, The SUBSEQUENT

XL. The Leader of a Phrase is the word used to introduce the Phrase—generally connecting its Subsequent to the Word which the Phrase qualifies.

XLI. The Subsequent of a Phrase is the Element which follows the Leading Word as its Object—depending on it for sense.

☞ Make Phrases and distinguish the *Leaders* from the *Subsequent*.

XLII. The Adjuncts may consist of { *Adjective* or *Adverbial* } { Words, Phrases, or Sentences.

☞ Make Sentences having Adjective *Words—Phrases—Sentences.*

XLIII. A Phrase is { Transitive or Intransitive.

XLIV. A Transitive Phrase is one whose Subsequent (Infinitive Verb or Participle) asserts an action which terminates on an Object.

☞ Make a Transitive Phrase; 1. *Participial*—2. *Infinitive.*

XLV. An Intransitive Phrase is one whose Subsequent is a Noun or a Pronoun, or a Verb or a Participle having no Object.

☞ Make an Intransitive Phrase; 1. *Prepositional*—2. *Participial*—3. *Infinitive*—4. *Independent.*

XLVI. A Phrase is, *in form,* { Prepositional, Participial, Infinitive, or Independent.

XLVII. A Prepositional Phrase is one that is introduced by a Preposition—having a Noun, a Pronoun (Word, Phrase, or Sentence), or a Participle, for its object of relation.

☞ Make a *Prepositional Phrase.*

XLVIII. A Participial Phrase is one that is introduced by a Participle, being followed by an Object of an action, or by an Adjunct.

☞ Make a *Participial Phrase.*

XLIX. An Infinitive Phrase is one that is introduced by the Preposition to—having a Verb in the Infinitive Mode as its Object of relation.

☞ Make an *Infinitive Phrase.*

L. An Independent Phrase is one that is introduced by a Noun or a Pronoun—having a Participle depending on it.

☞ Make an *Independent Phrase.*

LI. A PHRASE is COMPOUND when it has two or more Leaders or Subsequents.

☞ Make a *Compound Phrase*—Compound *Leaders*—Compound *Subsequent*.

LII. A PHRASE is COMPLEX when one of its Principal Parts is qualified by another Phrase.

☞ Make a *Complex Phrase*.

LIII. A Phrase is MIXED when it has one or more *Transitive*, and one or more *Intransitive* Subsequents.

☞ Make a *Mixed Phrase*.

REMARK 1.—Words combined into a Sentence, have a relation to each other—a relation which often determines their *forms*. The principal Modifications of words, as treated in PART II. of this work, are those of form—and these forms vary according to their relation to other words. Thus, in speaking of Frederick, I may say, "*he* assisted James." Here "he" stands for the name of Frederick; and that *form* of the Pronoun is used to denote that Frederick was the *agent* of the action—the *Subject* of the Verb. But if I say "him James assisted," I make quite a different assertion, not because I speak of different persons or of a different act, but because I use a different modification of the word "he."

But the *form* does not always determine the office of words in a Sentence.

I may say, "Frederick assisted James,"

and "James assisted Frederick."

Here, although I use the same words and the same *form* of those words, I make two widely different assertions. The difference in the assertions in these examples is caused by the change of *position* of the Words Hence, the laws of AGREEMENT and ARRANGEMENT of words in the construction of Sentences.

REM. 2.—As Diagrams are of great service in constructing Sentences, by serving as tests of the grammatical correctness of a composition, they are inserted in PART III. It is hoped that the Teacher will not fail to require the Class to write Sentences which shall contain words in every possible condition, and in every variety of modification. Young Pupils should be required to place the Sentences in Diagrams.

EXERCISES IN THE ANALYSIS OF SENTENCES.

EXERCISES ON THE CHART.

REM. 1.—The following *Exercises* will exhibit the proper method of using the Chart in Etymological Parsing.

REM. 2.—If the *large* Chart is used, the attention of the whole Class should be directed to it—one of the Students using a "pointer," as he repeats the construction of each word, according to the formulæ given below.

REM. 3.—It is well for beginners in Etymological parsing to have the Sentence to be parsed first placed in Diagram on the black board.

REM. 4.—In the following Exercises the words or parts of words which are printed in CAPITALS may be found on the Chart.

1. *Animals run.*

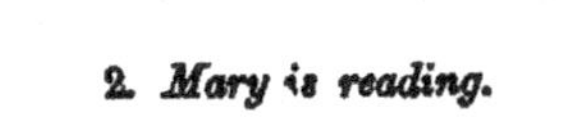

Animals. . . An Element in the SENTENCE—PRINCIPAL ELEMENT—SUBJECT—WORD—NOUN—COM. (*common*)—MAS. (*masculine*) Gender—THIRD Person—PLUR. (*plural*) Number—NOMINATIVE Case.

Run. . . . . . An Element in the SENTENCE—PRINCIPAL ELEMENT—PREDICATE—VERB—INDICATIVE MODE—PRESENT TENSE.

2. *Mary is reading.*

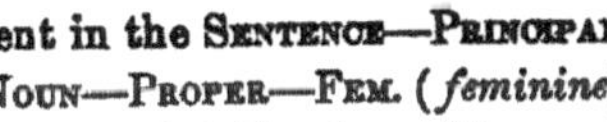

Mary . . . . . An Element in the SENTENCE—PRINCIPAL ELEMENT—SUBJECT—WORD—NOUN—PROPER—FEM. (*feminine*) Gender—THIRD Person—SING. (*singular*) Number—NOMINATIVE Case.

Is reading. . An Element in the SENTENCE—PRINCIPAL ELEMENT—PREDICATE—VERB and PART. (*participle*)—Verb is in the INDICATIVE Mode—PRESENT Tense.

Reading. . . An Element in the SENTENCE—PRINCIPAL ELEMENT—used in PREDICATE with "is."

3. *He might have been respected.*

He .... An Element in the SENTENCE—PRINCIPAL ELEMENT—SUBJECT—WORD—PRON. (*pronoun*)—PERS. (*personal*)—MAS. *masculine*) Gender—THIRD Person—SING. (*singular*) Number—NOMINATIVE Case.

Might have been respected } An Element in the SENTENCE—PRINCIPAL ELEMENT—PREDICATE—two VERBS and two PART. (*participles*)—Verb is in the POTENTIAL Mode—PRIOR PAST Tense.

4. *His palsied hand waxed strong.*

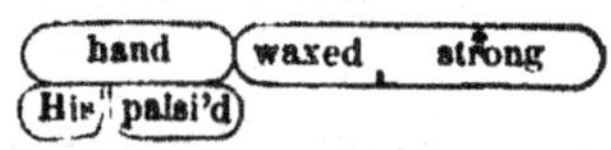

His............ An Element in the SENTENCE—ADJUNCT—PRIMARY—WORD—ADJECTIVE—SPEC. (*specifying*)—POSSES. (*possessive*).

Palsied......... An Element in the SENTENCE—ADJUNCT—PRIMARY—WORD—ADJECTIVE—VERBAL—INTRAN. (*intransitive*).

Hand.......... An Element in the SENTENCE—PRINCIPAL ELEMENT—SUBJECT—WORD—NOUN—COM. (*common*)—NEUT. (*neuter*) Gender—THIRD Person—SING. (*singular*) Number—NOMINATIVE Case.

Waxed strong.. An Element in the SENTENCE—PRINCIPAL ELEMENT—PREDICATE—VERB and ADJ. (*adjective*)—VERB is in the INDICATIVE Mode—PAST Tense.

Strong......... An Element in the SENTENCE—ADJ. (*adjective*) used in PREDICATE with "waxed."

5. *That good men sometimes commit faults, cannot be denied.*

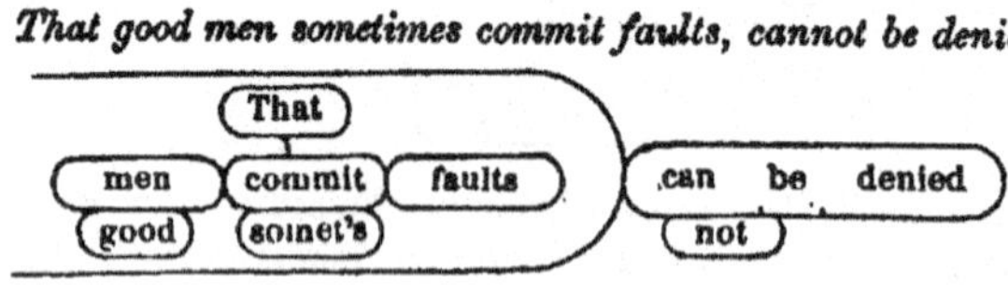

That good men sometimes commit faults, } is an Element in the SENTENCE—PRINCIPAL ELEMENT—SUBJECT—SENTENCE—SUBSTANTIVE—SIMPLE—TRANS. (*transitive*).

Cannot be denied......... } is an Element in the SENTENCE—PRINCIPAL ELEMENT—PREDICATE—two VERBS and a PART. (*participle*)—Verb is in the POTENTIAL Mode—PRESENT Tense.

Not ....is an Element in the SENTENCE—ADJUNCT—PRIMARY—WORD—ADVERB of Negation.

6. *He hears the thunder ere the tempest lowers.*

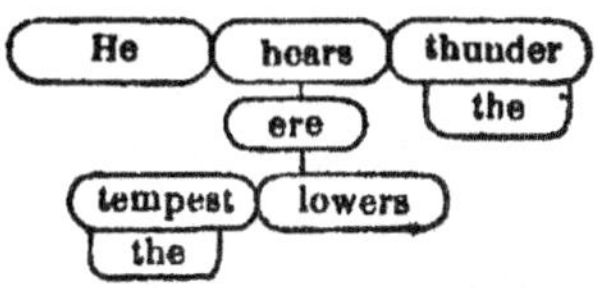

He ....Is an Element in the SENTENCE—PRINCIPAL ELEMENT—SUBJECT—WORD—PRON. (*pronoun*)—PERS. (*personal*)—MAS. (*masculine*) Gender—THIRD Person—SING. (*singular*) Number—NOMINATIVE Case.

Hears. .....Is an Element in the SENTENCE—PRINCIPAL ELEMENT—PREDICATE—VERB—INDICATIVE Mode—PRESENT Tense.

The ... .Is an Element in the SENTENCE—ADJUNCT—PRIMARY—WORD—ADJ. (*adjective*)—SPEC. (*specifying*)—PURE.

Thunder ....Is an Element in the SENTENCE—PRINCIPAL ELEMENT—OBJECT—WORD—NOUN—COM. (*common*)—NEUT. (*neuter*) Gender—THIRD Person—SING. (*singular*) Number—OBJECTIVE Case.

Ere the tempest lowers... } Is an Element in the SENTENCE—ADJUNCT—PRIMARY—SENTENCE—ADV. (*adverbial*)—SIMP. (*simple*) — INTRANS. (*intransitive*).

7. *Too low they build who build beneath the stars.*

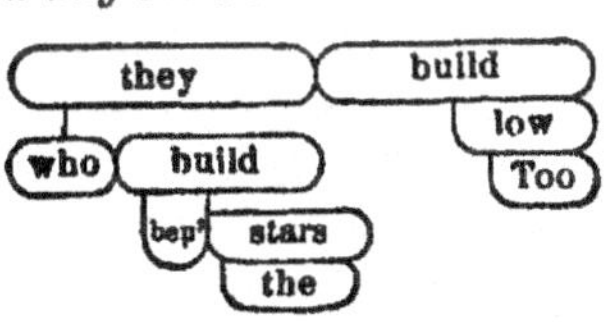

Too ....Is an Element in the SENTENCE—ADJUNCT—SECONDARY—WORD—ADVERB—of Degree.

Low...........Is an Element in the SENTENCE—ADJUNCT—PRIMARY—WORD—ADVERB—of Place.

They ....Is an Element in the SENTENCE—PRINCIPAL ELEMENT—SUBJECT—WORD—PRON. (*pronoun*)—PERS. (*personal*)—MAS. (*masculine*) Gender—THIRD Person—PLUR. (*plural*) Number—NOMINATIVE Case.

Build..........Is an Element in the SENTENCE—PRINCIPAL ELEMENT—PREDICATE—VERB—INDICATIVE Mode—PRESENT Tense.

Who build beneath the stars } Is an Element in the SENTENCE—ADJUNCT—PRIMARY—SENTENCE — ADJECT. (*adjective*) — SIMPLE—INTRANS. (*intransitive*).

Who ....Is an Element in the SENTENCE—PRINCIPAL ELEMENT—SUBJECT — WORD — PRON. (*pronoun*)—REL. (*relative*)—MAS. (*masculine*) Gender—THIRD Person—PLUR. (*plural* Number—NOMINATIVE Case.

Build..........Is an Element in the SENTENCE—PRINCIPAL ELEMENT—VERB—INDICATIVE MODE—PRESENT Tense.

Beneath the stars......... } Is an Element in the SENTENCE—ADJUNCT—SECONDARY—PHRASE—ADV. (*adverbial.*) — PREP. (*prepositional*) — INTRAN. (*intransitive*).

3. "*Scaling yonder peak,*
I saw an eagle wheeling near its brow."

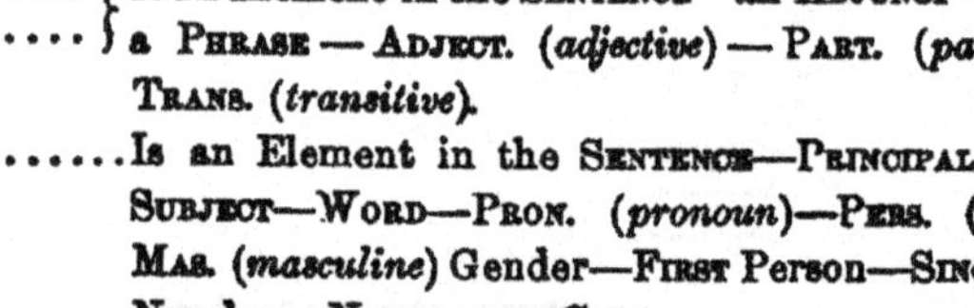

Scaling yonder peak,........ } Is an Element in the SENTENCE—an ADJUNCT—PRIMARY—a PHRASE — ADJECT. (*adjective*) — PART. (*participial*) — TRANS. (*transitive*).

I..............Is an Element in the SENTENCE—PRINCIPAL ELEMENT—SUBJECT—WORD—PRON. (*pronoun*)—PERS. (*personal*)—MAS. (*masculine*) Gender—FIRST Person—SING. (*singular*) Number—NOMINATIVE Case.

Saw ....Is an Element in the SENTENCE—PRINCIPAL ELEMENT—PREDICATE—VERB—INDICATIVE Mode—PAST Tense.

An............Is an Element in the SENTENCE—an ADJUNCT—PRIMARY—WORD—ADJECTIVE—SPEC. (*specifying*)—Pure.

Eagle..........Is an Element in the SENTENCE—PRINCIPAL ELEMENT—OBJECT—WORD—NOUN—COM. (*common*)—MAS. (*masculine*) Gender—THIRD Person—SING. (*singular*) Number—OBJECTIVE Case.

Wheeling near its brow ..... } Is an Element in the SENTENCE—an ADJUNCT—PRIMARY —PHRASE—ADJECT. (*adjective*)—PART. (*participial*)—INTRAN. (*intransitive*).

Near its brow...Is an Element in the SENTENCE—an ADJUNCT—SECONDARY —PHRASE—ADV. (*adverbial*) — PREP. (*prepositional*)— INTRAN. (*intransitive*).

REM.—In the analysis of a Complex Sentence (see OBS., p. 42) an Auxiliary Sentence is found to perform an individual office, and accordingly, it is parsed as *one Etymological Element* of the Principal Sentence. After it has been thus parsed, it should itself be analyzed, and the Words and Phrases of which it is composed, be parsed according to their respective offices. The same remark is applicable to Phrases. (See Exercise 7, above, and 2, below.)

ANALYSIS OF PHRASES BY THE CHART.

EXERCISES.

1. *In the beginning* (a Prepositional Phrase).

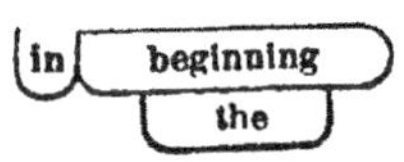

In ....Is an Element in the PHRASE — PRINCIPAL ELEMENT — the LEADER—a PREP. (*preposition*).

The........Is an Element in the PHRASE—an ADJUNCT—WORD—ADJ. (*adjective*).

Beginning..Is an Element in the PHRASE—PRINCIPAL ELEMENT—the SUBSEQUENT—a WORD—NOUN—OBJECT.

2. "*Scaling yonder peak*" (a Participial Phrase).

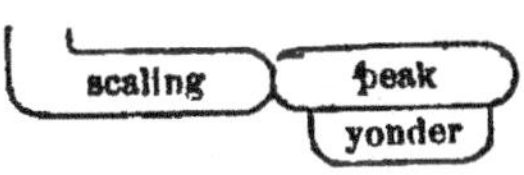

Scaling ....Is an Element in the PHRASE—PRINCIPAL ELEMENT—the LEADER—a PART. (*participle*)—TRANS. (*transitive*).

Yonder ....Is an Element in the PHRASE—an ADJUNCT—WORD— ADJ. (*adjective*).

Peak. ......Is an Element in the PHRASE—PRINCIPAL ELEMENT—th SUBSEQUENT—a WORD NOUN—OBJECT.

3 "*The time having arrived*" (an Independent Phrase).

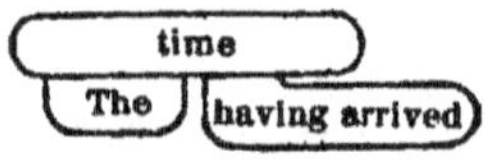

The ....Is an Element in the PHRASE—An ADJUNCT—WORD—ADJ. (*adjective*).

Time ......Is an Element in the PHRASE—PRINCIPAL ELEMENT—the LEADER—A NOUN—INDEPENDENT Case.

Having arrived.. } Is an Element in the PHRASE—PRINCIPAL ELEMENT—the SUBSEQUENT—a PART. (*participle*)—INTRAN. (*intransitive*).

4. *To bestow many favors* (an Infinitive Phrase).

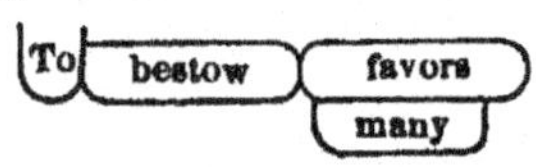

To.........Is an Element in the PHRASE—PRINCIPAL ELEMENT—the LEADER—a PREP. (*preposition*).

Bestow ....Is an ELEMENT in the PHRASE—PRINCIPAL ELEMENT—a part of the SUBSEQUENT—A VERB—INFIN. (*infinitive*) Mode—TRANS. (*transitive*).

Many......Is an Element in the PHRASE—an ADJUNCT—ADJ. (*adjective*).

Favors.....Is an Element in the PHRASE—PRINCIPAL ELEMENT—a part of the SUBSEQUENT—OBJECT—WORD—NOUN.

REM.—Exercises like the above are well calculated to *prepare* the Student for Exercises in Syntax; and when he shall have learned the Rules of Syntax, he should combine the above Exercises with the application of those Rules.

ADDITIONAL EXAMPLES—*Sentences and Phrases.*

1. "A mortal disease was upon her vitals, *before Cæsar had passed the Rubicon.*" (See Diagram, p. 41.)
2. "The fur *that warms a monarch*, warmed a bear."
3. "I have a temple in every heart *that owns my influence.*"
4. Much learning shows how little mortals know. (See p. 43.)
5. "He that getteth wisdom, loveth his own soul"

SYNTAX OF THE ELEMENTS OF SENTENCES.

I. *Of the Principal Elements.*

(1.) The Subject.

Rule 1.—The *Subject* of a Sentence must be in the *Nominative Case.*

Obs. 1.—The Subject of a Sentence is always *Substantive* in its *office.* (See p. 25, Obs. 2.)

Obs. 2.—The Subject of a Sentence may be { A *Word,* A *Phrase,* or A *Sentence.* }

EXAMPLES.

1. *A Word* { (*a*) *Noun*....1. "*Virtue* secures happiness." (*b*) *Pronoun*.2. "*He* plants his footsteps in the sea." }
2. *A Phrase*..............3. "*His being a minister,* prevented his rising to civil power."
   4. "*To give good gifts* and *to be benevolent,* are often very different things."
3. *A Sentence*............5. "*That all men are created equal,* is a self-evident truth."

Rem.—Whatever is *peculiar* to Pronouns, is discussed under the Rule for Pronouns. We now proceed to discuss what is common to Nouns, Pronouns, Phrases, and Sentences, considered as *Subjects of Sentences.*

Obs. 3.—The Subject of a Sentence may be ascertained by its answering to the Interrogatives *Who?* or *What?* placed before the Predicate. Thus, in the Examples above—

What "secures happiness?"..............Ans.—"*Virtue.*"
Who "plants his footsteps in the sea?"....Ans.—"*He.*"
What "prevented his rising to civil power?"............. } Ans.—"*His being a minister.*"
What "is a self-evident truth?"..Ans.—"*That all men are created equal.*"
What "are often different things?" Ans.—"*To give good gifts* and *to be benevolent.*"

SUBJECT WORD.

Obs. 4.—A Subject *Word* must be a *Noun* or a *Pronoun*.

(*a*.) The Form of the Nominative.

Obs. 5.—Because English Nouns are not varied in form to denote the Case (except for the Possessive), much attention is required in giving them their proper *position* in a Sentence. (See Remark 1, p. 180.)

(*b*.) Position of the Nominative.

Note 1.—In *position*, the Subject of a Sentence commonly precedes the Verb.

Examples.—1. *Animals* RUN.
2. *Resources* ARE DEVELOPED.
3. *Virtue* SECURES happiness.
4. "The *King* of Shadows LOVES a shining mark."
5. "The *sword* and the *plague-spot* with death STREW the plain."

Exception 1.—In *Interrogative Sentences*, the Subject is placed after the Verb, when the Verb constitutes a complete Predicate.

Example.—"*Heeds* HE not the bursting anguish?"

Exception 2.—When the Predicate consists of two Verbs, or a Verb and a Participle, Adjective, Noun, &c., the Subject is placed after the first word of the Predicate.

Examples.—*Is* HE injured?—*Is* SHE kind?—*Is* HE a scholar?—*Must* I leave thee?

Exception 3.—The Subject follows the Predicate, or the first Word of the Predicate, in the *declarative* Sentences.

When the Conjunction *if*, used to introduce a conditional or modifying Sentence, *is omitted*.

Example.—"*Dost* THOU not, Hassan, lay these dreams aside,
I'll plunge thee headlong in the whelming tide"

Exception 4.—When the word *there* is used to introduce the Sentence.

Examples.—1. "There *is* a CALM for those who weep."
2. ——— "There *breathes* not a SOUND,
While friends in their sadness are gathering round."

EXCEPTION 5.—When the Verb is in the Imperative Mode.

EXAMPLE.—"*Turn* YE, *turn* YE at my reproof."

EXCEPTION 6.—By the poets and public speakers, for rhetorical effect.

EXAMPLES.—1. "Loud *peals* the THUNDER."
2. "*Perish* the groveling THOUGHT."

OBS. 1.—But the Interrogatives, *who, which*, and *what*, used as Subjects, precede their Verbs.

EXAMPLES.—"WHO *will show* us any good?"
"WHAT *can compensate* for loss of character?"
"WHICH *shall be taken* first?"

OBS. 2.—When one word includes in its signification many others, expressed in the same connection, the general term is the proper Subject of the Verb; and the included terms may be regarded as explanatory, and, therefore, independent in construction. (See Independent Case, p. 85.)

EXAMPLE.—"*All* sink before it—*comfort, joy*, and *wealth*."

Some teachers prefer to supply the ellipsis—which is not improper.

OBS. 3.—The Subject of an Imperative Verb is commonly suppressed.

EXAMPLE.—"[ ] Take each man's censure, but [ ] reserve thy judgment."

OBS. 4.—But it is sometimes expressed.

EXAMPLE.—"Go *ye* into all the world."

OBS. 5.—It is sometimes accompanied by an explanatory word.

EXAMPLE.—"*Ye* rapid FLOODS, give way." (See "Independent Case.")

NOTE II.—Unnecessary repetition of the Subject should be avoided.

OBS. 1.—This principle is violated in the following Example:
"His teeth, *they* chatter, chatter still."

OBS. 2.—But this practice is allowable, when necessary to a proper rhetorical effect.

EXAMPLES.—Our *Fathers*, where are *they*? And the *Prophets*, do *they* live for ever?

OBS. 3.—The agent of an action expressed by an Infinitive Verb, may be in the Nominative or the Objective case.

1. I purpose *to go*.
2. I invited HIM *to go*.

OBS. 4.—The agent of an action expressed by a Participle, may be in the Possessive or the Objective Case.

1. I heard of YOUR *going* to Boston.
2. The *plowing* of the WICKED is sin.

REM.—But these "Agents" are not to be regarded as Subjects of Sentences.—[See "Infinitive" and "Participles," below.]

SUBJECT PHRASE.

1. "To steal is base."

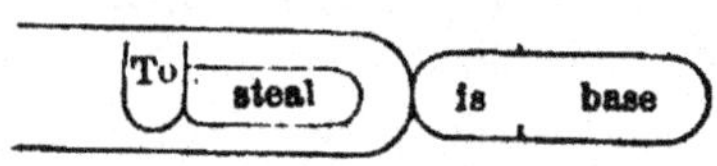

2. "Writing letters constitutes my most agreeable employment."

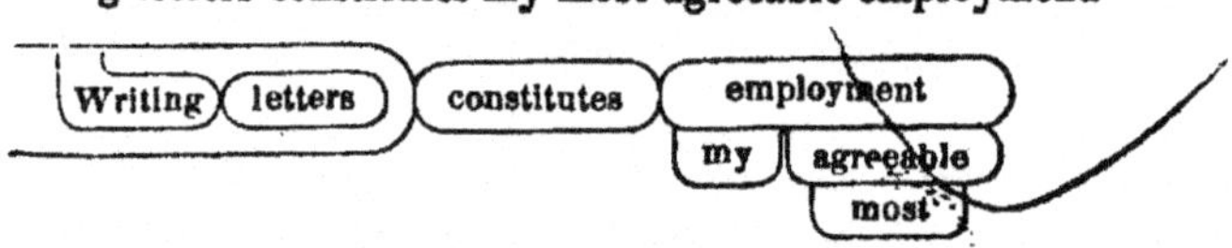

OBS. 5.—A Subject Phrase constitutes one distinct Element in the structure of a Sentence, and should be construed and parsed in the same manner as a Subject Word. Thus,

In Sentence (1), "To steal" is a Phrase—in *form*, *Infinitive;*
in *office*, *Substantive;* for it is the Subject of "is base."

"Writing letters" is a Phrase—in *form*, *Participial;*
in *office*, *Substantive;* for it is the Subject of "constitutes employment."

OBS. 6.—After a Phrase *as such* has been parsed, it should be analyzed, by resolving it into its constituent Elements. Thus, in the Phrase "to steal," "to" is a *Preposition*. The *Leader* of the Infinitive Phrase "steal," is a *Verb*, *Infinitive-Mode*—the Subsequent of the Phrase, and Object of the Preposition "to."

And, in the Phrase "writing letters," "writing" is a *Participle*—the *Leader* of the Participial Phrase. "Letters" is a Noun,—the Subsequent of the Phrase, and Object of the action expressed by "writing."

FORM OF THE SUBJECT PHRASE.

OBS. 7.—The Phrases commonly used as Subjects of Sentences, are the *Infinitive* and the *Participial*—Prepositional and Independent Phrases being seldom thus used.—(See CLARK'S ANALYSIS, page 109, *note*.)

POSITION OF THE SUBJECT PHRASE.

NOTE III.—In Position, the Subject Phrase commonly *precedes* its Predicate.

EXAMPLES.—1. *To do good* IS the DUTY of all men.
2. *Managing the household affairs* now CONSTITUTES the sum of my employments.

OBS. 1.—EXCEPTIONS.—The Subject Phrase sometimes *follows* its Predicate.

EXAMPLES.—"The sure WAY to be cheated IS *to fancy ourselves more cunning than others.*"

REM. 1.—"*To fancy ourselves more cunning than others,*" is the Subject. "Is way," is the Predicate.

REM. 2.—This position generally obtains, when the Indefinite Pronoun *it* is placed instead of the Phrase. "*It*" precedes, and the Phrase follows the Verb.

EXAMPLE.—IT is the duty of all, *to do good to others.*

REM. 3.—In parsing Examples like these, the Phrase is to be regarded as explanatory of the Pronoun *it*—used to define the Indefinite Word—and is, in its office, analogous to a Word used to explain a preceding Noun. (See Independent Case, Obs. 2, p. 85.)

SUBJECT SENTENCES.

"*That I have taken this old man's daughter,* is most true."

OBS. 1.—In Examples like the above we have two Sentences—one, *Principal,* the other *Auxiliary* or *Subordinate.* The Auxiliary Sentence is an Element in the Principal—the *Subject,* and should be parsed accordingly.

Thus, in the above Complex Sentence, the Principal Sentence is *Simple, Intransitive,* having one Subject—"*That I have taken this old man's daughter;*" one Predicate—"*is true;*" and one Adjunct—"*most.*"

OBS. 2.—After an Auxiliary Sentence has been parsed, as one Element in its Principal Sentence, it should be analyzed by resolving it into its constituent Elements. Thus, in the Auxiliary Sentence given above,

"That".......Introduces the Sentence: hence, a *Conjunction*.
"I"..........Is the Subject of its Sentence; hence, a *Substantive*.
"Have taken". Is the Predicate of its Sentence; hence, a *Verb* and *Participle*.
"This".......Is an Adjunct of "man"['s]; hence, an *Adjective*.
"Old"........Is an Adjunct of "man"['s]; hence, an *Adjective*.
"Man's"......Is an Adjunct of "daughter;" hence, an *Adjective*.
"Daughter"...Is the Object of "have taken;" hence, a *Substantive*.

OBS. 3.—The Subject Sentence is commonly—not always—introduced by the Conjunction "*that*." (See Examples below.)

POSITION OF SUBJECT SENTENCES.

NOTE IV.—A Subject Sentence is placed before its Predicate.

EXAMPLES.—1. "*That we differ in opinion* IS not STRANGE."
2. "*How he came by it*, SHALL BE DISCLOSED in the next chapter."

OBS. 2.—EXCEPTIONS.—When the Pronoun *it* is *substituted* for a Subject Sentence, the Pronoun *precedes*, and the Sentence for which it stands is placed *after* the Verb.

EXAMPLES.—"It is probable *that we shall not meet again*."

OBS. 2.—In parsing Sentences like the above, we are to parse "it" as the grammatical Subject of the Principal Sentence, and the whole Auxiliary Sentence as explanatory of the word "it"—a Logical Adjunct of "it." (See "Logical Adjunct," p. 29.)

EXERCISES.

☞ Let the Class make Sentences, which shall be correct examples of the several *Notes*, Observations, and Remarks, under Rule 1.

EXAMPLES FOR PARSING.

1. "*Friend* after friend departs;
2. *Who* has not lost a friend?
3. There is no *union* here of hearts,
That finds not here an end;
4. Were this frail *world* our final rest,
Living or dying *none* were blest.

5. Thus *star* by star declines,
 Till *all* are passed away;
6. As *morning* high and higher shines,
 To pure and perfect day:
7. Nor sink those *stars* in empty night,
 But hide themselves in heaven's own light."

FIRST MODEL.

"*Friend after friend departs.*"

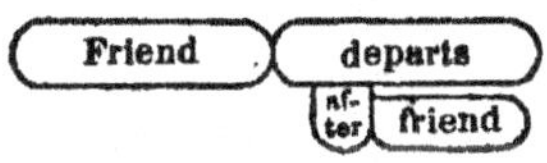

ANALYSIS.

Principal Parts { "Friend," ..Subject of "departs," } Simple Sentence,
{ "Departs,".Predicate of "friend," } Intransitive.

Adjunct........."After friend,"..Adjunct of "departs."

PARSING.

Friend.......Is a name, ...Hence, a Noun.
" Name of a class of persons,...Hence, Common.
[The gender is not indicated; and, whenever it is not, no mention of the gender should be made.]
" Spoken of,.................Hence, third person.
" Denotes but one, ...Hence, Singular Number.
" Subject of departs, ...Hence, Nominative Case.

After friend ..Modifies "departs"—denoting *time*, or *order of time*, ...Hence, an Adverb.

After........Expresses a relation of "departs" and "friend" ....Hence, a Preposition.

Friend.......Is a name, ...Hence, a Noun.
" Name of a class, ...Hence, Common.
" Spoken of, ...Hence, Third Person.
" Denotes but one, ...Hence, Singular Number.
" Object of the relation expressed by "after".................Hence, Objective Case.

Depart,......Expresses an action,.........Hence, a Verb.
" Action has no object, ...Hence, Intransitive.
" Simply declares,............Hence, Indicative Mode.
" Denotes present time,.......Hence, Present Tense.
" Predicate of "friend," ....Hence, { Third Person, Singular Number.

SECOND MODEL.

"*Who has not lost a friend?*"

ANALYSIS.

PRINCIPAL PARTS,	Who.....Subject, Has lost..Predicate, Friend ...Object,	Hence, a *Transitive Sentence*, Simple.
ADJUNCTS,.......	Not......Adjunct of "has lost." A........Adjunct of "friend."	

PARSED.

Who......Is a Pronoun—Interrogative—Third Person—Singular Number—Nominative Case to "has lost."

"The subject of a Sentence must be in the Nominative Case.

Has lost...Is a Verb—Irregular [lose, lost, losing, lost]—Transitive—Active Voice—Indicative Mode—Past Tense Indefinite—Third Person—Singular Number, to agree with its Subject "who."

Not.......Is an Adverb—Negative—Modifies "has lost."

A.........Is an Adjective—Specifying—Specifies "friend."

Friend.....Is a Noun—Common—Third Person—Singular Number—Objective Case to "has lost."

ADDITIONAL EXAMPLES.

1. "Rewarding and punishing actions by any other rule, would appear much harder to be accounted for by minds formed as he has formed ours."—*Bp. Butler.*

2. "*What time he took orders*, doth not appear."—*Life of Butler.*

3. "That every day has its pains and sorrows, is universally experienced."

4. "My hopes and fears start up alarmed."

5. "Who shall tempt, with wandering feet,
The dark, unfathomed, infinite abyss?"

6. "Not a drum was heard, nor a funeral note,"

7. "Not half of our heavy task was done."

8. "Few and short were the prayers we said."

9. "A chieftain's daughter secured the *maid*"

10. "Her satin snood, her silken plaid,
Her golden brooch, such birth betrayed."

II. THE PREDICATE.

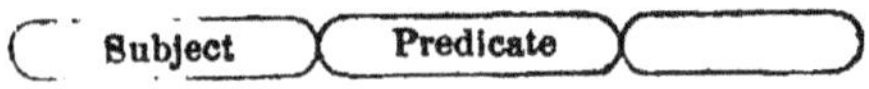

REM. 1.—In a Sentence, it is the office of the Predicate to make the assertion. It declares *existence*, *state*, *change*, or an *act*, performed or received.

REM 2.—A Predicate may consist of *one* Word or of a *combination* of Words. If of one Word, it must be a Verb.

Robert *studies*.

And, in addition, it may have

A second Verb,..........Robert *does study*.
A Participle,............Robert *is studying*.
An Adjective, ...Robert *is studious*.
A Noun,.................Robert *is a scholar*.
A Pronoun, ...It *is I*—If I *were you*.
A Preposition, ...Its idle hopes *are o'er*.

It may also consist of two Verbs and one or more Participles, &c.

We MIGHT HAVE WALKED—We MIGHT HAVE BEEN LOVED.

OBS. 1.—When a Predicate consists of more than one Word, the last constitutes the essential part of the Predicate. The other Words are Auxiliary, and are used to indicate *Voice*, *Mode*, *Tense*, and sometimes *Person* and *Number*. Thus, in the Sentence, "I may have been loved," the Word "loved" is the essential part of the Predicate:—"been," is an Auxiliary, the principal office of which is to denote the *Voice*; "have," denotes the *Tense*; "may," denotes the *Mode*.

OBS. 2.—Every complete Predicate must have a Subject, expressed or understood.

VERBS.

RULE 2.—A Verb must agree with its Subject in Number and Person.

REM.—This rule requires that the *form* of a Verb be determined by its Subject. Strictly speaking, Verbs have no Number and Person. The term is used to denote a variation in the form of a Verb to correspond with the Number and Person of its Subject. Thus,

In the Singular Number, no Suffix is used for the First Person; as, I walk.

Est or *st* is added for the Second Person, solemn style; as, Thou walk*est*.

S is added for the Third Person; as, John walks.

In the Plural Number, Verbs are not varied to denote the Person of their Subjects.

NUMBER.

NOTE I.—One Subject in the Singular Number requires its Verb to be in the Singular.

EXAMPLES.

Word Subjects....1. "EARTH *keeps* me here awhile."
2. "MAN *needs* but little here below."
3. "KNOWLEDGE *reaches* or *may reach* every home."
4. "HE *leaps* inclosures, *bounds* into the world."

Phrase Subjects ..5. "MY LEAVING HOME *does* not *please* you."
6. "TO DISPUTE THE DOCTOR *requires* fortitude."
7. "HIS BEING A SCHOLAR *entitles* him to respect."

Sentence Subjects..8. "THAT ALL MEN ARE CREATED EQUAL, *is* a self-evident truth."
9. "HOW HE CAME BACK AGAIN, *doth* not *appear*."
10. "THAT I HAVE TAKEN THIS OLD MAN'S DAUGHTER, *is* most true."

NOTE II.—Two or more Singular Subjects, indicating the same thing, require the Verb to be Singular.

EXAMPLE.—The SAINT, the FATHER, and the HUSBAND *prays*.

NOTE III.—Two or more Singular Subjects, taken separately, require the Verb to be Singular.

EXAMPLES.

Word Subjects....1. WILLIAM or WARNER *has* my knife.
2. "DISEASE OR POVERTY *follows* the lazy track of the sluggard."
3. "My POVERTY, but not my WILL, *consents*." *Shakspeare.*
4. "Every PHRASE and every FIGURE which he uses *tends* to render the picture more lively and complete."—*Blair.*

Phrase Subjects ..5. "WRITING LETTERS or READING NOVELS *occupies* her evening hours."

6. "TO BE OR NOT TO BE, *is* the question."

7. "TO SHOOT OR BE SHOT, *was* my only alternative."

Sentence Subjects..8. "*That my client aided in the rescue*, or *that he was present at the time of it*, DOES not APPEAR from the evidence adduced."

NOTE IV.—A Collective Noun, indicating *Unity*, requires its Verb to be in the Singular Number.

EXAMPLES.—1. "A NATION *has been smitten*."

2. "The SENATE HAS REJECTED the bill."

3. "Congress has adjourned."

NOTE V.—One or more Subjects of the Plural Number should have a Verb in the Plural.

EXAMPLES.

Word Subjects....1. "WOODS and GROVES *are* of thy dressing."—*Milton.*

2. "THEY *were forced* to eat what never was esteemed food."—*Josephus.*

3. "RULES and PRINCIPLES *are* of the greatest possible advantage."

4. "WINGS *were* on her feet."

NOTE VI.—Two or more Subjects of the Singular Number require the Verb to be in the Plural.

EXAMPLES.

Word Subjects..1. "The VIVACITY and SENSIBILITY of the GREEKS *seem* to have been much greater than ours."

2. "Even as the ROEBUCK and the HART *are eaten*."—*Bible.*

3. "Hill and valley boast thy blessing."—*Milton.*

Phrase Subjects.4. "*To be wise* in our own eyes, *to be wise* in the opinion of the world, and *to be wise* in the sight of our Creator, are three things so very different as rarely to coincide."—*Blair.*

5. "*Chewing tobacco* and *smoking cigars* disqualify a young man for mental improvement."—*Cutcheon.*

6. "To spin, to weave, to knit, and to sew, were once
a girl's employments;
But now to dress and to catch a beau, are all she
calls enjoyments."—*Lynn News.*

Sentence Subjects. 7. "Read of this burgess—on the stone *appear,*
How worthy he!—how virtuous!—and how dear!"
Crabbe.

8. "That friendship is a sacred trust,
That friends should be sincere and just,
That constancy befits them,
Are observations on the case,
That savor much of commonplace,
And all the world admits them."

NOTE VII.—A Collective Noun, indicating Plurality, requires its Verb to be in the Plural Number.

EXAMPLES.-1. "The PEOPLE *are* foolish, they have not known me."
2. "For the people speak but do not write."

OBS. 1.—Collective Nouns, which always require a Plural Verb, are the following:—

Gentry—mankind—nobility—people—peasantry.

OBS. 2.—Those which may have Verbs in the Singular or Plural, according to the sense, are the following:—

Aristocracy—army—auditory—committee—congress—church—meeting—public—school—remnant—senate.

OBS. 3.—The Logical Subject of a Sentence is sometimes the Object of a Phrase used to qualify the Grammatical Subject. Then, when the Object of the Phrase is plural in form, and indicates that the parts of which the number is composed are taken severally, the Verb should be plural.

EXAMPLE.—A *part* of the STUDENTS *have left.*

Here "students"—the name of many taken severally—is the Logical Subject of "have left," and requires the Verb to be Plural, although "part," the Grammatical Subject, is Singular.

OBS. 4.—When the Object of the Phrase is Singular, or the name of an aggregate number taken collectively, the Verb should be Singular.

EXAMPLE.—"*Two-thirds* of my HAIR *has* fallen off."

Here "hair"—the name of many taken collectively—is the Logical

Subject of "has fallen," and requires the Verb to be Singular, although "two-thirds," the Grammatical Subject, is plural.

Obs. 5.—But Nouns *not Collective* are not varied in number by their Adjuncts.

Examples.—1. "The *progress* of his forces *was impeded*."—*Allen.*

2. The *selection* of appropriate examples *requires* taste.

3. "All *appearances* of modesty are favorable and prepossessing."—*Blair.*

PERSON.

Note VIII.—Two or more Subjects, taken separately and differing in Person, should have separate Verbs, when the Verb is varied to denote the Person of its Subject.

Example.—*You* ARE in error, or *I* AM.

Obs.—But when the Verb is not varied to denote the person, it need not be repeated.

Examples.—1. *You* or *I* MUST GO.

2. The *doctors* or *you* ARE in error.

3. *Was* IT thou?

4. IT *was* the students.

Note IX.—When the Subject of a Verb differs in Person or Number (or both) from a Noun or Pronoun in Predicate, the Verb should agree with its Subject rather than with the word in Predicate.

Examples.—1. "THOU *art* the man."

2. "Who *art* THOU?"

3. "The wages of sin *is* DEATH."

4. CLOUDS *are* vapor.

5. A HORSE *is* an animal.

6. "And hoary peaks that proudly prop the skies, thy dwellings are."

Obs. 1.—The young Pupil often finds it difficult to decide which of the two Substantives is the Subject and which the Noun in Predicate. The following *test* will decide this point:—

When one term is *generic* and the other *specific*, the former belongs in Predicate—the latter is the Subject. Thus, in Example 5, "animal" is a generic term—"horse" is specific. We cannot say, *an animal is a horse*, for not every animal is a horse; but every horse is an animal. Hence, "horse" is the Subject, and "animal" is in Predicate.—(See Independent Case, p. 85, Obs. 5.)

MODE AND TENSE.

NOTE X.—That Mode and Tense of a Verb should be used which will most clearly convey the sense intended.

OBS. 1.—A Verb used to denote a conditional fact or a contingency should have the Subjunctive or the Potential form.

EXAMPLES.—"WERE *I Alexander*, I would accept the terms."
"So would I WERE *I Parmenio*."
"If we *would* improve, we must study."

OBS. 2.—But if the condition is assumed as unquestionable, the Verb may be in the Indicative Mode.

EXAMPLES.—"If thou *hadst* known."
If John *has offended* you, he will make due apology.

NOTE XI.—That form of the Verb should be used which will most clearly express the time intended.

OBS.—In constructing Complex Sentences, the Tense of the Principal Sentence does not necessarily control the Tense of the Verb in the Auxiliary Sentence.

EXAMPLES.—1. "I *said* in my haste, all men *are* liars."
2. "He *has been* so long *idle*, that he *knows* not how to work."
3. "Copernicus first *demonstrated* that the earth *revolves* upon its axis."
4. "He *called* so loud that all the hollow deep *resounded*."
5. "Those that *seek* me early *shall find* me."
6. "'And when we *are parted*, and when thou *art dead*,
O, where *shall* we *lay* thee?' his followers said."

OBS. 4.—The variations for the Potential Mode are rather variations of *form* than to indicate distinctions of *time*—this Mode being generally indifferent as to time.

EXAMPLE.—"O, *would* the scandal vanish with my life,
Then happy *were* to me ensuing death!"

OBS. 5.—The Infinitive Present generally indicates indefinite time—the Finite Verb on which it depends commonly determines its tense.

EXAMPLES.—"I *went* TO SEE him."—Present in form, but Past in sense.
"I *shall go* TO SEE him."—Present in form, but Future in sense.

OBS. 6.—But generally, to indicate past time, the Past Infinitive is used, *except when the Infinitive follows Verbs denoting purpose, expectation, wish, &c.*

EXAMPLES.—We *ought* TO HAVE GONE.
I *purposed* TO WRITE many days ago.
I *expected* TO MEET him yesterday.

FORM OF THE VERB.

NOTE XII.—That form of a Verb should be used which will correctly and fully express the fact intended.

Common Errors.—1. "There let him *lay*."—*Byron.*
2. "To you I *fly* for refuge."—*Murray.*

Corrected.—There let him *lie*.—To you I *flee* for refuge.

VOICE.

OBS. 7.—The form of the *Active Voice* is properly used when the agent of the action expressed is made the Subject of the Sentence.

EXAMPLES.—1. *Columbus* discovered America.
2. Cesar invaded Gaul.

OBS. 8.—The Passive form is used when the Object of the Act is made the Subject of the Sentence.

EXAMPLES.—1. America was discovered.
2. Gaul was invaded.

OBS. 9.—The Agent of the Action is made the Object of an Adjunct Phrase, when the Verb takes the Passive form.

EXAMPLES.—*Active Voice.*—1. William HAS SOLVED the *problem.*
2. Mary *gave* me a *rose.*
Passive Voice.—1. The *problem* has *been* solved by William.
2. A *rose* was given [to] me by Mary.

OBS. 1.—Action is *sometimes* improperly predicated of a Passive Subject.

EXAMPLES.

You *are mistaken.*
for.... .. ....You mistake.

The *house is building.*
for.............The *house is being built.*
which means....The house *is be*[com]*ing* built, i. e., people are at work upon it; but the house does not act.

REM.—This is one of the instances in which *Authority* is against *Philosophy.* For an *act* can not properly be predicated of a *Passive* Subject.

Many good writers properly reject this idiom.

"Mansfield's prophecy *is being realized.*"—*Michelet's Luther.*

TRANSITIVE AND INTRANSITIVE.

NOTE XIII.—A Verb which is necessarily Transitive requires an Object in construction, expressed or implied.

OBS. 1.—The appropriate Object of a Sentence should not be made the Object of a Phrase.

EXAMPLE.—"Transitive Verbs do not ADMIT of a *Preposition* after them."—*Bullion's Grammar,* p. 91.

CORRECTED.—Transitive Verbs do not admit Prepositions after them [to complete the Predicate].

NOTE XIV.—A Verb necessarily Intransitive should not have an Object, *except by poetic license or for other rhetorical purposes.*

EXAMPLE.—"I sit *me* down, a pensive hour to spend."

EXCEPTION 1.—But a small number of Verbs are used Transitively or Intransitively (See p. 107, Obs. 1.)

EXCEPTION 2.—Some Intransitive Verbs may have Objects of their own signification.

EXAMPLES.—1. "I *dreamed* a *dream* that was not all a dream."
2. "I have fought a good fight."

OBS. 1.—Some Verbs, commonly used Intransitively, become Transitive by virtue of a Prepositional Prefix.

EXAMPLES.—1. John *goes* to school.........."goes" is Intransitive.
2. John *undergoes* punishment.."undergoes" is Transitive.
3. The tower *looks* well......"looks" is Intransitive.
4. The tower *overlooks* the city. 'overlooks" is Transitive.
5. He *comes* from the field.
6. "Green *becomes* my complexion best."

OBS. 2.—In such examples of Compound Verbs in Predicate, it is generally—not always—the *Preposition in Composition* that makes the Verb Transitive. The Substantive following is, logically, the Object of the Preposition; but, grammatically considered, it is the Object of the Predicate, and should be parsed accordingly.

OBS. 3.—Verbs made Transitive by this use of Prefixes, can not elegantly be used in the Passive Voice.

EXAMPLES.—1. "John undergoes punishment."—We may not say punishment is undergone by John.
2. "The tower overlooks the city."—Nor, the city is overlooked by the tower.

OBS. 4.—Prepositions *not in composition*, used with Intransitive Verbs to introduce Adjunct Phrases, are construed with the Predicate when the Verb becomes Passive.

EXAMPLES.—1. "The children laughed at him."—He *was laughed at* by the children.
2. "We often thought of our friends at home."—Our friends at home *were* often *thought of.*

REM.—Such expressions are not often elegant, and should be avoided when the same thought can be otherwise expressed. Thus,

He was *derided* by the children.
Our friends at home were often remembered.

NOTE XV.—A Verb should not be used for its Participle in Predicate.

EXAMPLE.—James ought not to have *went.*

CORRECTED.—James ought not to have *gone.*

NOTE XVI.—A Participle should not take the place of its Verb.

EXAMPLE.—"The work is imperfect;—you *done* it too hastily."

CORRECTED.—"The work is imperfect; you *did* it too hastily."

OBS. 2.—Parts of the Predicate of a Sentence may be omitted by ellipsis.

1. The leading Word.

"If [ ] heard aright,
It is the knell of my departed hours."

2. The second Word.

"They may [ ] and should return to allegiance."

3. The whole Predicate.

"While [ ] there we visited the Asylum.

"To whom, thus Eve [ ]."—*Milton.*

EXERCISES IN ANALYSIS AND PARSING.

"*He maketh the storm a calm.*"

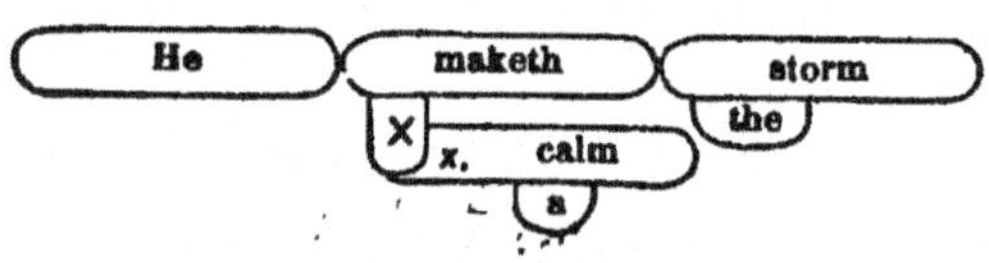

ANALYSIS.

PRINCIPAL PARTS . { He.......Subject, Maketh...Predicate, Storm....Object, } Simple Sentence—Transitive.

ADJUNCTS....... { The,................Adjunct of "storm." To become a calm,....Adjunct of "maketh." A,..................Adjunct of "calm."

PARSED.

He..................	Is used for a Noun,.....	Hence, a Pronoun.
"	Its form determines its Person.	Hence, Personal.
"	Spoken of.	Hence, Third Person.
"	Denotes but one.... ..	Hence, Singular Number
"	Subject of "maketh."...	Hence, Nominative Case.

RULE.—"*The Subject of a Sentence must be in the Nominative Case.*"

Maketh	Asserts an act	Hence, a Verb.
"	Act passes to an Object	Hence, Transitive.
"	Act done by its Subject	Hence, Active Voice.
"	Simply declares	Hence, Indicative Mode.
"	Denotes a present act	Hence, Present Tense.
"	Predicate of "he," which is of the Third Person, Singular Number	Hence, Third Person, Singular Number.

RULE.—"*A Verb must agree with its Subject in Person and Number.*

The	Describes "storm"	Hence, an Adjective.
"	Describes, by simply specifying	Hence, Specifying.
Storm	Is a Name,	Hence, a Noun.
"	Name of a class of things	Hence, Common.
"	Spoken of	Hence, Third Person.
"	Denotes but one	Hence, Singular Number
"	Object of action expressed by "maketh."	Hence, Objective Case.

RULE.—*The object of a Sentence must be in the Objective Case*

[To become] a calm	Modifies "maketh"—limiting the act to its result	Hence, an Adverb.
A	Describes "calm."	Hence, an Adjective.
"	Describes by simply specifying	Hence, Specifying.
Calm	Is a Name	Hence, a Noun.
"	Name of a class of things	Hence, Common.
"	Spoken of	Hence, Third Person.
"	Denotes but one	Hence, Singular Number
"	Used in Predicate with "become."	Hence, Independent Case

RULE.—*Note.*—"*A Noun or a Pronoun used in Predicate with a Verb, is in the Independent Case.*"

REM.—The above is the correct grammatical construction of the Sentence, and it is correctly parsed. But without the Adjunct Phrase "to become a calm," the word "maketh" could not properly have "storm" as its Object. "Storm" is the Object of the *modified* Predicate, "maketh [causeth to become] a calm."

GRAMMATICAL FALLACIES.

REM.—Let the Pupil correct the errors in the following Sentences, and give the authority for every criticism, by a proper reference to RULE 2, or to NOTES and OBSERVATIONS under the RULE.

1 "The rapidity of his movements *were* beyond example."—*Wells.*
2 "The mechanism of clocks and watches were totally unknown." *Hume.*
3. "The Past Tense of these Verbs are very indefinite with respect to time."—*Bullion's Grammar*, p. 31.
4. "Everybody are very kind to her."—*Byron.*
5. "To study mathematics, require maturity of mind."
6. "That they were foreigners, were apparent in their dress."
7. "Coleridge the poet and philosopher have many admirers."
8. "No monstrous height, or length or breadth appear."—*Pope.*
9. "Common sense, as well as piety, tell us these are proper." *Commentary.*
10. "Wisdom or folly govern us."—*Fisk's Grammar.*
11. "Nor want nor cold his course delay."—*Johnson.*
12. "Hence naturally arise indifference or aversion between the parties."—*Brown's Estimates.*
13. "Wisdom, and not wealth, procure esteem."—*Ib.*
14. "No company likes to confess that they are ignorant." *Student's Manual.*
15. "The people rejoices in that which should cause sorrow."
16. "Therein consists the force and use and nature of language."—*Berkley.*
17. "From him proceeds power, sanctification, truth, grace, and every other blessing we can conceive."—*Calvin.*
18. "How is the Gender and Number of the Relative known?" *Bullion's Practical Lessons.*
19. "Hill and dale doth boast thy blessing."—*Milton.*
20. "The Syntax and Etymology of the language is thus spread before the learner."—*Bullion's Grammar.*
21. "In France the peasantry goes barefoot, and the middle sort makes use of wooden shoes."—*Harvey.*
22. "While all our youth prefers her to the rest."—*Waller.*
23. "A great majority of our authors is defective in manner."—*J. Brown.*
24. "Neither the intellect nor the heart are capable of being driven." *Abbott.*

25. "Nor he nor I are capable of harboring a thought against your peace."—*Walpole.*
26. "Neither riches nor fame render a man happy."—*Day's Grammar.*
27. "I or thou art the person who must undertake the business."—*Murray.*
28. "The quarrels of lovers is a renewal of love."
29. "Two or more sentences united together, is called a compound sentence."—*Day's Grammar.*
30. "If I was a Greek, I should resist Turkish despotism." *Cardell's Grammar.*
31. "I can not say that I admire this construction, though it be much used."—*Priestly's Grammar*, p. 172.
32. "It was observed in Chap. iii. that the disjunctive *or* had a double use."—*Churchill's Grammar.*
33. "I observed that love constituted the whole character of God." *Dwight.*
34. "A stranger to the poem would not easily discover that this was verse."—*Murray.*
35. "Had I commanded you to have done this, you would thought hard of it."—*J. Brown.*
36. "I found him better than I expected to have found him." *Priestly's Grammar.*
37. "There are several faults which I intended to have enumerated." *Webster.*
38. "An effort is making to abolish the law."
39. "The Spartan admiral was sailed to the Hellespont."—*Goldsmith.*
40. "So soon as he was landed, the multitude thronged about him."—*Ib*
41. "Which they neither have nor can do."—*Barclay.*
42. "For you have but mistook me all the while."—*Shakspeare.*
43. "Who would not have let them appeared."—*Steele.*
44. "You were chose probationer."—*Spectator.*
45. "Had I known the character of the lecture, I would not have went."
46. "They don't ought to do it."—*Watkins.*
47. "Had I ought to place '*wise*' in Predicate with '*makes*'?—*Pupil.*
48. "Whom they had *sat* at defiance."—*Bolingbroke.*
49. "Whereunto the righteous *fly* and are safe."—*Barclay.*
50. "She *sets* as a prototype, for exact imitation."—*Rash.*

REM.—After correcting the above examples, the Pupil should analyze and parse them—using the MODEL given on p. 204–5, or that on p. 183–4.

III. *The Object of a Sentence.*

RULE 3.—The Object of an action or relation must be in the Objective Case.

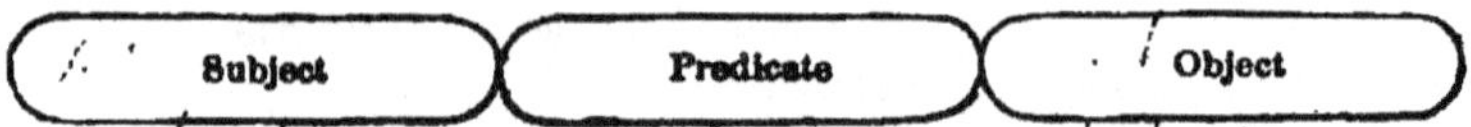

EXAMPLES.—1. "Virtue secures *happiness.*"
2. Mary and Anna are writing *letters.*
3. "*Him* from my childhood I have known."
4. *Them* that honor *me*, I will honor."

OBS. 1.—The Object of a Sentence may be—
1. *A Noun*....."Now twilight lets her *curtain* down,
2. *A Pronoun*.. And pins *it* with a star."
3. *A Phrase*...."I doubted *his having been a soldier.*"
4 *A Sentence*..."But Brutus says, *he was ambitious.*"

(1) OBJECT WORD.

"*Virtue secures happiness.*"

(*a*) FORM OF THE OBJECT.

OBS. 2.—The *forms* of Nouns do not distinguish the Objective Case from the Nominative or Subjective.

The Personal Pronouns and the Relative and the Interrogative *who* are the only Substantive Words that distinguish the cases by their *forms.*—(See Declension of Pronouns, page 89.)—Hence,

OBS. 3.—In constructing Sentences, special attention is required in giving to the Object of a Sentence its appropriate *position.*

POSITION OF THE OBJECT.

NOTE.—In *position*, the Object of a Sentence commonly follows the Predicate.

EXAMPLES.—1. "Virtue SECURES *happiness.*"
2. "The King of Shadows LOVES a shining *mark.*"
3. "In the beginning God CREATED the *heaven* and the *earth.*"

EXCEPTION 1.—By the poets and for rhetorical effect, the Object is often placed before the Predicate.

EXAMPLES.—1. "*Him*, from my childhood, I HAVE KNOWN."
2. "New ills that latter *stage* AWAIT."
3. "And all the *air* a solemn stillness HOLDS."

EXCEPTION 2.—A *Relative* Pronoun, being the Object of a Sentence, is placed before its Predicate.

EXAMPLES.—1. "The evil *which* he FEARED, has come upon him."
2. "Mount the horse *which* I HAVE CHOSEN for you."
3. "We serve a Monarch *whom* we LOVE,—
A God *whom* we ADORE."

TWO OR MORE OBJECTS.

OBS. 4.—A Sentence may have two or more Objects when they are connected in construction by Conjunctions, expressed or implied.

EXAMPLES.—1. "God CREATED the *heaven* and the *earth*."
2. 'Now twilight LETS her *curtain* down,
And PINS *it* with a star."
"For the Angel of Death SPREAD his *wings* on the blast,
And BREATHED in the face of the foe as he passed."

REMARK.—These are Compound Sentences. In Sentence (1), "heaven" and "earth" are Objects of the same Verb, "created." In Sentence (2), "curtain" is the Object of "lets," and "it" is the Object of "pins." Sentence (3) is also Compound; yet it has but one Object, "breathed" being Intransitive.

OBS. 5.—The Objects of a Compound Sentence sometimes consist of different Words, indicating the same being or thing.

EXAMPLES.—1. "By this dispensation, we HAVE LOST a *neighbor*, a *friend*, a *brother*."
2. "Thus she addressed the *Father* of gods, and *King* of men."

OBS. 6.—But one Word used to limit the signification of another, cannot be in the same construction; and hence, the two Words are not Objects of the same Verb, unless they are compounded and parsed as one Element.

EXAMPLES.—1. "We visited NAPLES, the *home* of our childhood."
2. Have you seen COLERIDGE, the *philosopher* and *poet*?
3. "And must I leave thee, Paradise?"

REM.—"*Home*" is a Noun, used to describe "Naples," not as an Adjective, but as an equivalent name of the same place.

"*Philosopher*" and "*poet*" are Substantive appellations of the man, "Coleridge."

"*Paradise*" limits the application of the word "*thee*."

(See "Logical Adjuncts" and "Independent Case," p. 85, Obs. 2, 3.)

OBS. 7.—The Verbs *appoint*, *call*, *choose*, *constitute*, *create*, *dub*, *elect*, *make*, *name*, and *proclaim*, sometimes have two Objects—one direct, and the other indirect.

EXAMPLES.—1. They named *him* JOHN.

2. The State Society elected *Rice* PRESIDENT,

3. And chose *Valentine* SECRETARY.

REM.—In Example (1), "him" is the *direct* Object—"John" the *remote* Object; and is, logically considered, a part of the Predicate—a *title* acquired by the action expressed by the Verb. The Verbs above given do not, in such examples, express the full Predicate, nor have we Verbs that *can*, unless, perhaps, in the following example:—

"They dubbed *him* KNIGHT."

Equivalent.—"They KNIGHTED *him*."

OBS. 8.—A Verb which, in the Active Voice, is followed by a direct and a remote object, retains the remote object as a part of the Passive Predicate.

EXAMPLES.—1. He *is named John*.

2. Rice *was elected President*.

REM.—This construction is analogous to that of Substantive in Predicate with a Neuter Verb.

Thou *art Peter*—He *is John*.

Thou art—what?—*Peter*. He is—what?—*named John*. The word "Peter" completes the Predicate; the words "named John" complete the Predicate.

OBS. 9.—The construction noticed in Obs. 7 should be carefully distinguished from that in which a Verb is followed by two Objects—one of the Verb and the other of a Preposition suppressed.

EXAMPLE.—"They *carried* the *child* home."

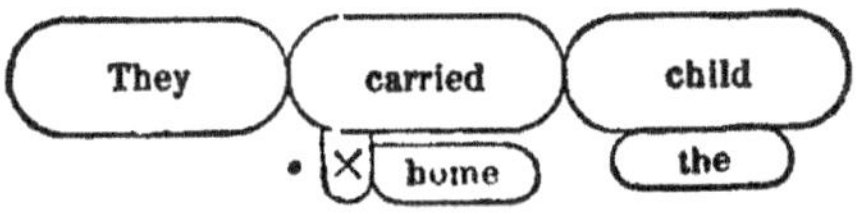

REM.—"Child" is the name of a young being, and, in this connection, is the proper object of "carried." But "home" is a name applied to a habitation, a building, and "they" probably did not "carry" that. They carried the child *to* some place—and that place was its *home*.

"He *told* ME his *history*."—He *related* TO ME his *history*.

I *asked him* his OPINION.

"Our dear Joachim has asked me for my opinion."—*Michelet's Luther.*

"He *gave* ME a book."—He *gave* a book to me."

REM.—In parsing examples like the above, the ellipsis should be supplied. Thus, "to his home" is an Adjunct of "carried." Hence, an Adverbial Phrase.

"Home," as a *Representative* of the Phrase, is an Adverb.

"Home," as an Element in the Phrase, is a Noun—Object of *to* understood. Hence, in the Objective Case.

OBS. 10.—The Verbs *make, esteem, regard, consider, elect, bid, dare, feel, hear, see,* and some others, are often followed by an Infinitive Phrase, having its Preposition (and sometimes the Verb) understood.

EXAMPLES.—1. "Lorenzo, these are thoughts that *make** *man* MAN."
Young.

.... these are thoughts that *make man* [TO BE] MAN.

2. "*Teach them* OBEDIENCE to the laws."

Teach them [TO YIELD] OBEDIENCE to the laws.

REM.—In examples like these the second Noun or Pronoun is the Object of the Verb understood or used in Predicate with it. Thus, "man" is used in Predicate with "to be," or "to become," understood; and "obedience" is the object of "yield."

EXAMPLES.—1. Intemperance makes a man [to become] a fool.

2. "He maketh the storm [ ] a calm." (See Diagram, p. 216.)

---

* The word make is generally thus used, when it signifies "to cause to be," "to cause to become."

NOTE IV.—Intransitive Verbs have no Object.

EXAMPLES.—I sit—Thou art—He sleeps.

OBS. 1.—But some Verbs, commonly used Intransitively, sometimes have Objects of their own signification.

EXAMPLES.—1. I have fought a good *fight*.
2. We ran a *race*.
3. He sleeps the sleep of death.
4. "Luther * * * * blew a *blast*."
5. "[They] shout their raptures to the clouldless skies."

NOTE V.—A few Verbs may be used Transitively or Intransitively.

EXAMPLES.—1. The sun *set* in the west.
2. He *set* the inkstand on the table.
3. Cool *blows* the wind.
4. The wind *blows* the dust.

POSITION OF THE OBJECT.

OBS. 1.—When a Transitive Verb is followed by two Objects—one, the Object of the Verb, and the other the Object of a Preposition suppressed, the Object of the Preposition is placed between the Verb and its Object.

EXAMPLES.—1. "Mary gave *me* a ROSE."
2. "Bring *home* my BOOKS."

REM.—"*Me*" is an abridged Adjunct of "*gave*" (see Adverbs by Representation, p. 23), and is placed next its Verb according to the Rule for the Position of Adverbs (see p. 259).

Exception.—When the indirect Object suggests the important thought, or when it is the emphatic word in the Sentence, it is placed *after* the direct Object.

EXAMPLE.—"They carried the CHILD *home*."

OBS. 2.—But, when the Preposition is expressed, the direct Object is placed next its Verb.

EXAMPLE.—"Mary GAVE a *rose* to me."

OBJECT PHRASE.

PRIN.—Transitive Verbs may have, as their Objects, *Substantive Phrases*.

EXAMPLES.—1. "I doubted *his having been a soldier.*"

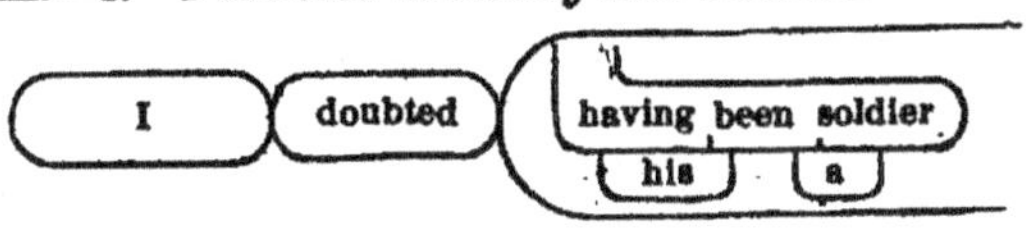

I doubted—*what?* Not "*his,*" nor "*having,*" nor "*been,*" nor "*a,*" nor "*soldier,*" but the fact asserted by the whole Phrase—"*His having been a soldier.*"

2. "His being a minister, prevented *his rising to civil power.*"

OBS. 1.—Object Phrases are limited, almost exclusively, to the *Participial Form,* Prepositional and Infinitive Phrases being commonly used as Adjuncts, and Independent Phrases as Logical Adjuncts. (See p. 20, Obs. 1; see also Clark's Analysis, p. 115.)

OBS. 2.—But Prepositional, Infinitive, and Independent Phrases may be used *technically* as Objects of Transitive Verbs.

EXAMPLES.—1. "The maniac repeated, '*on a bed of green sea-flowers,*' during the interview."

2. The damsel could not say "*to be loving,*" without embarrassment.

OBS. 3.—Infinitive Phrases following Verbs, commonly indicate *purpose* or *cause*, and serve to limit the signification or application of Verbs. Such are properly called Adverbs.

EXAMPLES.—1. Pupils are allowed *to read.*
2. Pupils appear *to read.*
3. Pupils assemble *to read.*
4. Pupils ought *to read.*
5. Pupils begin *to read.*
6. Pupils wish *to read.*

REM. 1.—In Sentences (1), (2), (3), and (4), the Phrase "*to read*" is plainly Adverbial, the Predicate Verbs being necessarily Intransitive.

In the analysis of Sentences like (5) and (6), two sentiments obtain with prominent grammarians—1, that "to read" is the Object of "begin" and "wish" (see Welch, p. 205, and others); 2d, that "begin" and "wish" are here Intransitive Verbs. (See Brown, p. 496, and others.)

The *test* given by these and other authors for determining the Object of a Verb, viz., the question *what?* does not seem to be appropriate.

Pupils beign—*what?*..............*to do what?*
Pupils wish—*what?* ....*to do what?*

If the question *what?* is more appropriate, "to read" is the Object of "wish." But,

If the question *to do what?* is more appropriate, "to read" is an Adjunct of "wish."

OBS. 4.—The Transitive Verbs having Objects expressed, are often limited by Infinitive Phrases.

EXAMPLES.—1. The teacher REQUESTED William *to recite.*
2. I BELIEVE the milk-man *to be honest.*

REM. 2.—"*To recite*" is a Phrase, Adjunct of "requested;" it *limits* the request. "William" is the Object of "requested."

"*To be honest*" is a Phrase Adjunct of "believe:" milk-man is the Object of the modified Predicate "believe to be honest."

OBS. 5.—This construction should be carefully distinguished from that in which the Infinitive Phrase is Adjunct of the Object.

EXAMPLES.—1. The general gave the ORDER *to fire.*

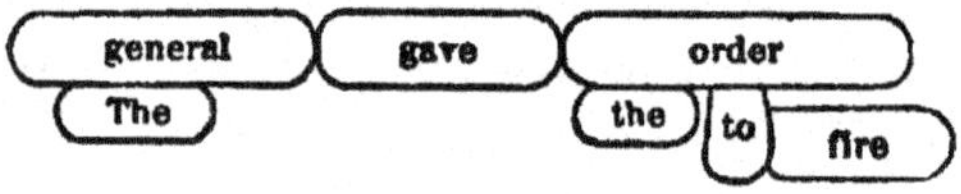

2. The subordinate manifested a DISPOSITION *to dictate.*
3. The truant manifested no inclination to return.
4. Idle pupils manifest little anxiety to improve.
5. "But half of our heavy task was done,
When the bell tolled the HOUR *for retiring.*"
6. "We have our various duties to perform."
7. "I have meat to eat that ye know not of."

REM. 3.—"*To fire*" limits "order;" hence, an Adjective.
"To dictate" limits "disposition;" hence, an Adjective.

☞ Let the Pupil place Sentences (2), (3), and (4) in the given Diagram; and vary the Diagram for (5), (6), and (7).

OBJECT SENTENCE.

PRIN.—Many Transitive Verbs have as their Objects *Substantive Auxiliary Sentences.*

OBS.—Object Sentences are distinguished as ***direct Objects*** and ***indirect Objects.***

EXAMPLES.

Direct.—1. "But Brutus says *he was ambitious.*"

2. "Nathan said unto David, *Thou art the man.*"

Indirect.—3. "The ancient Russians believed *that their northern mountains encompassed the globe.*"

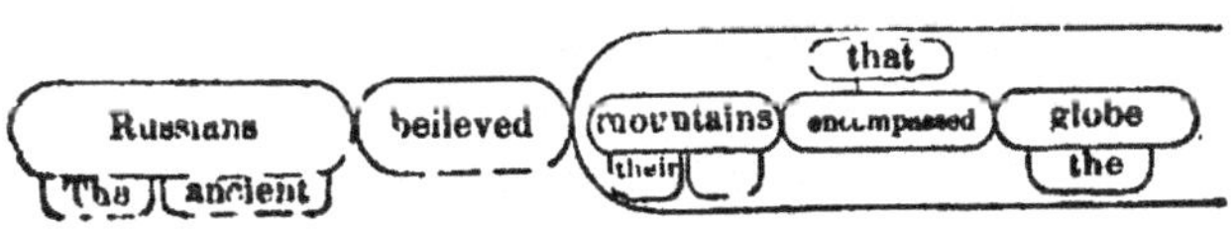

4. "God never meant *that man should scale the heavens by strides of human wisdom.*"
5. "Can you tell *where my Highland laddie's gone?*"
6. "He hastily demanded *why I came.*"
7. "The village all declared *how much he knew.*"
8. "Did you but know *to whom I gave the ring.*"
9. "He little dreamed *what dangers threatened him.*"
10. "We can not learn *who did it.*"

REM. 1.—The Pupil will notice that Sentences used as *Indirect Objects*, are introduced by a Word or a Phrase *which constitutes, logically, the essential part of the Object.* Thus in Sentence (4) "that" stands for the whole Proposition.

"Their northern mountains encompassed the globe."
"The ancient Russians believed *that.*"
"My Highland laddie has gone,"—can you tell *where?*
"I gave the ring,"—did you but know *to whom.*
"Dangers threatened him"—he little dreamed *what.*
"*Who* did it?"—we can not learn.

REM. 2.—Still we are to regard the *entire Auxiliary Sentence* as the Grammatical Object of the Principal Predicate.

OBS. 2.—This construction is to be carefully distinguished from Complex Sentences, in which the Object Sentences are introduced by the Double Relative *what.*

EXAMPLES.—1. "But here I stand and tell *what I do know.*"
2. "You have done what you should be sorry for."
3. "I can not tell what you think of this life."

REM. 3.—Here, "what I do know" is the *modified* Object of "tell."

OBS. 3.—By another construction, Auxiliary Sentences are placed after Predicates of Principal Sentences—not as Objects, but as Adjuncts of purpose, cause, &c.

EXAMPLES.—1. The pupil studies *that he may improve.*
2. "And I am glad *that he has lived thus long;*
3. And [ ] glad *that he has gone to his reward.*"

OBS. 4.—Another construction makes the Auxiliary Sentence a Logical Adjunct of a Substantive.

EXAMPLES.—"It is possible *that we have erred.*"

(See "Independent Case," and "Independent Sentence," in place.)

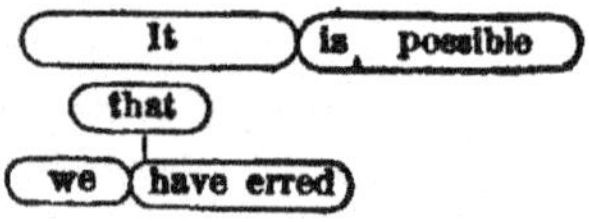

"We had strong suspicions *that Warner had the ring.*"

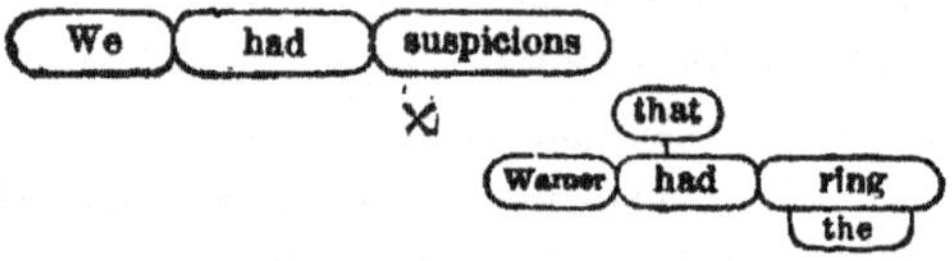

REM.—*What* were our suspicions?
Ans. *That Warner had the ring.*
Hence, "that Warner had the ring" is a logical Adjunct of "suspicions," and in the Diagram is placed under, but not attached to, "suspicions."

OBS. 5.—Sometimes a Principal Sentence *is thrown in* between the parts of an Objective Sentence.

EXAMPLES.—1. "Whose charms, *we thought,* could never fade."
2. "This explanation, *I doubt not,* will satisfy him."
3. "But confidence, *he added,* is a plant of slow growth."

THE OBJECTS OF PHRASES.

REM.—*Action* is expressed by *Verbs* and by *Participles*. *Relation* is expressed by *Prepositions*. Hence,

OBS. 1.—The Object of a Verb or a Participle is the Object of an *Action*, and must be in the Objective Case.

EXAMPLES.

Verb in Predicate.—"He that GETTETH *wisdom*, LOVETH his own *soul*."

Infinitive Verb.—"I came to BURY *Cesar*, not to PRAISE *him*."

Participle.—"He could not avoid GIVING *offense*."

OBS. 2.—The Object of a Preposition is the Object of a *Relation*, indicated by the Preposition, and should be in the Objective Case.

EXAMPLES.—1. "The time OF my *departure* is AT *hand*."
2. "FOR *me* your tributary stores *combine*."
3. "The boy stood ON the burning *deck*,
Whence all BUT *him* had fled."
4. "THAN *whom*, *Satan* EXCEPT, none higher sat."

NOTE I.—Nouns and Pronouns in the Objective Case, should have their appropriate forms.

EXAMPLES.—1. "Did you but know to *whom* I gave the *ring*."
2. "I call to *thee* with all my *voice*."
3. "It is not fit for such as *us*
To sit with rulers of the land."

EXCEPTION 1.—Rarely the Possessive form of Nouns and Pronouns in he Objective Case is used.

EXAMPLE—John is a friend of *mine*. (See p. 90.)

EXCEPTION 2.—Adjunct Sentences, introduced by the Conjunctions *as*, *before*, *than*, *till*, etc., are often contracted into Adjunct Phrases—the Subjects of the Sentences becoming the Objects of Phrases, often without a corresponding change of form. (See page 172.)

OBS.—The Objects of Phrases and Sentences may be *Words*, *Phrases*, or *Sentences*.

OBJECTS OF SENTENCES.

☞ Let the following Sentences be analyzed by the CHART, and parsed:

Word Objects.—1. "There thou shalt FIND my *cousin* Beatrice."—*Shaks.*
2. "His daring foe securely *him* DEFIED."—*Milton.*
3. "The broom its yellow *leaf* HATH SHED."—*Langhorn.*
4. "Did I REQUEST *thee*, Maker, from my clay,
To mould *me* man?"—*Milton.*

Phrase Objects.—5. "We may AVOID *talking nonsense* on these subjects."

6. "I DOUBTED *their having it.*"

Sentence Objects.—7. "They SAY, '*This shall be*,' and it is."

8. "Athens FOUND *that neither art nor science could avail against depravity of morals.*"

II. OBJECTS OF PHRASES—INFINITIVE.

Word Objects.—9. "How I love to SEE *thee*,
Golden, evening sun!"

10. "I come to BURY *Cæsar*, not to PRAISE *him*."

Phrase Objects.—11. "He endeavored to PREVENT *our being tossed about by every wind of doctrine*."

12. "It is difficult to DOUBT *his having seen military service.*"

Sentence Objects.—13. "This goes to PROVE *what strange creatures we are.*"

14. "The Governor commands me to SAY, *that he has no further business with the Senate.*"

PARTICIPIAL.

Word Objects.—15. "SCALING yonder *peak*, I saw an eagle."

16. "FINDING *fault*, never does any good."

Phrase Objects.—17. "By OPPOSING *your going to college*, your father abridged your usefulness."

Sentence Objects.—18. "The ceremonies concluded by the doctors' SAYING, '*Gentlemen, we will resume our studies at seven to-morrow.*'"

PREPOSITIONAL.

Word Objects.—19. "There came TO the *beach* a poor exile OF *Erin*."

20. "You are a much greater loser THAN *me* by his death."—*Swift.*

21. "The Jesuits had more interest at court THAN *him*."
Smollet.

22. "He suffers AS *them* that have no hope."
Maturin's Sermons.

Phrase Objects.—23. "In the matter OF *making and receiving presents*, much discretion is required."

24. "I had no knowledge OF *there being any connection between them.*"—*Stone.*

25. "To follow foolish precedents and wink
With both our eyes, is easier THAN *to think.*"

Sentence Objects.—26. "And all the air a solemn stillness holds—
SAVE *where the beetle wheels his droning flight.*"

QUESTIONS FOR REVIEW.

PAGE

208.—Repeat RULE III.—Make Examples to illustrate it.

The Object of a Sentence may consist of what? ....See Obs. 1.

What Object Words are distinguished by their *forms?* .See Obs. 2.

What is the usual *Position* of the Object?

209.—Mention the Exceptions, and give Examples.

When may two or more words be Objects of the same Verb?

Make Sentences to illustrate Obs. 4 and 5.

When may they not both be Objects of a preceding Verb?

Make Sentences to illustrate Obs. 6.

What Verbs may have *direct* and *indirect* Objects?

210.— Make Sentences to illustrate Obs. 7.

What Passive Verbs may have Objects?

Make Sentences to illustrate Obs. 8.

Make Sentences to illustrate Obs. 9

211.— Make Sentences to illustrate Obs. 10.

212.—What Verbs have no Objects? ....See Note IV

Make Sentences to illustrate Obs. 1.

What Verbs may be used Transitively or Intransitively?

Two Objects, one of a Verb and the other of a Preposition suppressed, have what *relative positions?*

Make Sentences to illustrate Obs. 2.

What position have the Objects when the Preposition is expressed?

Make Sentences to illustrate Obs. 3.

213.—What Phrases may be Objects of Sentences?

Make Sentences to illustrate Obs. 1.

215.—Make a Sentence having a sentence Object.

GRAMMATICAL FALLACIES.

☞ Let the Pupil correct the following Sentences, giving the proper authority for each correction:

1. "Let none touch it but those who are clean."—*Sale's Koran.*
2. "None but *thou*, O mighty prince, canst avert the blow."
3. "None but *thou* can aid us."
4. "No mortal man, save he, had e'er survived to say he saw."—*Scott.*
5. "We are alone; here's none but thee and I."—*Shakspeare.*
6. "Good Margaret, run *thee* into the parlor."—*Shakspeare.*
7. "He loves he knows not *who*."—*Addison.*

PRONOUNS.

Rule 4.—A Pronoun must agree with its Antecedent in Person and Number.

Note I.—A Pronoun should have a Singular form,

(1.) When it represents one Singular Antecedent.

Example.—*Henry* was quite well when I last saw him.

(2.) When it represents two or more Singular Antecedents taken separately.

Example.—"The *oil* of peppermint, or any other volatile *oil*, dropped on paper, will soon evaporate; no trace of it will be left."

Note II.—A Pronoun should have a Plural form,

(1.) When it has one Antecedent indicating Plurality.

Example. —Few *men* are as wise as they might be.

(2.) When it has two or more Antecedents taken collectively.

Example.—Mary and Anna always accomplish what they undertake.

PERSONAL PRONOUNS.

Note III.—The *form* of a Personal Pronoun should indicate its Person and Number.

Obs. 1.—The Pronouns *I* and *we* denote the person or persons speaking or writing—"I," Singular—"we," Plural. But,

Obs. 2.—"*We*" is used in the Singular by Editors and Emperors.

Examples.—"*We*, Nicholas I., Emperor of all the Russias."
"*We* shall present *ourself* as candidate at the next election."

Obs 3.—*Thou* is used in Solemn Style to denote a person addressed.

Example.—"*Thou* didst weave this verdant roof."

OBS. 4.—*You* was formerly limited to the Second Person Plural, but is now used in the Second Person Singular and Plural. Its Verb is commonly in the Plural form.

EXAMPLES.—"You *are come* too late."
You *have accomplished* your object.

OBS. 5.—But it has sometimes a Singular form.

EXAMPLES.—"On that happy day when you *was* given to the world."
Dod's Max
"When you *was* here comforting me."—*Pope.*
"Why *was* you glad?"—*Boswell's Life of Johnson.*

OBS. 6.—The Pronoun "*it*" often has an Indefinite or undetermined Antecedent; and may then represent any Gender, Person, or Number.

EXAMPLES.—"*It* snows." "*It* rains."
"IT was my *father.*"
"IT was the *students.*"
"A pleasant thing IT is, *to behold the sun.*"
"If ever there was a 'people's *man*,' in the true sense, IT was *Dr. Chalmers.*"—*B. B. Edwards.*

NOTE IV.—Pronouns of different Persons, used in the same connection, should have their appropriate position.

OBS. 1.—The Second Person is placed first—the Third next, and the First last.

EXAMPLE.—*You* and *James* and *I* have been invited.

OBS. 2.—But when a fault is confessed, this order is sometimes reversed.

EXAMPLE.—"*I* and *my people* have sinned."

OBS. 3.—This position obtains also when we acknowledge a defeat or a common calamity.

EXAMPLE.—"Then I and you and all of us fell down,
Whilst bloody Treason flourished over us."

NOTE V.—The Pronoun "*them*" should not be used Adjectively.

Incorrect.—Bring me *them* books.
Correct.—Bring me *those* books.

RELATIVE PRONOUNS.

OBS. 1.—A Relative Pronoun always performs a double office, and is used,

1. Substantively.

EXAMPLE.—He *who* studies, will improve.

"Who" relates to "he," and is the Subject of studies—hence, a Substantive.

2. Conjunctively—introducing an Adjective Sentence.

EXAMPLE.—He *who* studies, will improve.

"Who studies," is a Sentence used to describe "he."

"Who" introduces the Sentence—hence it is used Conjunctively.

OBS. 2.—*Who* and *whom* are applied to man, and to other intelligent beings; *which*, to things; *that*, to persons or things.

EXAMPLES.—1. "*He* THAT attends to his interior self, has business."

2. "Too low *they* build, WHO build beneath the stars."

3. "*He* WHOM sea-severed realms obey."

4. "The *books* WHICH I had lost have been returned."

5. ——— "where is the *patience* now
THAT you so oft have boasted to retain!"—*Lear*, III. 6.

OBS. 3.—But the name of a person, taken as a *name merely*, or as a title, may be represented by the Relative *which*.

EXAMPLE.—*Shylock*—WHICH is but another name for selfishness.

OBS. 5.—When the Relative "*what*" is used substantively, it bears a part in the structure of two sentences at the same time. It is always equivalent to "*that which*," or "*the things which*." The Antecedent part may be the Subject (A) or Object (B) of a Principal Sentence, the Object (C) of a Phrase in that Sentence, or used in Predicate (D). The Consequent or Relative part introduces an Auxiliary Sentence, which qualifies the Antecedent, and may be the Subject (E) or Object (G) of that Sentence, the Object of a Phrase (H), or used in Predicate with a Verb (I).

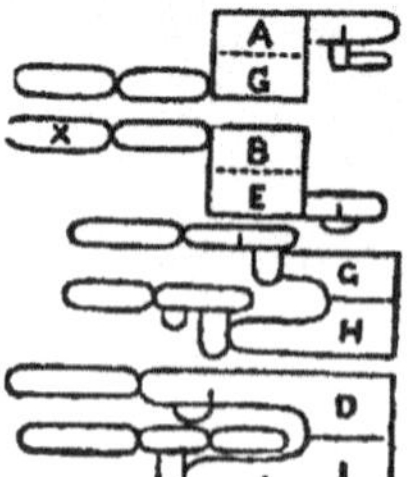

1. "WHAT reason weaves, by passion is undone." *Pope.*

2. 'Deduct WHAT is but vanity."—*Idem.*

3. "Each was favored with WHAT he most delighted in."

4. "It is not WHAT I supposed it to be."

OBS. 6.—*What* is sometimes a Simple Relative.

EXAMPLE.—"And *what* love can do, that dares love attempt."—*Romeo.*

OBS. 7.—*Whoever, whosoever, whatever, whatsoever,* and *who* (used for whoever), have a construction similar to *what.*

EXAMPLES.—"*Whatever* purifies, fortifies also the heart."

"*Who* lives to Nature, rarely can be poor;
Who lives to Fancy, never can be rich."

OBS. 8.—*What, which, whatever,* and *whatsoever,* are often used Adjectively.

EXAMPLES.—1. "*What* book have you?"
2. "*Whatever* object is most dear."
3. "*Whatsoever* things are honest."
4. "*Which* hope we have."

OBS. 9.—*That* is sometimes improperly used for the Relative *what.*

EXAMPLE.—"Take *that* is thine."

OBS. 10.—*What* is sometimes substituted for an Adverbial Phrase.

EXAMPLE.—"*What* [in what respect] shall it profit a man?"

OBS. 11.—*What* is sometimes used as an Exclamation.

EXAMPLE.—"*What!* Is thy servant a dog?"

OBS. 12.—The two words, *but what*—and also, *but that*—are sometimes improperly used for the Conjunction *that.*

EXAMPLES.—"I did not doubt *but what* you would come."
"I did not doubt *but that* you would come."

Corrected.—I did not doubt *that* you would come.

OBS. 13.—The Relatives *than* and *as* have Adjectives, or Adjective Pronouns, for their Antecedents.

As, when a Relative Pronoun, has for its Antecedent the word "*such*"—used Adjectively, or as an Adjective Pronoun.

Than follows *more,* or some other Adjective, in the Comparative Degree.

EXAMPLES.

1. "Nestled at his root
Is Beauty; *such* AS blooms not in the glare
Of the broad sun."—*Bryant.*

2. "We request *such* of you as think we overlaud the ode, to point out one word in it that would be better away."—*Wilson's Burns.*

3. "He has *less* discretion THAN he was famed for having."

4. "There is *more* owing her THAN is paid."—*All's Well,* i. 3.

REM.—Let it be remembered, that *than* and *as* are Substantives only when they constitute Subjects or Objects of Sentences. Most teachers would regard those words in the Examples above as thus used, but a rigid analysis of these sentences would require the ellipses to be supplied —then the words *as* and *than* would perform the office of Prepositions.

Beauty such as [that which] blooms not, &c.
Less discretion than [that which] he was famed for having.

POSITION.

NOTE IV.—The Position of Relative Pronouns should be such as most clearly to indicate their Antecedents.

OBS. 1.—When a Relative is the Subject or the Object of an Auxiliary Sentence, it should be placed next its Antecedent.

EXAMPLES.—1. "Can *all* THAT optics teach unfold
Thy form to please me so?"
2. "The *grave*, THAT never spoke before,
Hath found, at length, a tongue to chide."

EXCEPTION.—To this rule there are exceptions.
"O, *they* love least THAT let men know their love."—*Shakspeare.*

OBS. 2.—When the Relative is the Object of a Prepositional Phrase, it comes between its Antecedent and the Auxiliary Sentence with which that Phrase is construed.

EXAMPLE.—"We prize *that* most FOR WHICH *we labor* most."

REM.—"For which" modifies "labor"—"which" relates to "that."

OBS. 3.—The Relative *that*, used as the Object of a Preposition, is placed *before* the Preposition. *Whom*, *which*, and *what*, are placed after their Prepositions.

EXAMPLES.—1. "I have meat to eat *that* ye know not *of*."
2. "Withhold not good from them *to whom* it is due."
3. "The world *in which* we sojourn is not our home."
4. "We could not learn *for what* he came."

OBS. 4.—The Relative—whether the Subject or the Object of a Sentence, or the Object of a Phrase—can rarely be omitted without weakening the force of the expression.

EXAMPLES.—1. "For is there aught in sleep [ ] can charm the wise?"
2. "The time may come [ ] you need not fly."
3. "It is a question [ ] I can not answer."

OBS. 5.—But the suppression of the Relative is allowed when the position of the words is such as to prevent ambiguity or weaken the expression.

EXAMPLES.—1. "History is all the light we have in many cases; and we receive from it a great part of the useful truths we have."
2. "But they that fight for freedom, undertake
The noblest cause mankind can have at stake."

INTERROGATIVES.

NOTE V.—Interrogative Pronouns are construed like Personal Pronouns.

EXAMPLES.—1. As the Subject of a Sentence—WHO *has* the lesson?
2. As the Object of a Sentence—WHOM *seek* ye?
3. As the Object of a Phrase—*For* WHAT do we labor?

OBS. 1.—The Interrogative force of such Pronouns is commonly suppressed when they introduce Substantive Auxiliary Sentences.

EXAMPLES.—1. We shall soon ascertain *who has the lesson.*
2. Ye still refuse to tell *whom ye seek.*
3. We scarcely know *for what we labor.*

OBS. 2.—But the Principal Sentence may remain Interrogative.

EXAMPLES.—1. "*Who* shall decide *which shall have the pr*[illegible]"
2. *How* can you tell *whom the teacher wil*[illegible]
3. By *whom* did you learn *for whom I vo*[illegible]

OBS. 3.—The word which answers a question has [illegible] construction similar to that of the word which asks it.

EXAMPLES.—1. *Whose* book have you? *Mary's.*
2. *How* long was you going? *Three days.*
3. *Where* did you see him? *In Rochester.*
4. *Whence* came they? *From Ireland.*

REM.—"Mary's" specifies "book"—[during] "three days" modifies "was gone"—"in Rochester" modifies "did see"—"from Ireland" modifies "came."

OBS. 4.—The Interrogative *what*, followed by the Conjunctions *though*, *if*, and some others, commonly belongs to a Principal Sentence understood, and on which the following sentence depends for sense.

EXAMPLES.—1. "*What if* the foot aspired to be the head!"
What [would be the consequence] if the foot, &c.
2. "What though Destruction sweep these lovely plains!"
What [occasion have we to despair] though Destruction sweep these lovely plains!

ADJECTIVE PRONOUNS.

RULE 5.—Adjective Pronouns are *substituted* for the Nouns *which they qualify*.

NOTE I.—When used as Subjects, *each*, *either*, *neither*, *this*, *that*, and all other Adjective Pronouns indicating *unity*, require their Verbs to be in the *Singular* Number.

EXAMPLES.—1. "*Each believes* its own."
2. *Either* is sufficient.

NOTE II.—*These*, *those*, *many*, *others*, *several*, and other Adjective Pronouns indicating *plurality*, require their Verbs to be in the Plural.

EXAMPLES.—1. "*These* are the things which defile."
2. "*Those* were halcyon days."

NOTE III.—*Any*, *all*, *like*, *some*, *none*, *more*, and *such*, may have Verbs in the Singular or Plural, according as they indicate unity or plurality.

EXAMPLES.—1. "*None* but the upright in heart *are* capable of being true friends."—*Y. L. Friend.*
2. "*None has* arrived."
3. "*All are* but parts of one stupendous whole."
4. "What if the field be lost! *All is* not lost."
5. "The *like were* never *seen* before." "*Like produces* like."

6. "Objects of importance must be portrayed by objects of importance; *such* as *have* grace, by things graceful."

7. "Nestled at its root
Is Beauty; *such* as *blooms* not in the glare
Of the broad sun."

OBS. 1.—Qualifying and some Specifying Adjectives receive the definitive "*the*" before them, on becoming Adjective Pronouns. They may be qualified by *Adjectives* or *Adverbs*, according as the *thing* or the *quality* is to be qualified.

EXAMPLES.—1. "*The* GOOD alone are great."

2. "The *professedly* GOOD are not always *really* so."

3. "The *much* GOOD done by him will not soon be forgotten."

"Professedly" modifies the *quality*—hence, is an Adverb.

"Much" limits the *things* done—hence, is an Adjective.

OBS. 2.—In the analysis of a Sentence, *each other*, *one another*, and similar distributives, are properly parsed as single words.

But, in strict construction the parts perform different offices.

EXAMPLES.—They assisted each other.
They assisted—each [assisted] the other.

OBS. 3.—When two things are mentioned in contrast, and severally referred to by Adjective Pronouns—*this* and *these*, refer to the *latter*—*that* and *those*, to the *former*.

EXAMPLES.—1. "Here living tea-pots stand, *one arm* held out,
ONE bent; the handle THIS, and *that* the spout."—*Pope*

2. "Farewell, my *friends*; farewell, my FOES;
My peace with THESE, my love with *those*."—*Burns*.

3. "*Some* place the bliss in action; SOME, in ease:
Those call it pleasure; and contentment THESE."

EXERCISES.

"He that getteth wisdom, loveth his own soul."

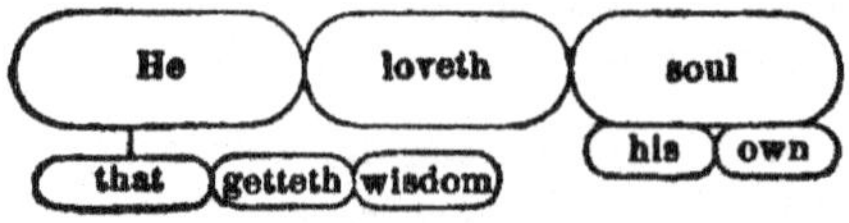

ANALYSIS.

PRINCIPAL PARTS ..	He .. ..Subject of "loveth."		Complex Sentence. Principal, Simple. Transitive.
	Loveth..Predicate of "he."		
	Soul ....Object of "loveth."		
ADJUNCTS...	That getteth wisdom	Adjunct of "he."	
	His.... ... own	Adjuncts of "soul."	
AUXILIARY SENTENCE	That....Subject of "getteth."		Auxiliary, Simple. Transitive.
	Getteth .Predicate of "that."		
	Wisdom.Object of "getteth."		

PARSED.

He ......Is used for a name..............Hence, a Pronoun.
" Its *form* denotes its Person.......Hence, Personal.
" Has the form of the Masculine. ..Hence, Masculine Gender.
" Spoken of.....................Hence, Third Person.
" Denotes but one................Hence, Singular Number.
" Subject of "loveth."............Hence, Nominative Case.

RULE 1.—"*The Subject of a Sentence must be in the Nominative Case.*"

That getteth wisdom } Is used to describe "He." ....Hence, an Adjective Sentence.

That.....Is used for a name..............Hence, a Pronoun.
" Introduces a sentence which qualifies its Antecedent.............Hence, Relative.
" Relates to "he" as its Antecedent. Hence, { Masculine Gender, Third Person, Singular Number.

RULE 4.—"*A Pronoun must agree with its Antecedent in Gender, Person and Number.*"

" Subject of "getteth."............Hence, Nominative Case.

RULE 1.—"*The Subject of a Sentence must be in the Nominative Case.*"

Getteth	..Expresses an action............	Hence, a Verb.
"	Act passes to an Object.........	Hence, Transitive.
"	Act done by ts Subject....	Hence, Active Voice.
"	Simply declares...........	Hence, Indicative Mode.
"	Denotes time present............	Hence, Present Tense.
"	Predicate of "that."............	Hence, { Third Person, Singular Number.

RULE 2.—"*A Verb must agree with its Subject in Person and Number.*

Wisdom	..Is a name......................	Hence, a Noun.
"	Name of a quality.	Hence, Abstract.
"	Spoken of.	Hence, Third Person.
"	Denotes but one................	Hence, Singular Number.
"	Object of "getteth."	Hence, Objective Case.

RULE 3.—"*The Object of an Action or Relation must be in th Objective Case.*"

Loveth	...Expresses an action............	Hence, a Verb.
"	Act passes to an Object.	Hence, Transitive.
"	Simply declares................	Hence, Indicative Mode.
"	Denotes a present act...........	Hence, Present Tense.
"	Predicate of "that."...........	Hence, { Third Person, Singular Number.

RULE 2.—"*A Verb must agree with its Subject in Person and Number*

His	......Describes "soul."...............	Hence, an Adjective.
"	Describes by specifying..........	Hence, Specifying.
"	Specifies by denoting possession...	Hence, Possessive.

Own	.....Describes "soul."	Hence, an Adjective.
"	Describes by specifying..........	Hence, Specifying.
"	Specifies by denoting possession. .	Hence, Possessive.

Soul	.....Is a name.	Hence, a Noun.
"	Denotes one of a class.	Hence, Common.
"	Spoken of......................	Hence, Third Person.
	Denotes but one................	Hence, Singular Numoer.
	Object of "loveth.".............	Hence, Objective Case.

RULE 3.—"*The Object of an Action or Relation must be in the Objective Cuse.*"

ADDITIONAL EXAMPLES.

1. The *man* WHO was present can give the particulars.
2. The *person* WHOM we met appeared very much alarmed.
3. I saw the *wretch* THAT did it.
4. We saw the *man* WHOM you described.
5. "Hesperus, that led
The starry host, rode brightest."—*Milton.*
6. "Memory and Forecast just returns engage—
That pointing back to youth, this on to age."
7. "There is something in their hearts which passes speech."—*Story*
8. "Behind the sea-girt rock, the star
That led him on from crown to crown
Has sunk."—*Pierpont.*
9. "The mountain-cloud
That night hangs round him, and the breath
Of morning scatters, is the shroud
That wraps the conqueror's clay in death."—*Idem.*
10. "Mount the horse
Which I have chosen for thee."—*Coleridge.*
11. "Few be they who will stand out faithful to thee."—*Idem.*
12. "For cold and stiff and still are they, who wrought
Thy walls annoy."—*Macaulay.*
13. "Ishmael's wandering race, that rode
On camels o'er the spicy tract that lay
Prom Persia to the Red Sea coast."—*Pollok.*
14. "The king granted the Jews which were in every city, to gather themselves together, and to stand for their life, to destroy, to slay, and to cause to perish, all the power of the people and province that would assault them."—*Bible.*
15. "We have more than heart could wish."
16. "My punishment is greater than I can bear."

INDEPENDENT CASE.

RULE 6.—A Noun or a Pronoun, not dependent on any other word in construction, is in the Independent Case.

REM.—As the grammatical Subject of a Sentence is limited to the Nominative Case of Nouns and Pronouns, so the Nominative Case is properly limited to the Subject of a Sentence. Hence the term "Nominative Case Independent" is inappropriate.

NOTE I.—The name of a person or thing addressed is in the Independent Case.

EXAMPLES.—1. "FRIENDS, ROMANS, COUNTRYMEN."
2. "Come, gentle SPRING—ethereal MILDNESS, come."

OBS. 1.—In the last example the word *thou*, understood, is the proper subject of "come." The words "spring" and "mildness" are addressed, and are independent in construction.

NOTE II.—A Noun or a Pronoun, used to explain a preceding Noun or Pronoun, is in the Independent Case.

EXAMPLES.—1. *Paul*, the APOSTLE, wrote to Timothy.
2. "Up springs the *lark*, shrill-voiced and shrewd,
The MESSENGER of morn."

OBS. 1.—This Note applies also to Phrases and Sentences.

EXAMPLES.—1. It is our *duty* to STUDY.
2. "*It* is possible THAT WE HAVE MISJUDGED."
3. "I shall be dignified with this high *honor*—TO BEAR MY LADY'S TRAIN."

(See p. 236.)

OBS. 2.—An Independent Noun or Pronoun is properly a logical Adjunct when it is used to describe or limit another word.

EXAMPLES.—*Paul* the APOSTLE.—*Peter* the GREAT.

REM.—"Apostle" describes "Paul," by limiting the application of that name to a particular individual.

NOTE III.—A Noun or a Pronoun, used as the Leader of an Independent Phrase, is in the Independent Case.

EXAMPLES.—1. *The* HOUR *having arrived*, we commenced the exercises

2. "Thus talking, HAND in hand, alone they passed
On to their blissful bower."

NOTE IV.—A Noun or a Pronoun, used in Predicate with a Verb, is in the Independent Case.

EXAMPLES.—"Thou art a *scholar.*" It is *I.* "God is *love.*"
"He maketh the storm a *calm.*"

OBS.—A Noun or a Pronoun used in Predicate, may have the *form* of the Nominative or the Objective Case.

EXAMPLES.—"I thought it to be *him;* but it was not *him.*"
"It was not *me* that you saw."

REM.—This idiom is established by good authority—ancient and modern—and grammarians can not well alter the custom.

"Nescire quid acciderit antequam natus es, est semper esse puerum."

"Not to know what happened before you was born, is always to be a boy."

Here, "puerum" (boy), has the form of the Accusative Case (Objective), and can not be the Nominative.

NOTE V.—A Noun or a Pronoun, used for Euphony, is in the Independent Case.

EXAMPLE.—"The moon *herself* is lost in heaven."

OBS.—In this Note are properly included Nouns and Pronouns, repeated for the sake of emphasis.

EXAMPLE.—"This, THIS is thinking free."

NOTE VI.—A Noun or a Pronoun denoting the Subject of remark—the title of a book—used in address, or in exclamation, etc., is in the Independent Case.

EXAMPLES.—1. "Our *Fathers!* where are they? and the *Prophets!* do they live forever?"

2. "Wright's *Orthography.*"

3. "Davies' *Mathematics.*"

4. *J. Q. Adams*, Quincy, Mass.

Adverbial Sentences are often elegantly condensed into Independent Phrases.

EXAMPLES.

Sentence.—When the hour had arrived, we commenced the exercises.

Phrase.—The hour having arrived, we commenced the exercises.

REM. 1.—"When the hour had arrived" is a Grammatical Adjunct of "commenced," an *Adverbial Sentence.* "*Hour*" is the subject of that Sentence: hence in the *Nominative Case.*

2. "The hour having arrived," is a Logical Adjunct of "commenced," an Independent Phrase. "*Hour*" is the Leader of that Phrase: hence in the *Independent Case.*

OBS. 7.—By a custom not to be recommended nor allowed, except by "poetic license," an Independent Phrase is sometimes preceded by a Preposition, which does not indicate a relation, nor properly connect it to an Antecedent.

EXAMPLES.—1. "WITH *arm in arm,* the forest rose on high,
And lessons gave of brotherly regard."

2. "UPON *our horse becoming weary,* we procured lodgings at a private house."

REM. 1.—"With" is not necessary to the grammatical construction of the Sentence—its affix being simply to preserve the rhythm.

2. The use of "upon" is unnecessary and improper.

EXERCISES IN THE USE OF THE INDEPENDENT CASE.

1. O Absalom! my son, my son!
2. Lend me your songs, ye *nightingales!*
3. How is IT possible *not to feel grateful for such benefits!*
4. Other things being equal, we prefer a fruit-growing climate.
5. Thou art the ruins of the noblest man
That ever lived in the tide of time.
6. Henceforth I never will be *Romeo.*
7. John dislikes to be called an idle *boy.*
8. That little indiscretion made him my *enemy.*
9. His teeth *they* chatter still.
10. Love and *love* only is the *loan* for love.
11. My *friends*—do THEY now and then send
A wish or a thought after me?
12. HE is the free *man* whom the truth makes free.

ADJUNCTS.

PRIN.—Adjuncts belong to the words which they modify or describe.

THE FORMS OF ADJUNCTS.

OBS. 1.—Adjuncts may consist of Words, Phrases, or Sentences.

EXAMPLES.—1. *A Word.*—We were walking *homeward.*

2. *A Phrase.*—We were walking *towards home.*

3. *A Sentence.*—"Let me stand here *till thou remember it.*" *Romeo.*

NOTE I.—In the use of Adjuncts, that form should be employed which will most fully convey the sense intended.

OBS. 1.—Many Adjunct *Words, Phrases,* and *Sentences* are interchangeable.

EXAMPLES.

Word Adjuncts.—1. "An *honest* MAN is the noblest work of God."

2. "*Dark* DAYS are remembered."

3. "The *wind's* low SIGH."

4. James CAME to school *early.*

Phrase Adjuncts.—5. A MAN *of honesty* is the noblest work of God.

6. Let him remember the DAYS *of darkness.*

7. The low SIGH *of the wind.*

8. James CAME to school *at an early hour.*

Sentence Adjuncts.—9. A MAN *who is honest,* is the noblest work of God.

10. DAYS *which are dark,* are long remembered.

11. The low SIGH *which the wind seems to make.*

12. James CAME to school *while it was yet early.*

OBS. 2.—But this interchange of Adjuncts is not always admissible.

EXAMPLES.

Correct.—"The TIME *of my departure* is at hand."

Incorrect.—My *departure's* TIME is at hand. (See Obs. 3, p. 245)

OBS. 3.—Adjuncts are often Complex. One Adjunct *Word* may be qualified or limited by another Word.

EXAMPLES.—*Two* HUNDRED dollars.

The CLOUD's deep voice. *The* WIND's low sigh.

OBS. 4.—An Adjunct *Word* may be limited by a *Phrase.*

EXAMPLES.—"From the shore, EAT *into caverns, by the restless wave.*"
"Wisdom is TOO high *for a fool.*"

OBS. 5.—An Adjunct *Word* may be limited by a *Sentence.*

EXAMPLES.—"He called so loud *that all the hollow deep resounded.*"
"OFT *as the morning dawns* should gratitude ascend."
(See Diagram, p. 42, and Diagram 3, p. 44.)

OBS. 6.—An Adjunct *Phrase* may be limited by a *Word.*

EXAMPLE.—Robert went *almost* TO BOSTON. (See Diagram.)

OBS. 7.—An Adjunct *Sentence* may be limited by a *Word.*

EXAMPLES.—"NOT *as the conqueror comes,*
They the true-hearted came."

THE OFFICES OF ADJUNCTS.

OBS. 1.—Adjuncts may be attached to any of the five Elements of Sentences.

1. *To the Subject.....*1. "*The* KING [*of shadows*] loves a shining mark."
(See Diagram, p. 39.)

2. *To the Predicate...*2. "And [*when its yellow luster smiled*
O'er mountains yet untrod],
Each mother HELD *aloft* her child,
To bless the bow of God."
(See Diagram, p. 62.)

3. *To the Object......*3. "One ink-drop, on a solitary thought,
Hath moved *the* MIND *of millions.*"
(See Diagram.)

4. *To the Adjective....*4. "The *truly* VIRTUOUS man is not REGARDLESS *of his reputation.*"
(See Diagram.)

5. *To the Adverb.....*5. "Wisdom is TOO high *for a fool.*"
(See Diagram.)

Hence,

PRIN.—All Adjuncts of *Substantives* are to be parsed as *Adjectives;* Adjuncts of *Verbs, Participles, Adjectives,* and *Adverbs,* are to be parsed as *Adverbs.*

OBS.—In addition to *Grammatical Adjuncts,* we have what may properly be called *Logical Adjuncts.* These are commonly Substantives, independent in construction, yet serving indirectly to limit or modify other Elements.

EXAMPLES.

1, PETER the *Hermit* resembled, in temperament, PETER the *Apostle*

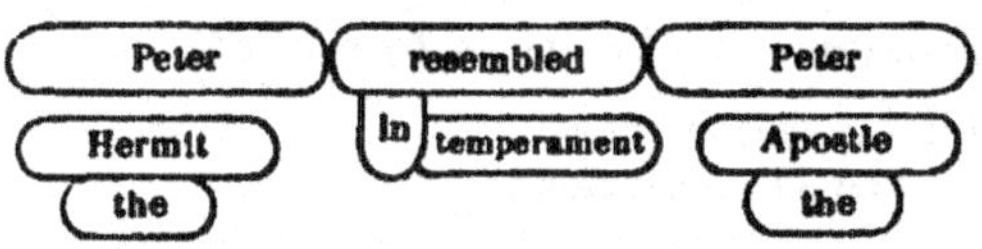

REM.—"Hermit" and "Apostle" are Nouns, yet serve to distinguish the two men named "Peter."

2. IT is possible *that we mistake.*"

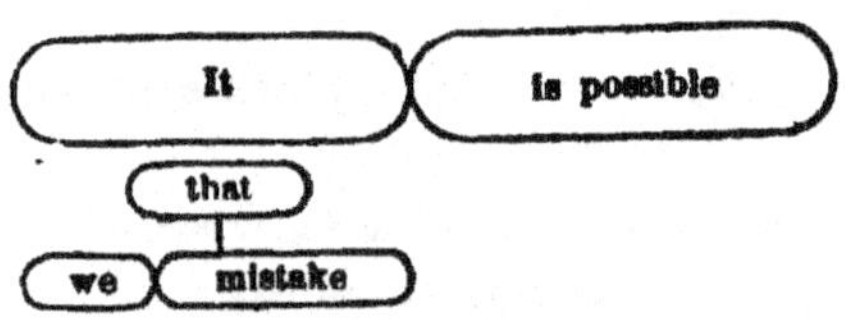

REM.—"*That we mistake*" limits the signification of the word "IT."

For further Observations on Logical Adjuncts, see "INDEPENDENT CASE," Part II., p. 85.

ADJECTIVES.

RULE 7. —Adjectives belong to Nouns and Pronouns which they describe.

OBS. 1.—It should be remembered that any word whose most important office is to specify, qualify, or otherwise describe a Noun or a Pronoun, is, *therefore,* an Adjective. (See Def. 97.) A word which is sometimes or generally used as some other "part of speech," may, in certain connections, be used Adjectively, and when thus used, it is an Adjective.

EXAMPLES.—An *iron fence*— *Working oxen.*

REM.—Every Adjective having its Substantive understood, becomes Pronominal (See Adjective Pronouns, p. 93.)

OBS. 2.—An Adjective may consist of a

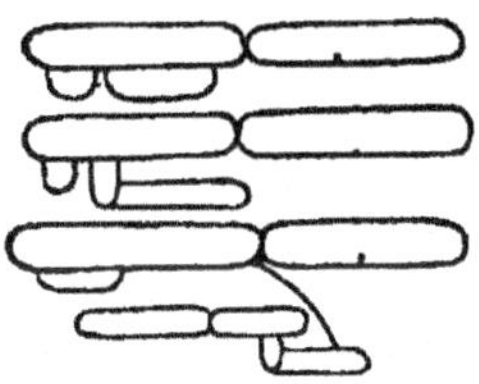

Word.—The *recitation* hour has arrived.

Phrase.—The hour *for recitation* has arrived.

Sentence.—The hour *in which we recite* has arrived.

ADJECTIVE WORDS.

OBS.—Adjectives describe Substantives in two distinct methods:

(1.) As an ordinary epithet, in which the attribute is not *asserted*, but *implied* or *assumed.*

EXAMPLES.—1. A *sweet* apple.

2. A *few* inhabitants.

3. "Night, *sable* goddess, from *her ebon* throne,
In *rayless* majesty, now stretches forth
Her leaden scepter o'er *a slumbering* world."

(2.) By *asserting* the attribute with the aid of a Verb or a Participle.

EXAMPLES.—4. The apple is *sweet.*

5. The inhabitants are *few.*

6. The world is *slumbering.*

7. "This latter mode of expression falls *short* of the force and vehemence of the former."—*Murray.*

THE FORMS OF ADJECTIVES.

REM. 1.—Many words in the English Language are, primarily, Adjectives.

EXAMPLES.—Hard—soft—sour—sweet—good—bad—old—young.

REM. 2.—But most words used as Adjectives, are Derivative Words

EXAMPLES.—Arabi*an*—virtu*ous*—hope*ful*—master*ly.*

REM. 3.—Many Adjectives have the same form as the Noun.

EXAMPLES.—A *silver* pencil—a *gold* pen—a *stone* bridge.

NOTE I.—That form of the Adjective should be used which is in accordance with reputable usage.

EXAMPLES.—1. A *gold* pen—not a *golden* pen.
2. A *silver* pencil—not a *silvery pencil.*
3. "*Golden* ears, though richly waving,
Must, in harvest, fall."
4. "The *silvery* tide will leave thee."

OBS. 1.—Two or more Adjectives are often used in common as Adjuncts of the same Substantive.

EXAMPLES.—1. "*The tall dark* MOUNTAINS and *the deep-toned* SEA."
2. "*A* TEMPER, *passionate* and *fierce*,
May suddenly your joys disperse,
At *one immense* EXPLOSION."

REM.—But the same Noun rarely has more than one *Specifying* Adjective. (See Specifying Adjectives below.)

OBS. 2.—When two or more Adjectives belong to the same Noun they may—

(1.) Severally qualify the Substantive only; or,

(2.) One Adjective may belong to the Noun as modified by the other.

EXAMPLES.—1. "He was a *tall, athletic, vigorous* man."
2. "Lamartine acted a conspicuous part in the *late French Revolution.*"

REM.—"Tall," "athletic," and "vigorous," are Adjectives—each standing in the same relation to the Word "man."

"French" describes or limits "Revolution;" "late" limits "French Revolution."

OBS. 3.—This construction should be distinguished from that in which the Adjective—and not the Adjective and the Noun combined—is modified by an Adverb.

EXAMPLES.—A *very* BEAUTIFUL flower. A *long-neglected* duty.

OBS. 4.—A Possessive Specifying Adjective may be limited by another Adjective.

EXAMPLES.—"He heard *the* KING'S command,
And saw *that* WRITING'S truth"
(See page 246.)

QUALIFYING ADJECTIVES.

COMPARISON.

REM.—As things are equal or unequal, similar or dissimilar, we have words indicating those differences. Hence,

1. COMPARISON OF EQUALITY.

OBS. 1.—Two or more things, similar in any given quality, are compared by the use of the word *As*, placed before the latter term.

EXAMPLES.—1. John is AS tall *as James.*
2. Warner is not so fair *as Arthur.*
3. "England can spare from her service SUCH men *as him.*"—*Lord Brougham.*

OBS. 2.—The *former* term of the comparison of equality may be preceded by *As* or *So*, and sometimes by *Such*. (See Examples above.)

2. COMPARISON OF INEQUALITY.

NOTE II.—In Comparisons of Inequality, when but two things are compared, the former term requires an Adjective of the *Comparative* Degree.

EXAMPLES.—1. "They are STRONGER *than lions* '—*Taylor.*
2. "Thou hast been WISER all the while *than me.*"—*Southey*
3. "Their instinct is MORE PERFECT *than that* of man."

EXCEPTION.—Some good writers employ the *Superlative.*

EXAMPLE.—"The largest boat of the two was cut loose."—*Cowper.*

OBS. 1.—The second term of comparison is commonly introduced by the word *Than.*
(See Examples above.)

OBS 2.—When the second term is a Substantive word, *Than* is a Preposition.

EXAMPLES.—1. "She suffers hourly more *than me.*"—*Swift.*
2. "*Than whom,* Satan except, none higher sat." —*Milton.*

OBS. 3.—When the second term is a Sentence, *Than* is commonly a Relative Pronoun.

EXAMPLES.—1. "He has MORE *than heart could wish.*"
2. "And there are LOVELIER flowers, I ween,
Than e'er in Eastern lands were seen."

(For other Observations on *Than*, see "Conjunctions.")

OBS. 4.—The second term of a Comparison may be suppressed, when the sense is not thereby obscured.

EXAMPLES.—1. "We both have fed as well."
2. "I have known *deeper* wrongs."—*Mitford.*

NOTE III.—Adjectives of the Superlative Degree are used when more than two things are compared.

EXAMPLES.—1. "The *richest* treasure mortal times afford is spotless reputation."
2. "Thou art the ruins of the *noblest* man
That ever lived in the tide of time."

OBS. 1.—Comparative and Superlative Adjectives require different constructions.

(1.) The Comparative Degree requires the former term to be excluded from the latter.

EXAMPLE.—*Iron* is more valuable than *all other metals.*

REM.—In this example, "*Iron*" is put as one term of comparison, and "*all other metals*" as the other term—two things are compared. Hence, the Comparative form.

(2.) The Superlative Degree requires the former term to be included in the latter.

EXAMPLE.—*Iron* is the most valuable of *all the metals.*

REM.—Here "*all the metals*" are taken severally. "*Iron*" is taken from the list, and put in comparison with the many others—more than two things are compared. Hence, the use of the Superlative form.

OBS. 2.—Adjectives whose significations do not admit of comparison, should not have the Comparative or the Superlative form.

EXAMPLES.—John's hoop is much more circular than mine.
Corrected.—John's hoop is much more nearly circular than mine.

OBS. 3.—Double Comparatives and Superlatives are improper.

EXAMPLE.—In the calmest and *most stillest* night.

OBS. 4.—But *Lesser* is often used by good writers.

EXAMPLE.—"The *lesser* co-efficient."—*Davies' Algebra.*

REM.—The Comparison of Adjectives is not commonly absolute, but relative. Thus, in saying this is the *sweetest* apple, I merely say that this apple possesses a higher degree of the quality than all other apples *with which it is compared.*

SPECIFYING ADJECTIVES.

NOTE IV.—Specifying Adjectives should be so used as clearly to signify the real intention of the speaker or writer.

REM. 1.—The peculiar province of Specifying Adjectives is to indicate the *individuality* of beings or things. Hence,

OBS. 1.—Specifying Adjectives should be used—

(1.) Before Nouns taken in a restricted sense.

EXAMPLES.—1. "*The* MAN of wealth and pride
Takes up *a* SPACE that *many* POOR supplied."
2. "He has betrayed *the* CONFIDENCE of *his* FRIENDS."
3. "*The* TRUTH of *that proposition* is self-evident."

REM. 2.—But Nouns may be restricted by the use of *Phrases.*

EXAMPLES.—1. "LOVE *of virtue* is exhibited in DEEDS *of charity.*"
2. "APPLICATION *to studies* secures EXCELLENCE *in scholarship.*"

OBS. 2.—Specifying Adjectives should not be used—

(1.) Before Nouns taken in a general sense.

EXAMPLES.—1. "*Man* needs but little here below."
2. "*Confidence* is a plant of slow growth."
3. "*Truth* crushed to earth shall rise again."

(2.) Before Proper Nouns.

EXAMPLES.—*Jackson* was the more skillful general
Webster, the greater statesman.

NOTE V.—A Specifying Adjective should be repeated when its omission would occasion ambiguity or obscurity.

OBS. 1.—We properly repeat the Specifying Adjective—

(1.) Before two or more Nouns specifically distinct.

EXAMPLES.—1. Man knows neither *the* day nor *the* hour of his departure.
2. *The* North and *the* South LINES are parallel.
3. "Bowen, *the* editor of 'The Teacher,' and *the* State Superintendent, will attend the Institute."

REM.—The omission of "*the*" before "State Superintendent" would imply that "Bowen" is the State Superintendent.

4. The teacher and the pupil.
5. "*My* poverty and not *my* will consents."

(2.) When two or more Nouns are joined in the same construction and taken severally,—especially if a part of the Nouns are suppressed.

EXAMPLES.—1. We have sold *the* black, *the* bay, and *the* white horse.
2. "*The* vain, *the* wealthy, and *the* proud,
In folly's maze advance."
3. *The* first, *the* third, and *the* fifth child, were sons.
4. "The honorable the Legislature of the State of New York."

NOTE VI.—Specifying Adjectives should not be repeated—

(1.) Before an additional Noun used as an epithet of the same principal Substantive.

1. "*The* HEAD and FRONT of my offending hath this extent."
2. "*The* North and South LINE is accurately drawn."

EXAMPLE.—RICE, *the* State Superintendent and President of the State Teachers' Association, will attend the Institute.

REM.—The Adjective "*the*" placed before the Noun "*President*," would imply that Rice is not State Superintendent.

NUMERAL ADJECTIVES.

NOTE VII.—In the use of Adjectives that imply Number, such should be employed as agree in Number with their Nouns.

EXAMPLES.—A book—one book—three books.
This book—that book—some books.

OBS. 1.—But a Noun having two or more Adjectives differing in Number, may agree in Number with the one placed next it.

EXAMPLE.—"Full *many* A GEM of purest ray serene."

OBS. 2.—One Numeral Adjective may qualify another Numeral.

EXAMPLES.—ONE *hundred* dollars—a *hundred* horses—FOUR *score* years—TWO *dozen* oranges.

NOTE VIII.—A Substantive should correspond *in form* to the Number indicated by its Adjective, when the Adjective is necessarily Singular or Plural.

EXAMPLES.—1. "The field is *two miles* long and *one mile* broad."
2. "*These hands* let useful skill forsake,—
3. *This voice* in silence die."

OBS. 1.—*Exception.*—A few Nouns are used technically or figuratively in the Singular Number, with Plural Adjectives.

EXAMPLES.—A *hundred head* of cattle—*fifty sail* of the line.

POSSESSIVE SPECIFYING ADJECTIVES.

RULE 8.—A Noun or a Pronoun in the Possessive Case is used Adjectively.

EXAMPLES.—*Webster's* Dictionary—*Our* neighbor.

OBS. 1.—The Possessive Case is a term applied by grammarians, with reference to the *form* of Nouns and Pronouns. Nouns and Pronouns in this Case, do not always indicate possession; and they may be in the Nominative, the Objective, or the Independent Case.

EXAMPLES.

1. The peddler deals in *boys'* caps and *children's* shoes.
2. "And they both beat alike—only, MINE *was* the quickest."
3. "He is a friend *of* MINE, and lives next door *to* SMITH'S."
4. "THINE is the kingdom."

OBS. 2.—The sign of the Possessive Case is not always annexed to the name of the Possessor.

(1.) It may be transferred to an attribute following the name of the possessor.

EXAMPLES.—1. The *Pope* of Rome's legate.
2. "Whether it be owing to the *Author* of nature's *acting* upon us every moment."—*Bp. Butler.*

(2.) When two or more Possessives, immediately following each other, are alike applicable to the same word, it is attached only to the last.

EXAMPLES.—1. George, James, and William's father.
2. A. S. Barnes and Co.'s publications.

OBS. 3.—But the sign of the Possessive should be repeated,

(1.) When one Possessive is used to specify another.

EXAMPLE.—Gould's Adam's Latin Grammar.

(2.) When the Possessives describe different things.

EXAMPLE.—"Heroes' and Heroines' shouts confusedly rise."

NOTE I.—Possessive Adjectives describe Nouns and Pronouns, by indicating possession, fitness, origin, condition, etc., etc.

EXAMPLES.

1. Boys' caps................"Boys'" denotes the size of the caps.
2. Webster's Dictionary. ......"Webster's" denotes the *author.*
3. "*Heaven's* immortal Spring shall yet arrive,
4. And *man's* majestic beauty bloom again,
Bright through the eternal year of *Love's* majestic reign."—*Beattie.*
5. "I heard of Peter's buying John's horse."

REM.—I heard of a certain *act*—an act of which Peter was the agent—hence, it was Peter's act. The act is expressed by the word "buying"—hence, the word "Peter's" limits the word "buying;" and is, therefore, an *Adjective.*

The object of Peter's act is "horse." The word "John's" is used to limit that object, not to a particular race, or color, or size, but to a particular *condition.* "John's," therefore, describes "horse"—hence, it is an *Adjective.*

OBS. 1.—A Noun or a Pronoun in the Possessive Case, is often equivalent to an Adjective Phrase.

EXAMPLES.

1. The *people's* will.................The will *of the people*.
2. *Webster's* Dictionary.............A Dictionary *written by Webster*.
3. *Boys'* caps.......................Caps *suitable for boys*.
4. "He heard the *king's* command,...The command *of the king*.
5. And saw that *writing's* truth."....The truth *of that writing*.

OBS. 2.—But they are not always equivalent.

EXAMPLES.—1. The love *of virtue*.....is not virtue's love.
2. The desire *of leisure*...is not leisure's desire.

Hence,

NOTE II.—Possessive Specifying Adjectives and Adjective Phrases should not be substituted the one for the other when they are not fully equivalent.

(See Examples above.)

OBS. 3.—The laws of interchange of Possessive Adjectives and their kindred Adjective Phrases are as follow:

(1.) When the Object of the Prepositional Phrase constitutes the *Agent* of an action, state, feeling, etc., *implied* in the Substantive limited, the Phrase and the corresponding Possessive Adjective are equivalent, and, therefore, interchangeable.

EXAMPLES.

1. The *people's* WILL............The WILL *of the people*.
2. The *sun's* RAYS..............The RAYS *of the sun*.
3. *Webster's* last SPEECH.........The last SPEECH *of Webster*.

(2.) When the Object of the Prepositional Phrase constitutes also the Logical *Object* of an action, state, feeling, etc., *implied* in the Substantive limited, the Phrase and the corresponding Possessive Adjective are not equivalent, and, consequently, cannot be interchanged.

EXAMPLES.

Correct.—"The DOCTRINE *of Divine sovereignty*."
Incorrect.—Divine *sovereignty's* DOCTRINE.

(3.) When the Object of the Prepositional Phrase may be the Logical Subject or Logical Object of the action, state, etc., implied in the Substantive limited, the use of the Phrase generally occasions ambiguity and is inadmissible without the addition of some other Element.

EXAMPLE.—"The love of God shall make their bliss secure."

REM.—This may mean God's love to them or their love to God.

OBS. 4.—If we intend the former, the ambiguity may be removed by the Phrase *to them*, placed after the word "God," or, if the latter, by the word *their* in place of the word "the." Thus,

1. The love of God *to them* shall make their bliss secure.
2. *Their* love of God shall make their bliss secure.

OBS. 5.—Adjectives derived from Nouns and Pronouns in the Possessive Case, often retain their Substantive character, and may be qualified by other Adjectives.

EXAMPLE.—"He saw *that* WRITING's truth." "That" specifies "writing." He saw the truth *of that writing*.

REM.—This observation is also applicable to other Adjectives derived from Nouns.

"*A cast* IRON hinge." "Cast" qualifies "iron;" and "iron" is an Adjective.

OBS. 6.—A word in the Possessive form is often used to specify a Phrase.

EXAMPLES.—1. "Upon MR. TALBOT's *being made Lord Chancellor*."

Life of Butler

2. "From OUR *being born into the present world*. . . ."

Butler's Analogy

OBS. 7.—In constructions like the above, the Possessive sign should not be omitted.

Correct construction.—All presumption of DEATH's *being the destruction of living beings*, must go upon the supposition that they are compounded.—*Bp. Butler.*

Incorrect construction.—1. "Nor is there so much as any appearance of our LIMBS *being endued with a power of moving*," etc.

Bp. Butler.

2. "A fair wind is the cause of a VESSEL *sailing*."

Graham's Synonyms.

REM.—In the last example, the author intended to say that *wind* is the cause of an act—an act expressed by the word "sailing."

But he makes himself say that *wind* is the cause of a *thing*—a thing named by the word "vessel."

Corrected.—Wind is the cause of a VESSEL's *sailing*.

Obs. 8.—Possessive Adjectives are sometimes qualified by Sentences introduced by Relative Pronouns and by Phrases.

Examples.—1. "How various HIS employments *whom the world calls idle.*"—*Willson's Burns.*
2. "I have spoken of HIS eminence *as a judge.*"
3. "Heaven be THEIR resource *who have no other but the charity of the world.*"

Rem.—It is the Substantive Element in the Possessive Adjective that is thus limited by the Auxiliary Sentence. Thus, "his" is equivalent to "*of him;*" and "*him*" is limited by the Sentence "*whom the world calls idle.*"

Position of the Possessive.

Obs. 9.—When the Possessive is used Adjectively, it is placed before the Noun or the Pronoun which it specifies.

Examples.—1. The WIDOW'S *mite.*
2. The CULPRIT'S *confession.*
3. OUR *father* and OUR *mother.*

Obs. 10.—Like other Specifying Adjectives, it precedes Qualifying Adjectives belonging to the same Noun or Pronoun.

Examples.—1. "The BROOK'S *bright* wave."
2. "The WIND'S *low* sigh."
3. OUR *devoted* father and OUR *affectionate* mother.

Obs. 11.—Possessive Adjectives, in addition to their primary office, sometimes introduce Auxiliary Sentences.

Examples.—1. "All are but parts of one stupendous WHOLE,
Whose body Nature is, and God the soul."—*Pope.*
2. "There are a sort of MEN *whose* visages
Do cream and mantle like a standing pond."
Shakspeare.

Rem.—In Sentence (1), "*whose*" is an Adjunct of "body," and it is used also to introduce the Adjunct Sentence "Whose body Nature is, and God the soul."

Obs. 12.—The Possessive Adjective is often the *Logical* Subject of a Participle.

EXAMPLES.—1. "I have an engagement which prevents *my staying* longer with you."

2. "I allude to *your inviting* me to your forests."—*Pope.*

Who invited me?—*you.*

This observation also applies to Substantives.

EXAMPLE.—The boy's mistake. *Who* mistook?—the boy.

ADJECTIVES IN PREDICATE.

NOTE III.—An Adjective, like a Participle, may be used in Predicate, with a Verb, when the Verb requires its aid to make the assertion.

EXAMPLES.—1. "His palsied hand *waxed strong.*"

2. "Canst thou *grow sad* as Earth *grows bright*?"

3. Vanity often *renders* man *contemptible.*

4. Virtue always *makes* man *happy.*

OBS. 1.—Many English Verbs contain the signification of such Adjectives in themselves. Thus,

"Waxed strong"....has its equivalent, *strengthened.*
"*Grows bright*" ..... " " *brightens.*
"*Makes happy*" ..... " " *happifies.*

OBS. 2.—But not all Predicate Adjectives have their equivalent Verbs. Thus, for the Predicate, "Renders contemptible," we have not the Verb, *contemptibleize.*

OBS. 3.—Participles, like Verbs, sometimes require the use of Adjectives to complete the sense. Adjectives thus used are said to be "*in Predicate.*"

EXAMPLES.—1 "The desire of *being happy* reigns in all hearts."

2. Her highest happiness consists in *making* others *happy.*

OBS. 4.—Adjectives may be in Predicate—

(1.) With Transitive Verbs—Active Voice.

EXAMPLES.—1. "They'll *make* me *mad,* they'll *make* me *mad.*"

2. "The study of science tends to *make* us *devout.*"

(2.) With Passive Verbs.

EXAMPLES.—1. "He *was made wretched* by his own folly."

2. "The children *were rendered miserable* by the sins of the father."

(3.) With Neuter and other Intransitive Verbs.

EXAMPLES.—1. "How *dear* to my heart *are* the scenes of my childhood
2. "*Be* not therefore *grieved* nor *angry* with yourselves."

(4.) With Verbs—Infinitive Mode.

EXAMPLES.—1. "The study of science tends to *make* us *devout*."
2. "Dost thou well to *be angry?*"
3. "I own it made my blood *run cold*."

(5.) With Participles as Adjectives.

EXAMPLES.—1. "*Falling short* of this, we cannot succeed."
2. "Our horse *becoming frightened*, we leaped from the carriage."

(6.) With Participles as Verbal Nouns.

EXAMPLES.—1. "Her life was spent in *making* others *happy*."
2. "*Becoming angry* at trifles is indicative of a weak mind."

OBS. 5.—This construction of the Adjective should be carefully distinguished from that in which it is used as a *representative* of an Adverbial Phrase.

EXAMPLES.—1. "Caled entered every day *early* and returned *late*."
2. "The surging billows and the gamboling storms come *crouching* to his feet."
3. "The mind was well informed, the passions [were] held *subordinate*, and diligence was choice."

"Early"............is substituted for *at an early hour.*
"Late"............. " " *at a late hour.*
"Crouching"........ " " *in a crouching attitude.*
"Subordinate" ...... " " *in a subordinate condition*

Hence, "early," "late," "crouching," and "subordinate," are to be parsed—

(1.) As Adverbs—being used as *representatives* of Adverbial Phrases.

(2.) But in the analysis of these Phrases, these words are to be parsed, in their *individual* capacity, as Adjectives, qualifying their Substantives understood.

REM.—For Substantives in Predicate, see "*Independent Case.*"

FORM.

NOTE IV.—Adjectives used in Predicate should not take the Adverbial form.

EXAMPLES.

Incorrect.—1. William feels *badly* to-night. 2. I feel *sadly.*
3. How *beautifully* it looks! 4. It appears *strangely* to me.
Corrected.—William feels *bad* to-night. I feel *sad.*
How *beautiful* it looks! It appears *strange* to me.

REM.—It will be noticed that the Adjective in Predicate does not *modify* the Verb. It describes the Subject by the aid of the Verb. Hence,

OBS. 1.—Adverbs are not used as a part of the Grammatical Predicate.

OBS. 2.—The Verb used in Predicate with an Adjective is sometimes suppressed.

EXAMPLES.—1. "No position, however *exalted*, could satisfy his ambition."
2. "A man may grow rich by seeming *poor.*"

REM.—"Exalted" is in Predicate with "*may be*," suppressed.
"Poor" " " "*be.*"

POSITION OF ADJECTIVES.

OBS. 3.—An Adjective *Word* is commonly placed before its Noun and after its Pronoun: an Adjective *Phrase* or *Sentence* after its Noun or Pronoun

EXAMPLES.—1. An *influential* man.
2. A man *of influence.*
3. A man *who possesses influence.*

OBS. 4.—But when an Adjective Word is limited or modified by a Phrase, it is commonly placed after its Noun.

EXAMPLES.—1. "Seest thou a man DILIGENT *in his business.*"
2. "Truth, CRUSHED *to earth*, will rise again."
3. "From the shore,
EAT *into caverns by the restless wave,*
And forest-rustling mountains, comes a voice,
That, solemn-sounding, bids the world prepare."

OBS. 5.—When the same word is qualified by two or more Adjectives, the one denoting the most definite quality should be placed next it; and, when one Adjective *specifies* and the other *qualifies*, the Qualifying Adjective is placed next the Noun.

EXAMPLES.—1. An *industrious* YOUNG man.
2. A *large* SWEET apple.
3. "Sound *the* LOUD timbrel o'er *Egypt's* DARK sea."

NOTE V.—An Adjective in Predicate is placed immediately after its Verb or Participle.

EXAMPLES.—1. "Which MAKETH *glad* the heart of man."
2. "Canst thou GROW *sad* as earth GROWS *bright?*"
3. "His palsied hand WAXED *strong.*"
4. "And the eyes of the sleepers WAXED *deadly* and *chill.*"
5. "How various his employments whom the world CALLS *idle.*"

OBS. 1.—EXCEPTION.—When the Verb is Transitive, its Object is sometimes—not always—placed between it and the Adjective in Predicate.

EXAMPLES.—1. "Vanity often RENDERS man *contemptible.*"
2. "Winter MAKETH the light heart *sad.*"

OBS. 2.—EXCEPTION 2.—For the sake of euphony, for emphasis, or for rhythm, the Adjective is sometimes placed before the Verb.

EXAMPLES.—1. "*Hard* IS my fate, cried the heart-broken stranger."
2. "*Bloodless* ARE these limbs, and cold."
3. "*Hard, hard,* indeed, WAS the contest for freedom."

OBS. 3.—This construction should be carefully distinguished from that in which the Adjective qualifies the Object of the Verb.

EXAMPLES.—1. "But we left HIM *alone* with his glory."

EXERCISES IN REVIEW.

PAGE

234.—What is an *Adjunct?*

What may be the *forms* of Adjuncts?

1. "A man *who has talents*, will succeed in business."

Condense this by replacing the *Sentence* Adjunct by a *Phrase.*

Replace the *Phrase* by an equivalent *Word.*

Are all Adjunct *Words, Phrases,* and *Sentences* interchangeable?

235.—What Elements of Sentences may be affected by Adjuncts?

How are Adjuncts of Substantives to be parsed?

236.—How are *Logical Adjuncts* commonly construed?

Repeat RULE 7.—Make Sentences to illustrate.

In what distinct methods do Adjectives describe Substantives?

Is Word used Adjectively in one Sentence, always an Adjective?

Wherein do Adjectives commonly differ *in form* from Substantives of similar signification?

238.—Repeat NOTE I.—Make Sentences to illustrate.

What Adjectives are commonly used in *Comparisons of Equality?*

239.—What Word introduces the second term of the Comparison?

Supply the proper Words omitted in the following Sentences.

2. "Anna is—tall as Clarissa."

3. "Rachel is not—tall as Mary."

Repeat NOTE II.—Make Sentences to illustrate.

What Word introduces the second term of a *Comparison of Inequality?*

4. "Delia is taller—Isabella, but not fairer—Helen."

Supply the proper Words in the above Sentence.

240.—Repeat NOTE III.—Make Sentences to illustrate.

Correct the following Sentences, and give proper authority for each criticism:

5. "Shakspeare is more faithful to the true language of Nature, than any writer."—*Blair.*

6. "Cibber grants it to be a better poem of its kind than ever was written."—*Pope.*

7. "The Christian religion gives a more lovely character of God, than any religion ever did."—*Murray.*

8. "Of all other nations, ours has the best form of government: It is, of all others, that which most moves us."—*Sheridan.*

PAGE

241.—Repeat Note IV.—Make Sentences to illustrate.

Correct the following errors by the Note, or by the Observations:

9. "Northern Spy is fine specimen of an apple."
10. "Lawrence is abler mathematician than a linguist."
11. "The highest title in the State is that of the Governor."
12. "Organic chemistry treats of the animal and vegetable kingdom."
13. "The north and south poles are indicated on the map."
14. "Mary, widow of the late Col. Clark, and the mother of the Governor, resides with us."

242.—Repeat Note V.—Make Sentences to illustrate.

15. "Substitutes have three Persons; the First, Second, and the Third."—*Pierce's Grammar.*
16. "In some cases we can use either the Nominative or Accusative, promiscuously."—*Adam's Latin Grammar.*
17. "I doubt his capacity to teach either the French or English languages."
18. "The passive and neuter verbs I shall reserve for some future consideration."—*Ingersoll's Grammar.*
19. "*E* has a long and short sound."—*Bicknell's Grammar.*
20. "The perfect participle and imperfect tense ought not to be confounded."—*Murray.*
21. "There is, however, another, and *a* more limited sense." *Adam's Rhetoric.*
22. "Novelty produces in the mind a vivid and *an* agreeable emotion."—*Blair.*
23. "Jewell the poet and the professor of English literature has criticised it."

243.—Repeat Note VII.—Make Sentences to illustrate.

Correct the following errors:

24. "I have not been in London *this* five years." *Webster's Grammar*
25. "If I had not left off troubling you about those kind of things."—*Swift.*
26. "They are these kind of gods which Horace mentions." *Addison.*
27. "Many things are not that which they appear to be." *Sanborn's Grammar*

PAGE

243.—Repeat Note VIII.—Make Sentences to illustrate.

Correct the following errors:

28. "The wall is ten foot high."—*Harrison's Grammar.*

29. "A close prisoner, in a room twenty foot square."—*Locke.*

30. "These verses consist of two sort of rhymes."—*Formey.*

31. "'Tis for a thousand pound."—*Cowper.*

Repeat Rule 7.—Make Sentences to illustrate.

Correct the following errors:

32. "I have neither John nor Eliza's books."—*Nixon.*

33. "James relieves neither the boy nor the girl's distress."

34. "Which, for distinction sake, I shall put down severally."

35. "King James translators merely revised former translations."—*Frazee's Grammar.*

244.—Repeat Note I.—Make Sentences to illustrate.

245.—Repeat Note II.—Make Sentences to illustrate.

Correct the following errors:

36. "The General in the army's name, published a declaration."—*Hume.*

37. "The bill passed the Lord's house, but failed in the Commons."

38. "It is curious enough that this Sentence of the bishop is, itself, ungrammatical."—*Cobbett's Grammar.*

39. "We should presently be sensible of the melody suffering."

40. "This depends on their being more or less emphatic, and on the vowel-sound being long or short."

41. "Whose principles forbid them taking part in the administration of the government."—*Liberator.*

248.—Repeat Note III.—Make Sentences to illustrate.

250.—Repeat Note IV.—Make Sentences to illustrate.

Correct the following errors:

42. "The group of little misses appeared most lovely and beautifully."

43. "Heaven opened *widely* her everlasting gates."
Milton, perverted.

44. "The poor girl feels very badly about it."—*Hawley.*

45. "The sight appeared terribly to me."

46 "Did not Lois look most beautifully at the lecture?"

ADVERBS.

RULE 9.—Adverbs belong to Verbs, Adjectives, and other Adverbs which they modify.

OBS. 1.—An Adverb may consist of a *Word*, a *Phrase*, or a *Sentence*.

EXAMPLES.

1. I shall go *soon*.

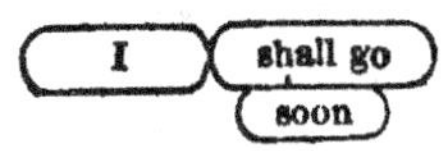

2. I shall go *in a short time*.

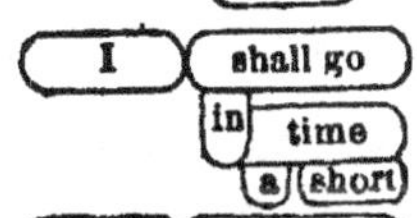

3. I shall go *ere day departs*.

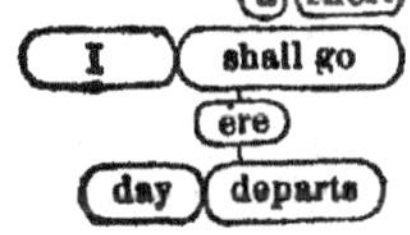

OBS. 2.—An Adverb may modify a *Word*, a *Phrase*, or a *Sentence*.

EXAMPLES.

1. William STUDIES *diligently*.

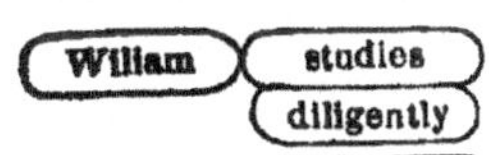

2. Arthur went *almost* TO BOSTON.

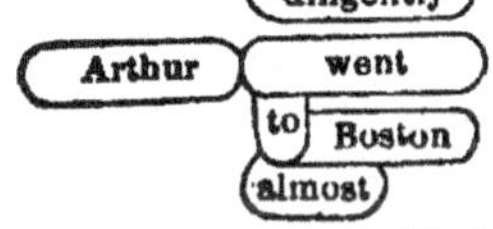

3. "*Not* AS THE CONQUEROR COMES,
They, the true-hearted, came."

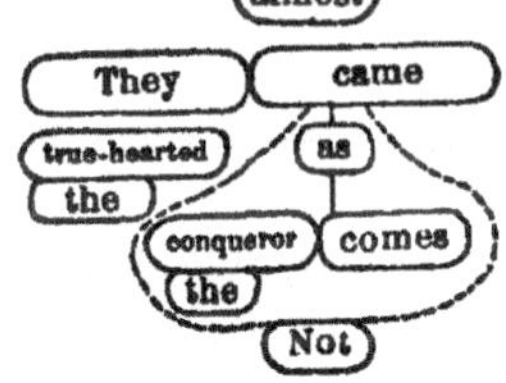

ADVERBIAL WORDS.

NOTE I.—In the use of Adverbs, that form should be adopted which is in accordance with the best authority.

OBS. 1.—Most Adverbs are *derivative words*, and are generally formed by adding *ly* (formerly written lie—a contraction of like) to its Primitive.

EXAMPLES.—A *just* man will deal *justly*.
A *foolish* man will act *foolishly*.

OBS. 2.—When an Adjective supplies the place of an Adverb, *by representation*, the Adjective form should be retained.

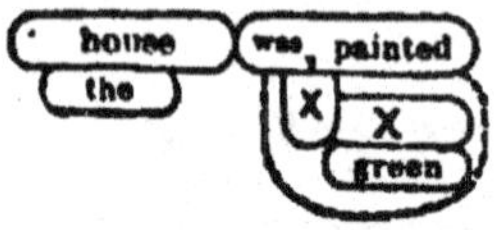

EXAMPLES.

1. The house was painted *green*.
2. Open thy mouth *wide*.

Expanded.—1. The house was painted *with green paint*.
2. Open thy mouth *to a wide extent*.

"*Green*" and "*wide*" are Adverbs by representation.

OBS. 3.—This construction should be carefully distinguished from that of Adjectives in Predicate.

EXAMPLES.

Correct.—1. The orange *tasted sweet*.
2. Velvet *feels smooth*.
3. Some *deemed* him wondrous *wise*.

Incorrect.—1. The orange tasted *sweetly*.
2. Velvet feels *smoothly*.
3. Some deemed him wondrous *wisely*.

OBS. 4.—The words which Adverbs properly modify are sometimes suppressed.

EXAMPLES.—"Thou canst but add one bitter wo
To those [ ] *already there*."

OBS. 5.—Adverbs sometimes supply the place of Verbs which they modify.

EXAMPLES.—1. "*Back* to thy punishment, false fugitive."
2. "*I'll away* to the pleasant land."

OBS. 6.—Many words, commonly used as Adverbs, often take the place of Nouns, and become *Pronouns*.

EXAMPLES.—1. Till *then*—for till that time.
2. From thence—for from that place.
3. And I have made a pilgrimage from *far*.—*Hosmer.*
4. "O, let the ungentle spirit learn from *hence*,
A small unkindness is a great offense."

OBS. 7.—Participles become Adverbs whenever they indicate the manner of an action or modify a quality.

EXAMPLES.—"'Tis strange, 'tis *passing* strange."
"A virtuous household, but *exceeding* poor."

OBS. 8.—But most Participial Adverbs have the suffix *ly* added, or they become Adverbs by *representation*.

EXAMPLES.—1. "He spoke *feelingly* on that subject."
2. "She conducted herself most *lovingly* throughout the play."
3. "Now it mounts the wave,
And rises, *threatening*, to the frowning sky."
4. "The surging billows and the gamboling storms
Come, *crouching*, to his feet."

"Come" *in a "crouching" attitude.* (See Obs. 2, above.)

OBS. 9.—A few words, commonly employed as Prepositions, are sometimes used Adverbially.

EXAMPLES.—1. "Thou didst look *down* upon the naked earth."
2. "And may, at last, my weary age
Find *out* the peaceful hermitage."
3. "Master Sir Philip, you may come *in*."

NEGATIVE ADVERBS.

NOTE II.—But one Negative Word or Particle should be used in asserting a negative proposition. For,

OBS. 1.—Two Negatives applied to the same act or quality, make it affirmative.

EXAMPLES.—1. "*Not* with*out* cause."
2. "Such occurrences are *not* *un*frequent."
3. "*Nor* did he *not* perceive them."
4. "He did not forget not to pay for the books."

OBS. 2.—Negative Prefixes in derivative words have the same force as Negative Adverbs.

EXAMPLES.—1. "He was *not* *un*mindful of his obligations."
2. "Such expressions are *not* *in*elegant."
3. "That costume would *not* be *in*appropriate to the occasion."

REM. 1.—Such expressions have not always the full force of the corresponding affirmative assertions, but serve to negative the negative assertion.

OBS. 3.—Negative Adverbs are used primarily to modify Verbs.

EXAMPLE.—1. "They *wept* NOT."

(2.) To modify Adjectives.

EXAMPLES.—2. NOT *one* of the family was there

3. "NOT *every* one that saith unto me, 'Lord! Lord!' shall enter into the kingdom of heaven."

(4.) To modify other Adverbs.

EXAMPLES.—4. He is NOT *generally* in error.

5. "They died NOT *by hunger or lingering decay,*
The steel of the white man hath swept them away."

6. "NOT *as the conqueror comes,*
They, the true-hearted, came."

REM. 1.—The influence of the Negatives, *not*, *neither*, etc., is often exerted on Nouns, Phrases, and whole Sentences. And, generally, when a Negative occurs in connection with other Adjuncts, the influence of the Negative reaches the whole proposition, including the other Adjuncts. Thus, in Example (5), "*not*" modifies the phrase, "*by hunger or lingering decay.*" And in Example (6), "*not*" negatives the sentence "*as the conqueror comes.*"

OBS. 4.—The Adverbs, *yes*, *yea*, *no*, *nay*, are independent in construction.

REM. 1.—The relation of these words to others in the sentence or period is *logical* rather than grammatical. Their grammatical relation is generally to Elements in Sentences suppressed.

POSITION OF ADVERBS.

NOTE III.—The Position of Adverbs should be such as most clearly to convey the sense intended.

OBS. 1.—Adverbs which modify Verbs generally precede a Single Verb in Predicate.

EXAMPLES.—1. "Man *naturally* SEEKS his own happiness."

2. "*Then*, when I am thy captive, TALK of chains."

3. "*Now* FADES the glimmering landscape on the sight."

OBS. 2.—When the Predicate consists of more than one word, the Adverb is commonly placed after the first word in Predicate.

EXAMPLES.—1. "We CAN *not* HONOR our country with too deep a reverence."

2. "I HAVE *always* BEEN an admirer of happy human faces."

3. "I WILL *never* LEAVE thee nor FORSAKE thee."

OBS. 3.—Adverbs modifying Adjectives are placed before their Adjectives.

EXAMPLES.—1. "We can not honor our country with *too* DEEP a reverence."

2. "We can not love her with an affection *too* PURE and FERVENT."

3. "The *very* RICH man can never be *truly* HAPPY."

4. "The selfish man can never be *truly* POLITE."

Exception.—The word *enough*, used Adverbially, is commonly placed after its Adjective.

OBS. 4.—Adverbs are placed before other Adverbs which they modify.

EXAMPLES.—1. "*How* LIGHTLY mounts the muse's wing."

2. "*Too* LOW they build, who build beneath the stars."

3. "*How* ARDENT I seized it with hands that were glowing."

OBS. 5.—Adverbial Phrases are commonly placed after the words which they modify.

EXAMPLES.—1. "There CAME *to the beach* a poor exile of Erin."

2. "Time SLEPT *on flowers* and LENT his glass *to Hope.*"

3. "The firmament GROWS BRIGHTER *with every golden grain.*"

OBS. 6.—Adverbial Sentences are commonly placed after the words which they modify.

EXAMPLES.—1. "The firmament grows brighter with every golden grain,
As handful after handful falls on the azure plain."

2. "And I am GLAD *that he has lived thus long.*"

REM.—To the above rules for the Position of Adverbial Elements, there are numerous exceptions. No specific rules can be given, which will always be applicable. The judgment and taste of the writer are required to decide as to the Position of all the Elements of Sentences.

QUESTIONS FOR REVIEW.

PAGE

255.—Repeat RULE 8.

An Adverbial Element may consist of what?

Make Sentences to illustrate Obs. 1.

Adverbs may modify what Elements of a Sentence?

Make Sentences to illustrate Obs. 2.

Repeat NOTE I.

How are Adverbs, derived from Adjectives and Nouns, formed?

256.—When may the Adjective *form* be retained?

Make Sentences to illustrate Obs. 2.

"Cora feels happily to-night."

Correct that Sentence by Obs. 3. (See also p. 250.)

When are Participles used Adverbially?

Make Examples adapted to Obs. 7.

257.— Make Examples adapted to Obs. 8.

Make Examples adapted to Obs. 9.

NEGATIVE ADVERBS.

Repeat NOTE II.

"I have not seen none of your books."

Correct that Sentence by Obs. 1.

"Warner was not unwilling to go to school."

Make an equivalent Sentence. (See Obs. 2.)

258.—What is there peculiar in the use of Negative Adverbs?

Make Sentences to illustrate Obs. 3.

POSITION OF ADVERBS.

Repeat NOTE III.

What is the usual position of Adverbial Words?

William studies commonly diligently very.

Correct that Sentence by Obs. 1 and 4.

"*I never will disturb my quiet with the affairs of state.*"

Correct that by Obs. 2.

259.—"*The day was pleasant very, and the wind fair exceedingly.*"

Correct that by Obs. 3.

What is the usual position of Adverbial Phrases?

Make Sentences to illustrate Obs. 5.

What is the usual position of Adverbial Sentences?

Make Complex Sentences to illustrate Obs. 6.

EXERCISES IN ANALYSIS.

"How dear to my heart are the scenes of my childhood,
When fond Recollection presents them to view."

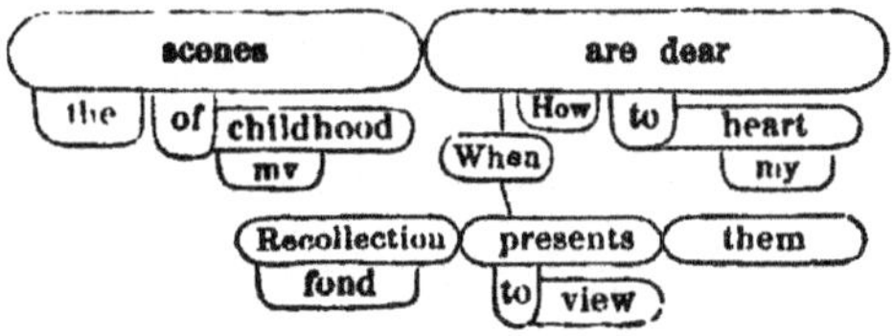

ANALYSIS.

PRINCIPAL ELEMENTS { *The Subject,*............"Scenes" / *The Predicate,*.........."Are dear" } INTRANSITIVE SENTENCE.

ADJUNCTS.
- *Of the Subject,*....
  - "The" ....*a Word.*
  - "Of my childhood" ......*a Phrase.*
- *Of the Predicate,*..
  - "How" ....*a Word.*
  - "To my heart" ....*a Phrase.*
  - "When fond Recollection presents them to view" *a Sentence.*

PARSED BY THE CHART.

"How"..........An Element in the Sentence—Adjunct—Primary—Word—Adverb—of Degree.—(Repeat RULE 8.)

"Dear" ....An Element in the Sentence—Principal Part—"in Predicate"—Adjective.—(Repeat NOTE III. to RULE 7.)

"To my heart"..An Element in the Sentence—Adjunct—Phrase—Adverbial—Prepositional—Intransitive.—(Repeat RULE 8.)

"Are" ....An Element in the Sentence—Principal Part—in Predicate—Verb—Indicative Mode—Present Tense—agreeing in Person and Number with "scenes."—(Repeat RULE 2.)

"The" ....An Element in the Sentence—Adjunct—Word—Specifying—Pure.—(See RULE 7.)

"Scenes" ....An Element in the Sentence—Principal Part—Subject—Word—Noun—Common—Third Person—Plural Number—Nominative Case.—(Repeat RULE 1.)

"Of my childhood" .... An Element in the Sentence—Adjunct—Phrase—Adjective—Prepositional—Intransitive.—(Repeat RULE 8.)

"When fond Recollection presents them to view" .... An Element in the Principal Sentence—Adjunct—Sentence—Adverbial—Simple—Transitive,—(Repeat RULE 8.)

REM. 1.—For the Analysis of the Phrases, "To my heart," and "Of my childhood," see p. 185.

REM. 2.—The Auxiliary Sentence, "When fond Recollection presents them to view," may now be analyzed by the above formula, as a distinct Sentence.

PARTICIPLES.

Rule 10.—A Participle has the same construction as the "part of speech" for which it is used.

I. Participles used as Nouns.

Note I.—A Participle used as a Noun may be—

(1.) The Subject of a Sentence.

Examples.—1. "The BEGINNING of strife *is* as when one letteth out water."

2. "The PLOWING of the wicked *is* sin."

3. "*Taking a madman's sword*, to prevent his doing mischief, CAN NOT BE REGARDED as robbing him."

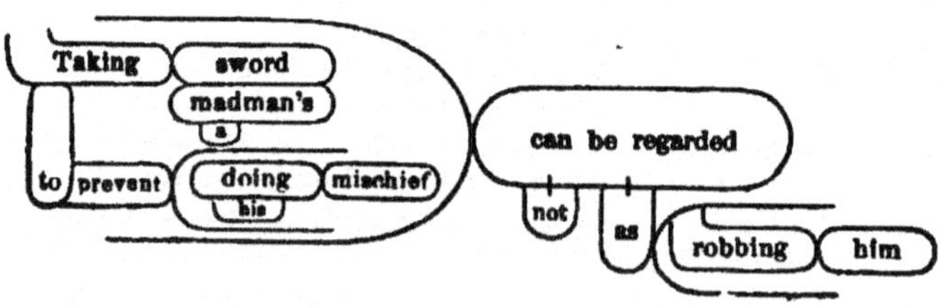

(2.) The Object of a Verb.

Examples.—4. "I doubted *his having been a soldier.*"

5. "While you strive *to bear* BEING LAUGHED AT."

Young Ladies' Friend.

6. "Taking a madman's sword to PREVENT *his doing mischief*, cannot be regarded as robbing him."

(3.) The Object of a Preposition.

Examples.—7. "*In* the BEGINNING."

8. "Poverty turns our thoughts too much *upon* the SUPPLYING of our wants: Riches, *upon* ENJOYING our superfluities."—*Addison.*

9. "Taking a madman's sword to prevent his doing mischief, cannot be regarded AS *robbing him.*"

NOTE II.—A Participle used as a *Noun*, i. e., as the name of an action, retains its Verbal character, and may be followed by an Object when it is the leader of a Participial Phrase.

EXAMPLES.—1. "They could not avoid GIVING *offense*."
2. "Its excesses may be restrained without DESTROYING its *existence*."
3. RECEIVING *goods*, known to be stolen, is a criminal offense.
4. We have succeeded in MAKING A BEGINNING.

REM.—"Giving offense" is a Substantive Phrase—Object of the Verb "avoid." "Giving" is the Leader of the Phrase: "Offense" is the Subsequent—Object of "giving."

In Sentence (4), "Making a beginning" is a Substantive Phrase—Object of the Preposition "in." "Making" is the Leader of the Participial Phrase; "beginning" is the Subsequent—Object of "making."

(See also the preceding diagram.)

OBS. 1.—A Participle, being the Leader of a Participial Phrase, often has its Subject suppressed.

REM.—In Sentence (1), above, "they" is the *implied* agent of the action expressed by "giving."

In Sentences (2) and (3), the agents of "destroying" and of "receiving" is neither expressed nor implied.

In Sentence (4), "we" is the implied Subject of "making."

NOTE III.—The agent of an action expressed by a Participle, is sometimes expressed, and is generally in the *Possessive Form*.

EXAMPLES.—1. "We have heard of *his* GOING to the Falls."
2. "I doubted *his* HAVING BEEN a soldier."
3. "Mr. Burton objected to his *son's* JOINING the army."

NOTE IV.—The sign of the Possessive Case of Nouns and Pronouns, used as the Logical Subjects of Participles, should not be omitted.

EXAMPLES.

Improper Construction.—1. "A fair wind is the cause of a *vessel sailing.*"
Graham's Synonyms.

2. He opposed *me* going to college.

Corrected.—1. A fair wind is the cause of a *vessel's* sailing.

2. He opposed *my* going to college.

OBS. 1.—The Logical Subject of a Participle may be in the Objective Case *only as the Object of a Preposition.*

EXAMPLES.—1. "The PLOWING of the *wicked* is sin."

2. "By the CROWING of the *cock*, we knew that morning was nigh."

REM.—"*Cock*" is the Object of the Preposition "of," and is therefore in the Objective Case. But it is also the Agent of the Action implied in the word "crowing;" and is, therefore, the Logical Subject of the Verbal Noun "crowing."

OBS. 2.—Phrases thus used as Adjuncts of Participles, are sometimes equivalent to Possessive Specifying Adjectives, and, therefore, are interchangeable.

EXAMPLES.—1. The crowing *of the cock.*—The *cock's* crowing.

2. "We listened to the singing *of the children.*"
We listened to the *children's* singing.

OBS. 3.—The Definitive, *the*, should be placed before a Verbal Noun whose Logical Subject is the Object of the Preposition *of.*

EXAMPLE.—"The PLOWING of the *wicked* is sin."

OBS. 4.—The Definitive, *the*, should not be placed before a Verbal Noun whose Logical Subject is in the Possessive Case.

EXAMPLE.—"You object to *my* PLOWING the garden so early."
Not to my *the* plowing.

OBS. 5.—In the Analysis of a Participial Phrase, the Participle indicates the office of the Phrase, and is to be parsed accordingly. Thus,

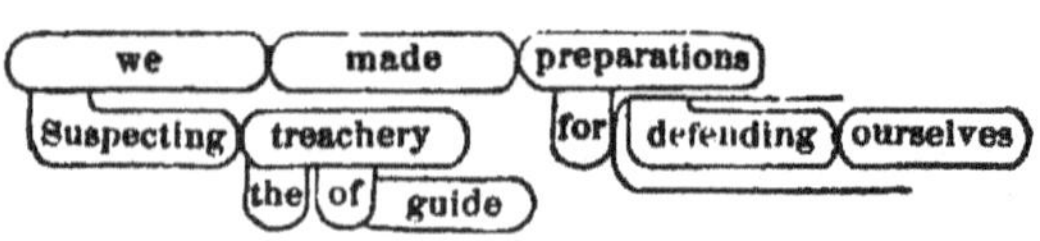

1. "*Suspecting the treachery of our guide,* WE made PREPARATIONS *for defending ourselves* from any hostile attacks."

Here "*suspecting*" and "*defending*" are Participles, each used to introduce a Participial Phrase; but

"*Suspecting the treachery of our guide*" shows a condition of "WE." Hence, an Adjective Phrase.

"Suspecting" describes "we," by expressing, incidentally, an act of "we." Hence, a Verbal Adjective.

"*For defending ourselves*" limits the action expressed by "PREPARATIONS." Hence, an Adjective Phrase.

"*Defending*" is the *name* of an act, Object of the Preposition "for." Hence, a Verbal Noun.

2. *Suspicious* of the treachery of our guides, WE made preparations for *defense*.

"*Suspicious*" describes "*we*," by expressing a condition or state of "*we*." Hence, an Adjective.

"*Defense*" is a *name*, Object of the Preposition "for." Hence, a Noun.

II. PARTICIPLES USED AS ADJECTIVES.

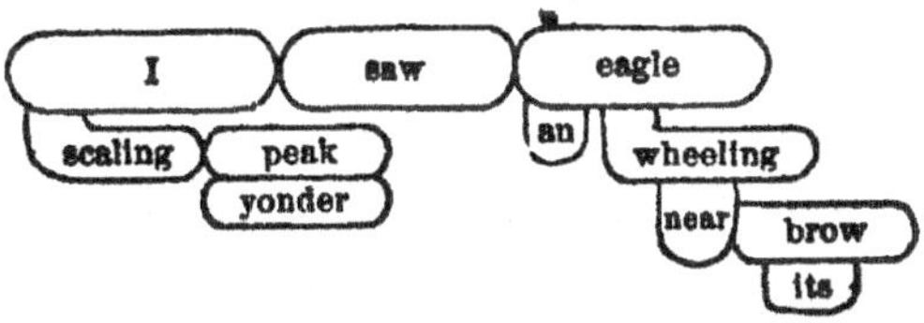

NOTE V.—A Participle used as an Adjective belongs to a Noun or a Pronoun which it describes; and may be modified by Adverbs.

EXAMPLES.—1. "Whose visages
Do cream and mantle like a STANDING *pond*."

2. "*Scaling yonder peak*, I saw an EAGLE
Wheeling near its brow."

3. "We saw IT *plunging* 'mid the billowy strife,
And *dashing* madly on to fearful doom."

REM. 1.—"Scaling yonder peak" is a Phrase—Adjunct of "I"; hence, *Adjective*. "Wheeling near its brow" is a Participial Phrase—Adjunct of "eagle"; hence, *Adjective*. "Near its brow" is a Prepositional Phrase—Adjunct of "wheeling"; hence, *Adverbial*.

In Sentence (3), "Mid the billowy strife" is an Adjunct of "plunging." "Madly," and "on," and "to fearful doom" are Adjuncts of "dashing"; hence, are *Adverbs*.

OBS. 1.—The Participle, used as an Element in an Independent Phrase, may be suppressed when the sense is not thereby rendered obscure.

EXAMPLES.—1. "Thus talking, hand [ ] in hand, alone they passed
On to their blissful bower."—*Milton.*

2. "Now, *man to man* and *steel to steel*,
A chieftain's vengeance thou shalt feel."

REM. 2.—It should be remarked, that such omissions of Participles occur only when they have Adjuncts.

REM. 3.—In analysing and parsing such Adjuncts, it is necessary to restore the Participles to which they belong. Thus, "in hand" is a Phrase—Adjunct of *being*, understood; hence, an Adverbial Phrase. "To man" is an Adjunct of *being opposed*, understood.

III. PARTICIPLES USED AS ADVERBS.

NOTE VI.—A Participle used Adverbially, belongs to Verbs, Adjectives, or Adverbs, which it modifies.

EXAMPLE.—'Tis strange! 'tis PASSING *strange!*

OBS. 2.—Participles are seldom used Adverbially without the termination *ly*.

EXAMPLE.—"He *spoke* FEELINGLY on that subject."

IV. PARTICIPLES USED AS PREPOSITIONS.

NOTE VII.—A Participle used as a Preposition, shows a relation of its object to the word which its Phrase qualifies.

EXAMPLE.—"He *said* nothing CONCERNING his temporal *affairs*."

OBS. 3.—The young scholar often finds it difficult to determine whether a Participle is used as a Preposition or an Adjective. His difficulties on this subject will vanish when he recollects that—

1. *A Participle used as a Preposition, does not relate to a Noun or a Pronoun—it generally introduces an Adverbial Phrase.*

2. *A Participle used as an Adjective, always relates to a Noun or a Pronoun—it generally introduces an Adjective Phrase.*

V. PARTICIPLES USED IN PREDICATE WITH VERBS.

NOTE VIII.—A Participle used in Predicate, asserts an act, being, or state, and may be modified by Adverbs.

EXAMPLE.—"We are *anxiously* EXPECTING to hear from William."

NOTE IX.—In the use of Participles in Predicate, the proper modification should be used.

(1.) When an action is to be predicated of the Subject, *i. e.*, when the Subject performs the act, the Active Participle should be used.

EXAMPLES.—1. *Henry* is RECITING his lesson.
2. People are building the church.

(2.) When the Subject is to be represented as receiving the action, the Passive Participle should be used.

EXAMPLES.—1. Henry's *lesson* is BEING RECITED.
2. The church is being built.

NOTE X.—The Participial Phrase should not be employed when the use of the Infinitive Phrase would be more elegant.

EXAMPLES.—1. "If the case stands thus, 'tis dangerous *drinking*." *Collier.*

Better.—If the case stands thus, 'tis dangerous *to drink.*

2. "It deserves *remarking*."—*Harris's Hermes.*

Better.—It deserves *to be remarked.*

3. "He refused *complying* with the regulations."

Better.—He refused *to comply* with the regulations.

NOTE XI.—The Participial Phrase should be used in preference to a Sentence, or any other more complicated construction, which would express the same idea.

EXAMPLES.

Sentence.—1. *As I was scaling yonder peak*, I saw an eagle, *which was wheeling near its brow.*

Complex Prepositional Phrase.—2. *On scaling yonder peak*, I saw an eagle *in the act of wheeling near its brow.*

Participial Phrase.—3. *Scaling yonder peak*, I saw an eagle *wheeling near its brow.*

REM.—These Sentences are all grammatically correct; but the last gives the sentiment fully, and has the advantage of being the most concise, and is therefore to be preferred.

OBS.—The Logical Subject of a Participle may be suppressed only when the construction is sufficiently clear without it.

EXAMPLES.

Incorrect.—1. "Having resigned his commission, the company was disbanded."

2. "Counting the women and the children, the company was ascertained to be too large for the accommodations."

Correct.—1. (*a*) *He* having resigned his commission, the company was disbanded.

or (*b*) The captain having resigned his commission, the company was disbanded.

2. (*c*) On counting the women and the children, the company was found to be too large for the accommodations.

or (*d*) The women and the children being counted, the company was found to be too large for the accommodations.

or (*e*) Counting the women and the children, we found that the company was too large for the accommodations.

EXERCISES IN REVIEW.

☞ Let the *errors* in the following Sentences be corrected by a proper application of the NOTES and OBSERVATIONS under RULE 9.

1. "It requires no nicety of ear as in the distinguishing of tones, or measuring time."—*Sheridan.*
2. "He mentions Newton's *writing of a commentary.*"
3. "The cause of their salvation doth not so much arise from their embracing of mercy, as from God's exercising of it."
Pennington.
4. "Those who accuse us of denying of it, belie us."—*Bently.*
5. "In the choice they had made of him for restoring of order."
6. "The Governor's veto was writing while the final vote was taking in the Senate."
7. "To prevent *it* bursting out with open violence."—*Robertson.*
8. "This must prevent any regular proportion of time being settled."
Sheridan.
9. "The compiler proposed *publishing* that part by itself."—*Adams*
10. "Artaxerxes could not refuse pardoning him."—*Goldsmith.*
11. "They refused doing so."—*Harris.*
12. "Entering the cars, the seats were found to be all occupied."

THE INFINITIVE VERB.

RULE 11.—A Verb in the Infinitive Mode, is the Object of the Preposition *to*, expressed or understood.

OBS. 1.—The Infinitive Verb partakes much of a Substantive character, generally expressing the *name* of an act, being, or state.

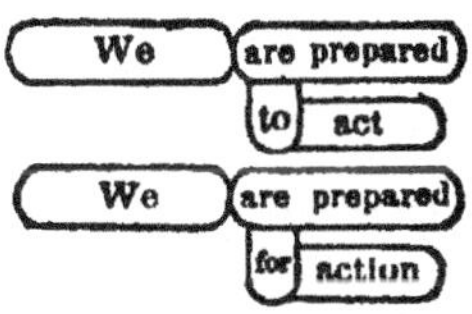

EXAMPLES.

We are prepared to act.

Equivalent.—We are prepared for action.

OBS. 2.—The Infinitive Verb is never used as a *grammatical* Predicate; hence, it has no grammatical Subject. But it is often the *logical* Predicate of a Noun or a Pronoun, which may be in the Nominative or the Objective form.

EXAMPLES.—1. *We* love to *study*.
2. We requested *him* to *speak*.

REM.—"*We*," the *grammatical* Subject of "love," is also the *logical* Subject of "*study*."

"*Him*," the *grammatical* Object of "requested," is the *logical* Subject of "speak."

NOTE I.—Infinitive Verbs following the Verbs *bid*, *but*, *dare*, *feel*, *hear*, *let*, *make*, *need*, *see*, and sometimes *behold*, *have*, *help*, *know*, *observe*, *perceive*, and some others, do not require the Preposition *to*.

EXAMPLES.—1. "I plunged in and BADE him *follow*."
2. "He DARES not *touch* a hair of Catalina."
3. "LET me *hear* thy voice *awake*."
4. "Clara HELPED me *work* that problem."
5. "I can not BUT *suspect* that she assisted Cora too."
6. "I would not HAVE you *go* to-day."
7. "Necessity COMMANDS me *name* myself."

OBS. 3.—The Infinitive Verb, with its Preposition, is often suppressed.

EXAMPLES.

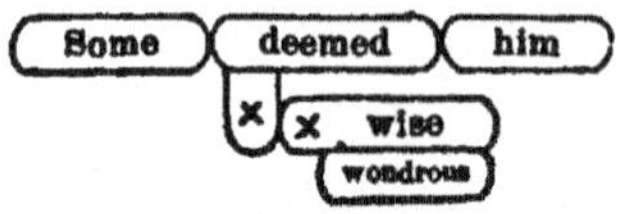

1. "Some deemed him wondrous wise."
2. "Intemperance makes a man [ ] a fool."

OBS. 4.—The Infinitive is sometimes elegantly used for other Modes

EXAMPLES.

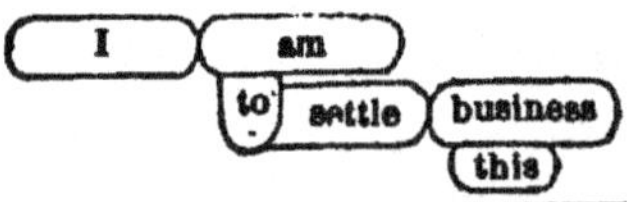

1. "I am *to settle* this business."
Arthur.

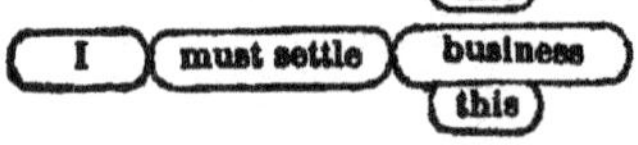

Equivalent.—I *must settle* this business

THE INFINITIVE PHRASE.

OBS. 5.—The Infinitive Verb, with its Preposition constitutes an Infinitive Phrase, and may be construed as a *Substantive*, an *Adjective*, or an *Adverb*.

EXAMPLES.

1. "*To be*, contents his natural desire."

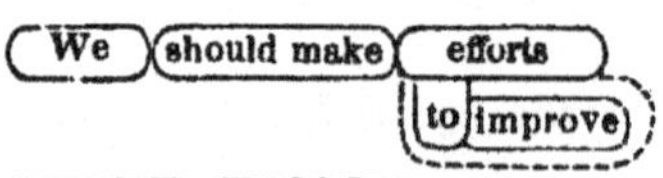

2. We should make efforts *to improve*

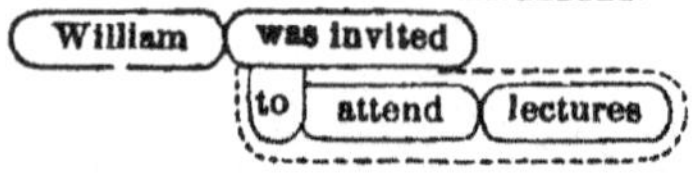

3. William was invited *to attend lectures.*

OBS. 6.—An Infinitive Phrase, used Substantively, may be—

1. The *Subject* of a Sentence.
   "*To be able to read well*, is a valuable accomplishment."
2. The *Object* of a Preposition.
   "We were ABOUT *to retire.*"
   "Be so kind AS *to place that in diagram.*"
3. A *Logical Adjunct.*
   "IT is our duty *to make good use of our time.*"

REM.—In the opinion of some grammarians, the Verbs *love, desire, wish, expect*, and some others, take Infinitive Phrases after them *as Objects*. (See pp. 213, 214.)

OBS. 7.—An Infinitive Phrase used Adjectively, may be the Adjunct of—

1. *The Subject of a Sentence.*
   "A constant PURPOSE *to excel* marked his whole career."
2. *The Object of a Sentence.*
   William has made EFFORTS *to improve* in speaking.
3. *The Object of a Phrase.*
   "He arrived in TIME *to give his vote.*"
4. *A Substantive in Predicate.*
   That is the BUSINESS next *to be done.*

OBS. 8.—An Infinitive Phrase used Adverbially, may be the Adjunct of—

1. *A Verb in Predicate.*
   William EXPECTS *to obtain the prize.*
   Will you ALLOW me *to place this in diagram?*
2. *An Adjective in Predicate.*
   We are READY *to depart.*
3. *An Adverb.*
   We were TOO late *to take the cars.*

OBS. 9.—The Infinitive, like other Phrases, is sometimes independent in construction.

EXAMPLE.—And, *to be plain with you,* I think you the more unreasonable of the two.

OBS. 10.—The Infinitive Phrase often follows the Words *as* and *than.*

EXAMPLES.—1. "An object so high *as* TO BE INVISIBLE."
2. "He said nothing farther *than* TO GIVE an apology for his vote."

REM.—In the above and similar examples, *as* and *than* are to be regarded as Prepositions, having for their objects the Infinitive Phrases following. In like manner it sometimes follows other Prepositions.

EXAMPLE.—We are *about* TO RECITE. (See Obs. 6, above.)

PREPOSITIONS.

Rule 12.—A Preposition shows a relation of its Object to the word which its Phrase qualifies.

Obs. 1.—The Object of a Preposition may be—

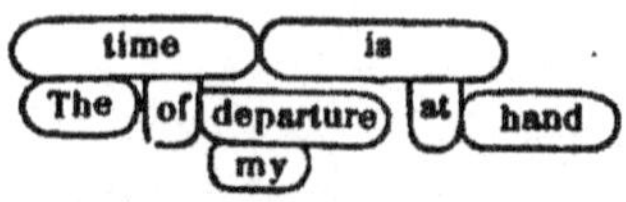

1. A Word.
"The time of my *departure* is at *hand*."

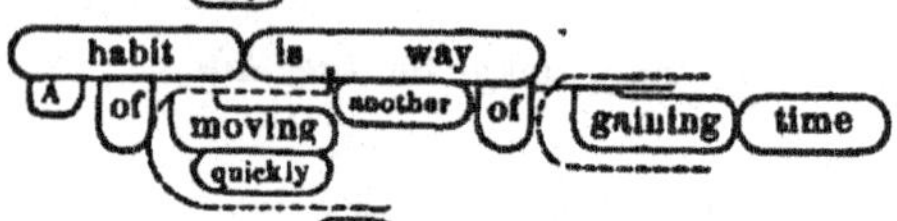

2. A Phrase.
"A habit of *moving quickly* is another way of *gaining time*."

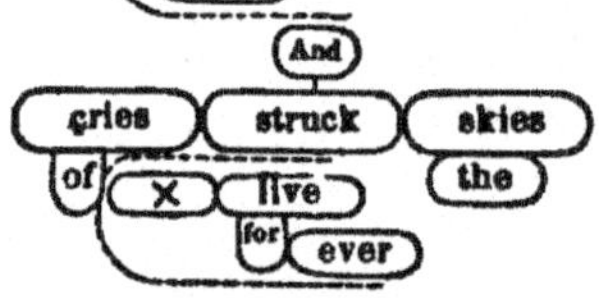

"And cries of '*live for ever*' struck the skies."

Obs. 2.—A Word, a Phrase, or a Sentence, being the Object of a Preposition, is, in its office, *Substantive*.—(See "departure," "hand," "moving quickly," "gaining time," and "live for ever," in the Examples above.)

Obs. 3.—Words which follow Prepositions as their Objects of relation are Nouns or Pronouns, and commonly have the Objective form.

Rem.—For Exceptions, see p. 172.

Obs. 4.—But Words commonly used as Adjectives or Adverbs, often become Objects of Prepositions, and are then properly parsed as Substantives, in the Objective Case.

Examples.—1. "He has faded from earth like a star from on *high*."
2. John is a friend of *mine*.
3. "As *yet* the trembling year is unconfirmed."

Obs. 5.—Scholars often find it difficult to determine the Antecedent term of a relation expressed by a Preposition—examples sometimes occur in which the relation of the Object of a Preposition seems to exist, not to any word, but to the whole Sentence. Generally, however, this question can be settled by ascertaining *which word is qualified by the Phrase* introduced by a Preposition—that word is the Antecedent term of relation.

Example.—"A *flood* of *glory bursts* from all the *skies*."

REM.—Here the Phrase "of glory" specifies "flood;" hence "flood" is the Antecedent term of the relative expressed by "of"; and the Phrase is Adjective.

"From all the skies" modifies "bursts"; hence "bursts" is the Antecedent term; and the Phrase is Adverbial.

OBS. 6.—Double Prepositions are sometimes allowed.

EXAMPLES.—1. "*Out of* every grove the voice of pleasure warbles."
2. "There can be no question *as to* which party must yield."

OBS. 7.—But two Prepositions should not be used, when one of them will fully express the sense intended.

EXAMPLES.—1. "*Near to* this dome is found a path so green."—*Shenstone.*
2. "Not *for to* hide it in a hedge."—*Burns.*

OBS. 8.—POSITION.—The proper place for a Preposition is (as its name implies) before the Phrase which it introduces.

EXAMPLES.—1. "IN *dread*, IN *danger*, and alone,
Famished and chilled THROUGH *ways* unknown."

OBS. 9.—But, by the poets, it is often placed after its Object.

EXAMPLE.—"From peak to peak, the rattling *crags* AMONG,
Leaps the live thunder."

OBS. 10.—And sometimes in colloquial style.

EXAMPLE.—"You will have no mother or sister to go *to*."—*Abbott.*

REM.—This idiom is inelegant, and not to be recommended.

OBS. 11.—A Preposition commonly indicates the office of the Phrase which it introduces.

EXAMPLE.—See page 160.

OBS. 12.—Many words commonly used as Prepositions, are sometimes employed, not as Elements of Phrases, but as Word Elements in Sentences. These are commonly Adverbs.

EXAMPLES.—1. "Come *on*, my brave associates."
2. "Lift *up* thy voice like a trumpet."
3. "*Down, down*, the tempest plunges on the sea,
4. And the mad waves rise *up* to buffet it."

NOTE I.—Care should be exercised in the choice of Prepositions.

OBS. 13.—The particular Preposition proper to introduce a given Phrase depends—

1. Usually on the word which the Phrase is to qualify.
2. Sometimes on the Object of the Phrase.

EXAMPLES.

Accommodate *to.*	Die *by* violence.	Abhorrence *of.*
Accord *with.*	" *of* a disease.	Agreeable *to.*
Accuse *of.*	Differ *from.*	Compliance *with.*
Acquainted *with.*	Diminish *from.*	Conformable *to.*
Ask *of* a person.	Dissent *from.*	Difficulty *in—with.*
" *for* a thing.	Insist *upon.*	Eager *in—for.*
Bestow *upon.*	Made *of* a thing.	Need *of.*
Boast *of.*	" *by* a person.	True *to.*
Concur *with—in.*	" *in* a place.	Value *upon.*
		Worthy *of.*

OBS. 14.—When the second term of a Comparison is expressed by a Phrase—

After a *Superlative*, the Preposition *of* is commonly used.

After a *Comparative*, the Preposition *than* is commonly used.

EXAMPLES.—Grammar is the most interesting *of* all my studies.

Grammar is more interesting *than* all my other studies.

OBS. 15.—When the second term of a *Comparison of equality* is a Noun or a Pronoun, the Preposition *as* is commonly used—sometimes *like* is used.

EXAMPLES.—1. "He hath died to redeem such a rebel AS *me*."—*Wesley*

2. "An hour LIKE *this*, may well display the emptiness of human grandeur."

OBS. 16.—Some writers improperly substitute the words *for* and *with* for *as*.

EXAMPLE.—"It implies government of the very *same* kind WITH THAT which a master exercises over his servants."—*Bp. Butler.*

OBS. 17.—A Preposition and its Subsequent constitute a Phrase, generally constituting an Adjective or an Adverbial Adjunct.

EXAMPLES.

Adjective Element.—1. "The KING *of Shadows* loves a shining mark."

Adverbial Element.—2. "Time SLEPT *on flowers*, and LENT his glass *to Hope*."

REM. 1.—The Prepositional Phrase is rarely used as a Substantive Element in a Sentence.—(See CLARK'S ANALYSIS, p. 115.)

REM. 2.—In the analysis of a Sentence, a Phrase contained in it is to be parsed, first, as one distinct element in the structure of its Sentence; then the Phrase is to be analysed, and each of its distinct Elements pointed out. (See p. 185.)

CONJUNCTIONS.

RULE 13.—Conjunctions connect Words, Phrases, and Sentences.

EXAMPLES.

Words.....1. "In the beginning, God created the HEAVEN *and* the EARTH."

Phrases....2. "TO GIVE GOOD GIFTS *and* TO BE BENEVOLENT, are often different things."

Sentences...3. "Thou art perched aloft on the beetling crag,
And the waves are white below."

OBS. 1.—*Words* connected by Conjunctions have a similar construction.

EXAMPLES.—1. "God created the *heaven* AND the *earth*."
2. "Time *slept* on flowers, AND *lent* his glass to Hope."
3. "A *great* AND *good* man has fallen."

REM.—"Heaven" and "earth" are alike Objects of "created."—"Slept" and "lent" are Predicates of "Time."—"Great" and "good" describe "man."

OBS. 2.—But they have not necessarily similar modifications.

EXAMPLE.—"Every teacher *has* AND *must have* his own particular way of imparting knowledge."—*McElligott.*

REM.—"Has" and "must have" are Predicate of "teacher"—but they are not of the same Mode.

OBS. 3.—Phrases and Sentences used as Elements in the structure of a Principal Sentence, have a similar construction, when connected by Conjunctions.

EXAMPLES.—1. "He served his country *in the cabinet* AND *in the field*."
2. "*To eat* AND *to sleep*, constitute the sum of his employments."
3. "*While I am his* AND *he is mine*,
I'm ever safe from ill."

OBS. 4.—But Conjunctions may introduce Principal Sentences, without connecting them to any Word or Sentence in construction.

EXAMPLES.—1. "*And* who says this?"
2. "*That* I have taken this old man's daughter is most true."
3. "*And* I am glad *that* he has lived thus long."

OBS. 5.—Conjunctions introducing Adjunct Sentences, connect their Sentences to the Word modified by such Auxiliaries.

EXAMPLES.—1. "And, IF I sought,
Think'st thou no other *could be brought?*"
2. "As ye journey, sweetly *sing.*"
3. "How *dear* to my heart *are* the scenes of my childhood,
WHEN fond recollection presents them to view."

(See Diagram, p. 000.)

OBS. 6.—But Auxiliary Substantive Sentences are simply *introduced* by Conjunctions.

EXAMPLES.—1. "THAT all men are created equal, is a self-evident truth."
2. "He knew not THAT *the chieftain lay*
Unconscious of his son."

(See Diagram, p. 229.)

OBS. 7.—The *Position* of Sentences often determines their connection, without the use of Conjunctions.

EXAMPLES.—1. "The time may come *you need not run.*"—*Thomson.*
2. "Milton! thou shouldst be living at this hour—
[For] England hath need of thee."
3. "But Brutus says, *he was ambitious.*"

OBS. 8.—Auxiliary Adjective Sentences are commonly introduced by Relative Pronouns and by Possessive Adjectives derived from them.

EXAMPLES.—1. "He WHO *filches from me my good name,*
Robs me of that WHICH *not enriches him.*"
2. "Lo the poor Indian, WHOSE *untutored mind*
Sees God in clouds or hears him in the wind."
3. "Thou hadst a voice WHOSE *sound was like the sea.*"
4. "A voice, *from* WHENCE *I knew not,* spake these words."

OBS. 9.—Conjunctions that introduce Auxiliary Adverbial Sentences, and some others, indicate the *offices* of the Sentences which they introduce.

If, Unless, etc., indicate *condition.*—*As, When, Before,* etc., indicate *time.*—*For, Hence, Therefore,* etc., indicate an *inference* or *cause.*—*But, Yet, Nevertheless,* etc., indicate *restriction* or *opposition.*—*Nor, Neither,* etc., indicate a *negation.*

EXAMPLES.—1. "*If sinners entice thee,* consent thou not."
2. "Speak of me *as I am*—nothing extenuate,
Nor set down aught in malice."
3. "Then, *when* I AM THY CAPTIVE, talk of chains."
4. "I go, *but* I return."

OBS. 10.—Conjunctions may be omitted only when the connection is sufficiently clear without them.

EXAMPLES.—1. "Unnumbered systems, [ ] suns, and worlds,
Unite to worship thee;
2. While thy majestic greatness fills
Space, [ ] Time, [ ] Eternity."

OBS. 11.—The Adverb "how" is sometimes improperly used instead of the Conjunction "that."

EXAMPLE.—"She tells me how, with eager speed,
He flew to hear my vocal reed."—*Shenstone.*

OBS. 12.—Conjunctions sometimes introduce the remnant of a Sentence.

EXAMPLE.—*Though* [ ] *afflicted,* he is happy.

OBS. 13.—POSITION.—The proper place for a Conjunction is before the Sentence which it introduces, and between the Words or Phrases which it connects.

EXAMPLES.—"And there lay the rider, *distorted* AND *pale,*
With the *dew* on his brow AND the *rust* on his mail."

OBS. 14.—But in Complex Sentences, the Conjunction introducing the Principal Sentence is commonly placed first, and that introducing the Auxiliary Sentence immediately following.

EXAMPLE.—"And *when* its yellow *luster smiled,*
O'er mountains yet untrod,
Each MOTHER HELD aloft her CHILD
To bless the bow of God."

But to this rule there are exceptions.

EXAMPLES.—1. "They kneeled BEFORE *they fought.*"
2. "How vain are all these glories, all our pains,
UNLESS *good sense preserve what beauty gains.*"—*Pope.*

CORRESPONDING CONJUNCTIONS.

OBS. 15.—Many Conjunctions correspond to Adverbs, to Prepositions, and to other Conjunctions.

As.......so......" *As* is the mother, *so* is the daughter."
So........as......"Mary is not *so* cheerful *as* usual."
Both ....and ...." *Both* good *and* bad were gathered in one group."
Either ...or......" *Either* you mistake, *or* I was misinformed."
Neither ..nor....." *Neither* Alice *nor* Caroline has been here to-day."
Whether .or......" I care not *whether* you go *or* stay."
So.......that...."He called *so* loud *that* all the hollow deep."
Such.....that...." My engagements are *such that* I can not go."
If ...... then...." *If* you will take the right, *then* I will go to the left."
Not only. but also." She was *not only* vain, *but also* extremely ignorant."
Though ..yet....." *Though* man live a hundred years, *yet* is his life as vanity."
Because .therefore." *Therefore* doth my father love me, *because* I lay down my life."

REM.—The Antecedent corresponding word is sometimes expletive.

OBS. 16.—Double Conjunctions are sometimes used.

EXAMPLES.—1. " *As though* he had not been anointed with oil."

2. *And yet*, fair bow, no fabling dreams,
But words of the Most High
Have told why first thy robe of beams
Was woven in the sky."

OBS. 17.—But they may not be used when one of them would fully express the connection.

EXAMPLE.—" There would be no doubt *but that* they would remain."
The word " *but*" is unnecessary and improper.

EXCLAMATIONS.

RULE 14.—Exclamations have no dependent construction.

OBS.—Exclamations may be followed by Words, Phrases, or Sentences.

EXAMPLES.—1. " O Scotia! my dear, my native soil!"
2. " Wo! wo! to the riders that trample thee down."
3. " O that I could again recall
My early joys, companions all!"

WORDS OF EUPHONY.

PRIN.—Words of Euphony are, in their offices, chiefly rhetorical.

REM.—The Principles of Euphony are much required in the structure of all languages; for Euphony, words are altered in form, position, and office—and they are, for Euphony, created or omitted.

OBS.—Euphony allows—

(1.) The Transposition of Words in a Sentence.

EXAMPLE.—"From peak to peak, the rattling *crags* AMONG,
Leaps the live thunder."

(2.) The omission of a letter or syllable.

EXAMPLE.—"Hark! *'tis* the breeze of twilight calling."

(3.) The substitution of one letter for another.

EXAMPLES.—1. Collect, for *Con*lect.
2. Syllogism, " *Sun*logism.
3. Immigrant, " *In*migrant.

(4.) The addition of a letter, syllable, or word.

EXAMPLE.—"It was his bound*en* duty thus to act."

(5.) A word to be separated into parts, and another word inserted between them.

EXAMPLE.—"*How* MUCH *soever* we may feel their force."

(6.) A word to be used not in its ordinary office.

EXAMPLES.—1. "And there lay the steed with his nostril ALL *wide*."
2. "The more I see of this method, THE *better* I like it."

POSITION.

NOTE.—Words of Euphony should be placed in their appropriate connection.

OBS. 1.—In the following examples, this principle is violated:—

1. "To think of others, and not *only* of himself."

Here "only" is used to render "himself" emphatic. A better position would be—". . . .and not of himself *only*."

"Joyous Youth and manly Strength and stooping Age are *even* here."

Better—Joyous Youth and manly Strength and *even* STOOPING AGE are here.

"When our hatred is violent, it sinks us *even* beneath those we hate."

Better—. . . . it sinks us beneath *even* THOSE WE HATE.

OBS. 2.—A Word *repeated* in the same connection is to be regarded as a word of Euphony.

EXAMPLES.—"Down! *down!* the tempest plunges on the sea."
"For life! *for life*, their flight they ply."

GENERAL RULES.

1. In constructing a Sentence, such Words should be chosen as will most clearly convey the sense intended—regard being had also to variety and other principles of taste.

2. In expressing Complex ideas, judgment and taste are to be exercised in the use of Phrases and Sentences, when they may equally convey the sense.

3. That Modification of Words should be adopted which is in accordance with the most reputable usage.

4. The relative *Position* of Words, Phrases, and Sentences should be such as to leave no obscurity in the sense.

5. Involved Complex Sentences should not be used, when Simple or Independent Sentences would better convey the sense.

RECAPITULATION OF THE RULES OF SYNTAX.

RULE 1.—THE SUBJECT OF A SENTENCE—NOUN OR PRONOUN.

The Subject of a Sentence must be in the Nominative Case.

RULE 2.—PREDICATE OF A SENTENCE—VERB.

A Verb must agree with its Subject in Person and Number.

RULE 3.—THE OBJECT OF A SENTENCE OR PHRASE—NOUN OR PRONOUN.

The object of an action or relation must be in the Objective Case.

RULE 4.—PRONOUNS.

A Pronoun must agree with its Antecedent in Gender, Person, and Number.

RULE 5.—ADJECTIVE PRONOUNS.

Adjective Pronouns are substituted for the Nouns which they qualify.

RULE 6.—INDEPENDENT CASE—NOUN OR PRONOUN.

A Noun or a Pronoun not dependent on any other word in construction, is in the Independent Case.

RULE 7.—ADJECTIVES.

Adjectives belong to Nouns and Pronouns which they describe.

RULE 8.—POSSESSIVE SPECIFYING ADJECTIVES.

A Noun or a Pronoun in the Possessive Case is used Adjectively.

RULE 9.—ADVERBS.

Adverbs belong to Verbs, Adjectives, and other Adverbs which they modify.

RULE 10.—PARTICIPLES.

A Participle has the same construction as the "part of speech" for which it is used.

RULE 11.—VERBS—INFINITIVE.

A Verb in the Infinitive Mode is the Object of the Preposition TO, expressed or understood.

RULE 12.—PREPOSITIONS.

A Preposition shows a relation of its Object to the word which its Phrase qualifies.

RULE 13.—CONJUNCTIONS.

Conjunctions introduce Sentences and connect Words and Phrases.

RULE 14.—EXCLAMATIONS.

Exclamations have no dependent construction.

ADDITIONAL EXAMPLES FOR PARSING.

1. "He was stirred
With such an agony he sweat extremely."—*Henry VIII*, ii. 2.

2. "But it is fit things be stated as they are considered—as they really are."—*Bp. Butler.*

3. "He whose soul
Ponders this true equality, may walk
The fields of earth with gratitude and hope."—*Wordsworth.*

4. "Before we passionately desire anything which another enjoys, we should examine into the happiness of its possessor."

5. "They say 'this shall be,' and it is,
For ere they act, they think."—*Burns.*

6. "My heart is awed within me, *when I think* of the great miracle that still goes on in silence round me."

7. "Take good heed,
Nor there be modest, where thou shouldst be proud."—*Young.*

8. "Ambition saw that stooping Rome could bear
A master, *nor* had virtue to be free."—*Thomson.*

PART IV.

DEF. 1.—That part of the Science of Language which treats of *utterance*, is called *Prosody*.

OBS.—Utterance is modified by *Pauses*, *Accent*, and the laws of *Versification*.

PAUSES.

DEF. 2.—Pauses are cessations of the voice in reading or speaking.

OBS. 1.—Pauses are { Rhetorical and Grammatical.

OBS. 2.—Rhetorical Pauses are useful chiefly in arresting attention. They are generally made after or immediately before emphatic words.

They are not indicated by marks.

EXAMPLES.—There is a calm   for those who weep,
A rest   for weary pilgrims found.

OBS. 3.—Grammatical Pauses are useful—in addition to their Rhetorical effect—in determining the sense.

They are indicated by

MARKS OF PUNCTUATION.

They are—

The Comma ...... ,	The Period........ .
The Semicolon.... ;	The Interrogation.. ?
The Colon........ :	The Exclamation... !

The Dash —

OBS. 4.—In its Rhetorical office,

The Comma requires a short pause in reading.

The Semicolon, a pause longer than the Comma.

The Colon, a pause longer than the Semicolon.

The Period requires a full pause.

The Dash, the Marks of Exclamation and Interrogation, require pauses corresponding with either of the other marks.

REM.—In the use of Marks of Punctuation, good writers differ; and it is exceedingly difficult for the Teacher to give Rules for their use, that can be of general application.

The following Rules are the most important:

COMMA.

RULE 1.—When more than two words of the same construction occur consecutively, the Comma should be repeated after each.

EXAMPLES.

Correct.—1. "Veracity, justice, and charity, are essential virtues."

2. "There is such an exactness in definition, such a pertinence in proof, such a perspicuity in his detection of sophisms, as have been rarely employed in the Christian cause."—*B. B. Edwards.*

Incorrect.—3. "The dripping rock the mountain's misty top,
Swell on the sight and brighten with the dawn."

4. Fame wisdom love and power were mine.

OBS.—EXCEPTION.—The Comma is not placed between an Adjective and its Noun, although preceded by other Adjectives of the same construction.

EXAMPLES.

Correct.—1. "David was a brave, martial, enterprising prince."

2. "With that dull-rooted, callou[illegible]dence."

Incorrect.—3. "The tall, dark, mountain[illegible]-toned sea."

4. [illegible] how unjust to Nat[illegible]
[illegible]ughtless, thank[illegible]man!

RUL[illegible] parts of [illegible] separ[illegible]omma. [illegible] Prin[illegible]nce.

[illegible]

RULE 3.—An Adjunct Phrase or Sentence, used to express an incidental fact, and placed between the parts of the Principal Sentence, is separated by Commas.

EXAMPLES.

Correct.—1. "The grave, *that never spoke before,*
Hath found, *at length,* a tongue to chide."
Incorrect.—2. "Truth crushed to earth will rise again."
3. "Rise sons of harmony and hail the morn."

OBS.—But when an Adjunct Phrase or Sentence which is indispensable in perfecting the sense, immediately follows the word which it qualifies, the Comma should not intervene.

EXAMPLES.

Correct.—1. "Every one *that findeth me,* shall slay me."
2. "Let school-taught pride dissemble all it can."
Incorrect.—3. "The fur, that warms a monarch, warmed a bear."

RULE 4.—Words, Phrases, and Sentences, thrown in between the parts of a Principal Sentence, are separated by Commas.

EXAMPLES.

Correct.—1. "Go, *then,* where, *wrapt in fear and gloom,*
Fond hearts and true are sighing."
2. "Now, *therefore,* I pray thee, let thy servant abide."
Incorrect.—3. "It is a clear lake the very picture *ordinarily* of repose."

RULE 5.—A Phrase or a Sentence used as the Subject of a Verb, requires a Comma between it and the Verb.

EXAMPLES.

Correct.—1. *To do good to others,* constitutes an important object of existence.
2. *That we are rivals,* does not necessarily make us enemies.
Incorrect.—3. "That all men are created equal is a self-evident truth."
"His being a minister prevented his rising to civil power."

RULE 6.—Words used in direct address, should be separated by a Comma.

EXAMPLES.

Correct.—1. 'Thou, whose spell can raise the dead,
Bid the prophet's form appear;

Incorrect.—2. Samuel raise thy buried head
King behold the phantom seer!"

RULE 7.—Adjunct Sentences, Phrases, and sometimes Words, not in their natural position, should be separated by a Comma.

EXAMPLES.

Correct.—1. "Into this illustrious society, he whose character I have endeavored feebly to portray, has, without doubt, entered."

2. "He, like the world, his ready visit pays,
Where Fortune smiles."

Incorrect.—3. "To him who in the love of Nature holds
Communion with her visible forms
She speaks a various language."

SEMICOLON.

RULE 8.—The Semicolon is used at the close of a Sentence, which, by its terms, promises an additional Sentence.

EXAMPLES.

Correct.—1. "The Essayists occupy a conspicuous place in the last century; but, somehow, I do not feel disposed to set much store by them."

Incorrect.—2. "It thunders! but I tremble not
My trust is firm in God."

3. "Wisdom is better than rubies,
It can not be gotten for gold."

OBS.—By many writers, the Semicolon is used to separate short Sentences, which have not a close dependence to each other.

EXAMPLES.

Correct.—1. "He was a plain man, without any pretension to pulpit eloquence, or any other accomplishment; he had no gift of imagination; his language was hard and dry; and his illustrations, homely."

Incorrect.—2. "I had a seeming friend—I gave him gifts and he was gone
I had an open enemy I gave him gifts, and won him—
The very heart of hate melteth at a good man's love.'

COLON.

RULE 9.—The Colon is used at the close of a Sentence, when another Sentence is added as a direct illustration or inference.

EXAMPLES.

Correct.—1. "Let me give you a piece of good counsel, my cousin: follow my laudable example: write when you can: take Time's forelock in one hand and a pen in the other, and so make sure of your opportunity."

Cowper.

Incorrect.—2. 'From the last hill that looks on thy once holy dome,
I beheld thee, O Sion! when rendered to Rome
'Twas thy last sun went down, and the flames of thy fall
Flashed back on the last glance I gave to thy wall."

Hebrew Melodies.

REM.—The Colon is not much used by late writers—its place being supplied by the Semicolon, the Dash, or the Period.

PERIOD.

RULE 10.—The Period is used at the close of a complete or independent proposition.

OBS.—The Period is also used after initial letters and abbreviations.

EXAMPLES.

Correct.—J. Q. Adams, LL. D., M. C.

Incorrect.—A S Barnes and Co 51 John St N Y.

DASH.

RULE 11.—The Dash is used to indicate—

1. An abrupt transition.
2. An unfinished sentence.
3. A succession of particulars.

EXAMPLES.

Correct.—1. "They met to expatiate and confer on state affairs—to read the newspapers—to talk a little scandal—and so forth—and the result was—as we have been told—considerable dissipation."—*Wilson's Burns.*

Incorrect.—2. "To me the 'Night Thoughts' is a poem, on the whole, most animating and delightful amazingly energetic full of the richest instruction improving to the mind much of it worthy of being committed to memory some faults obscure extravagant tinged occasionally with flattery."

OBS. 1.—The Dash is often used instead of the Parenthesis.

EXAMPLE.—"As they disperse they look very sad—and, no doubt they are so—but had they been, they would not have taken to digging."

OBS. 2.—Many modern writers use the dash in place of the Semicolon and the Colon—and sometimes with them.

EXAMPLE.—"Ye have no need of prayer;—
Ye have no sins to be forgiven."—*Sprague.*

EXCLAMATION.

RULE 12.—The mark of Exclamation is used after a Word, Phrase, or Sentence, whose prominent office is, to express sudden or intense emotion.

EXAMPLES.

Correct.—1. "Hark! a strange sound affrights mine ear."
2. "To arms!—they come!—the Greek, the Greek!"

Incorrect.—3. "O my coëvals, remnants of yourselves."
4. "Poor human ruins tottering o'er the grave."

INTERROGATION.

RULE 13.—The mark of Interrogation is used after a Word, Phrase, or Sentence, by which a question is asked.

EXAMPLES.

Correct.—1. "Why is my sleep disquieted?"
2. Who is he that calls the dead?

Incorrect.—3. "Is it for thee the lark ascends and sings."
4. "What pleasing study cheats the tedious day."

REM.—When the Interrogation or Exclamation is used, the Comma, Semicolon, Colon, or Period, is omitted.

GRAMMATICAL AND RHETORICAL SIGNS.

OBS.—The signs used in writing are—

1. The Apostrophe	'	8. Inflections { Rising	ˊ
2. The Quotation	" "	Falling	ˋ
3. The Hyphen	-	Circumflex	ˆ
4. The Bracket	[ ]	9. Measures { Long	¯
5. The Parenthesis	( )	Short	˘
6. References	* †	10. Caret	^
7. The Brace	}	11. Dieresis	¨
		12. Index	☞
		13. Section	§
		14. The Paragraph	¶

DEF. 3.—*The Apostrophe* (') is used to indicate the omission of a letter, and to change a Noun into a Possessive Specifying Adjective.

EXAMPLES.—1. "Hearts, from which *'twas* death to sever;
2. Eyes, this world can *ne'er* restore."
3. "How lightly mounts the Muse's wing."

DEF. 4.—*The Quotation* (" ") is used to inclose words taken from some other author or book.

EXAMPLES.—"Southey, among all our living poets," says Professor Wilson, "stands aloof and 'alone in his glory.'"

REM.—A Quotation quoted is indicated by single marks.

EXAMPLE.—(See the latter part of the Example above.)

DEF. 5.—The *Hyphen* (-) is used between two elements of a compound word.

EXAMPLES.—Money-market—ink-stand—black-board.

REM.—It is also used at the end of a line, when the word is not finished. (See this remark.)

DEF. 6.—*The Bracket* [ ] is used to inclose a letter or mark, given as an explanatory example; or a Word, Phrase, or Sentence, thrown in by a reviewer, and not a part of the original sentence.

EXAMPLE.

"Mr. Secor found means to have Mr. Butler recommended to him [Lord Talbot] for his chaplain."

DEF. 7.—*The Parenthesis* ( ) is used to inclose a Phrase or Sentence, explanatory of, or incidental to, the main Sentence.

EXAMPLE.—"Come, my Ambition! let us mount together,
(To mount Lorenzo never can refuse,)
And, from the clouds where pride delights to dwell,
Look down on earth."

REM.—Modern writers often use the Dash for the same purpose.

EXAMPLE.—"The monotony of a calm—for the trade-wind had already failed us—was agreeably relieved yesterday, by the neighborhood of two ships, etc."—*Malcolm.*

DEF. 8.—*References* (* † ‡ §) direct attention to notes at the margin or the bottom of the page.

REM.—The letters of the Latin or Greek alphabets, and sometimes figures, are used for the same purpose.

DEF. 9.—*The Brace* (}) is used to include many species in one class.

EXAMPLE.—Adjectives are distinguished as { Qualifying, Specifying, Verbal.

REM.—By the old poets, the Brace was also used to join the lines of a triplet.

DEF. 10.—*Inflections* (ˊ ˋ ˇ) indicate elevations or depressions of the key-note in reading.

EXAMPLES.—"Do you go to Albanyˊ?" "I go to Uticaˋ."

Def. 11.—*Measures.* { (¯) indicates the long sound of a Syllable, as lāte, mēte, nōte.
(˘) indicates the short sound of a Syllable, as lĕt, mĕt, nŏt. }

Def. 12.—*The Caret* (^) is used between two Words, to indicate the place of words omitted, and placed above the line.

Example.—"The proper study ^ (of mankind) is man."

Def. 13.—*Dieresis* (¨) is placed over the second of two vowels, to show that they belong to different syllables.

Examples.—Preëmption—Coëval.—Reëducate.

Obs.—The Hyphen is sometimes placed between the vowels for a similar purpose.

Example.—Co-operate.

Def. 14.—*The Index* (☞) is used to point out a word or sentence considered worthy of special notice.

Def. 15.—*The Section* (§) marks the divisions of a chapter or book.

Def. 16.—*The Paragraph* (¶) is used when a new subject of remark is introduced.

Rem.—The sign of the Paragraph is retained in the Holy Scriptures; but in other compositions, the Paragraph is sufficiently indicated by its commencing a new line on the page.

Def. 17.—*Accent* is a stress of voice placed on a particular syllable, in pronouncing a word.

Def. 18.—*Emphasis* is a stress of voice placed on a particular word in a Sentence.

Obs.—This mark is indicated—

1. In manuscript, by a line drawn under the emphatic word.
2. On a printed page, by the use of *Italic* letters—CAPITAL letters are used to indicate words still more emphatic.

PART IV.—PROSODY.

COMPOSITION.

DEF. 19.—Composition—as the word implies—is the art of *placing together* words, so as to communicate ideas.

OBS.—Composition is of two kinds—

PROSE AND VERSE.

In *Prose Composition*, Words and Phrases are arranged with a primary reference to the *sense*.

In *Verse*, the Sound and Measure of Words and Syllables determine their position.

OBS.—Among the various kinds of Prose Compositions, may be mentioned the following:

Narrative, Descriptive, Didactic, Historical, Biographical.

VERSE.

DEF. 20.—Verse consists of words arranged in measured lines, constituting a regular succession of accented and unaccented Syllables.

OBS.—Verse is used in Poetry. The different kinds of Poetry are—

Lyric,	***Charade,***	***Sonnet,***
Dramatic,	***Ballad,***	***Pastoral,***
Epic,	***Epigram,***	***Elegiac,***
Didactic,	***Epitaph,***	***Madrigal.***

DEF. 21.—LYRIC POETRY is—as its name imports—such as may be set to music. It includes the "Ode" and the "Song."

OBS. 1.—Lyric Poetry is of three kinds, the Ode, the Hymn, and the Song.

OBS. 2.—The *Ode* is generally longer than the other kinds of Lyric Poetry, and is often irregular in its structure.

Familiar Examples.—"Alexander's Feast," by *Dryden.*
"Ode on the Passions," " *Collins.*
"Immortality," " *Wordsworth.*

☞ **Let the Pupil give other Examples.**

OBS. 3.—The *Hymn* is shorter, and is arranged in regular stanzas adapted to sacred worship.

Familiar Examples.—"The Psalms and Hymns" in general use in Christian Congregations.

OBS. 4.—The *Song* is also short, but is more varied in its stanzas, and is adapted to secular uses.

Familiar Examples.—"Irish Melodies," by *Moore.*
"Songs," " *Barry Cornwall.*

☞ Let the Pupil give other Examples.

REM.—English Lyric Poetry makes use of Rhyme exclusively.

DEF. 22.—EPIC POETRY is a historical representation—real or fictitious—of great events.

REM.—*Epic Poetry* may employ either rhyme or blank verse.

EXAMPLES.—*Rhyme.*—"Lady of the Lake," by *Scott.*
"Curse of Kehama," " *Southey.*
Blank Verse.—"Paradise Lost," " *Milton.*
"Course of Time," " *Pollock.*

☞ Let the Pupil give other Examples.

DEF. 23.—DRAMATIC POETRY is a poem descriptive of scenes, events, or character, and is adapted to the stage.

OBS. 1.—It includes { The Tragic and The Comic.

EXAMPLES.—*Tragic.*—"Othello," by *Shakspeare.*
Comic.—"All's well that ends well."—*Shakspeare.*

☞ Let the Pupil give other Examples.

DEF. 24.—DIDACTIC POETRY is that style adapted to the inculcation of science or duty.

EXAMPLES.—"Pleasures of the Imagination," by *Akenside.*
"Art of Preserving Health," " *Armstrong.*

☞ Let the Pupil give other Examples.

DEF. 25.—The CHARADE is a short poem, usually in a Lyrical form, containing a *Riddle.*

DEF. 26.—An EPIGRAM is a witty poem, short, and generally abounding in ludicrous expressions.

EXAMPLES.—"Swans sing before they die: 'twere no bad thing,
Should certain persons die before they sing."

DEF. 27.—An EPITAPH is a poetic inscription to the memory of some departed person.

EXAMPLES.—"Underneath this stone doth lie
As much beauty as could die,
Which in life did harbor give
To more virtue than doth live."—*Jonson.*

DEF. 28.—ELEGIAC POETRY is that species used to commemorate the death of some person.

EXAMPLES.—"Lysidas," by *Milton.*
"Elegy," " *Gray.*

DEF. 29.—The SONNET is a Poem devoted to the development of a single thought, in rhyming verse of a peculiar structure, and generally of fourteen lines.

DEF. 30.—The MADRIGAL is a Lyric Poem of an amatory nature, and of a lively species of verse.

DEF. 31.—PASTORAL POETRY relates to rural life, and is generally a song.

EXAMPLES.—"Rural Sports," by *Gay.*
"The Falls of the Passaic," by *Irving.*

DEF. 32.—The BALLAD is a Lyric Poem, of a Narrative cast, in a simple or rude style of composition.

EXAMPLES.—"Battle of Brunnenberg," by *Ferris.*

VERSIFICATION.

DEF. 1.—VERSIFICATION is the art of making verse—*i. e.*, the proper arrangement of a certain number of Syllables in a line.

PRIN.—There are two prominent distinctions in Verse,

1. *Blank Verse.*
2. *Rhyme.*

DEF. 2.—BLANK VERSE consists in measured lines of ten Syllables each, and which may or may not end with the same sound.

EXAMPLE.—"'Tis midnight's holy hour; and silence now
Is brooding, like a gentle spirit, o'er
The still and pulseless world. Hark! on the winds
The bell's deep tones are swelling; 'tis the knell
Of the departed year."

DEF. 3.—RHYMING VERSE consists of measured lines, of which two or more end with the same sound.

EXAMPLES.

Rhymes successive.—"Thou bright glittering star of even!
Thou gem upon the brow of heaven!
Oh! were this fluttering spirit free,
How quick 'twould spread its wings to thee!"

Rhymes alternating.—"Oh! sacred star of evening, tell
In what unseen celestial sphere,
Those spirits of the perfect dwell—
Too pure to rest in sadness here."

DEF. 4.—A line in Poetry is technically called a *Verse.*

EXAMPLE.—"And I am glad that he has lived thus long."

REM.—Verses are of different lengths.

DEF. 5.—A half verse is called a *Hemistich.*

EXAMPLE.—"I, too, will hasten back with lightning speed,
To seek the hero."

DEF. 6.—Two rhyming verses which complete the sense, are called a *Couplet.*

EXAMPLES.—1. "Look round our world; behold the chain of love,
Combining all below and all above."
2. 'And more true joy Marcellus exiled feels,
Than Cæsar with a senate at his heels."

DEF. 7.—Three verses which rhyme together, are a *Triplet.*

EXAMPLE.—"So fair, so sweet, withal so sensitive,
Would that the little flowers were born to live,
Conscious of half the pleasure which they give."

DEF. 8.—Four lines or more are called a *Stanza.*

EXAMPLE.—"Full many a gem, of purest ray serene,
The dark unfathomed caves of ocean bear;
Full many a flower is born to blush unseen,
And waste its sweetness on the desert air."

PRIN.—Verses may end with { Rhyming *Syllables*, or Rhyming *Words.* }

EXAMPLE.—" We come, we come, a little band,
As children of the nation;
" We are joined in heart, we are joined in hand,
To keep the Declaration."

REM.—In the above stanza, the first and third lines end with Rhyming *Words*—the second and fourth, with Rhyming *Syllables.*

DEF. 9.—A collection of Syllables is called a *Foot.*

PRIN.—A Foot may consist of { two Syllables, or three Syllables. }

DEF. 10.—Feet of two Syllables are the

Trochee, . . . first long, second short. . . . — ⏑
Iambus, . . . first short, second long, . . . ⏑ —
Pyrrhic . . . both short . . . . ⏑ ⏑
Spondee . . . both long . . . . — —

Feet of three syllables are the

Dactyl . . . . one long and two short. . . . . — ⏑ ⏑
Anapest . . . two short and one long . . . . ⏑ ⏑ —
Amphibrach. first short, second long, third short. ⏑ — ⏑
Tribrach . . . three short . . . . ⏑ ⏑ ⏑

REM.—Most English Poetry is written in Iambic, Trochaic, or Anapæstic Verse.

TROCHAIC VERSE.

1. *Hexameter*, or *six feet.*

"On a | mountain | stretched be | neath a | hoary | willow,
Lay a shepherd swain, and viewed the rolling billow."

2. *Pentameter*, or *five feet.*

"Rouse him | like a | rattling | peal of | thunder."

3. *Tetrameter*, or *four feet.*

On the | mountain's | top ap | pearing,
Lo, the sacred herald stands!

4. *Trimeter*, or *three feet.*

"How I | love to | see thee,
Golden evening sun."

5. *Dimeter*, or *two feet.*

Rich the | treasure,
Sweet the pleasure.

6. *Monameter*, or *one foot.*

Ringing.
Singing.

IAMBIC VERSE.

1. *Six feet.*

The praise | of Bac | chus then | the sweet musi | cian sung

2. *Five feet.*

Oh, I | have loved | in youth's | fair ver | nal morn,
To spread | ima | gina | tion's wild | est wing.

3. *Four feet.*

There is | a calm | for those | who weep,
A rest | for wea | ry pil | grims found.

4. *Three feet.*

What sought | they thus | afar!
Bright jew | els of | the mine!

5. *Two feet.*

"I am | the grave."

6. *One foot.*

"My home."

ANAPÆSTIC VERSE.

1. *Four feet.*

' But we stead | fastly gazed | on the face | of the dead.

2. *Three feet.*

"And I loved | her the more | when I heard
Such tenderness fall from her tongue."

3. *Two feet.*

"Fŏr thĕ nīght | only drāws
A thin veil o'er the day."

DACTYLIC VERSE.

1. *Four feet.*

Come, ye dis | consolate, | where'er ye | languish.

2. *Three feet.*

Earth has no | sorrows that | Heaven can not | heal.

3. *Two feet.*

Free from anx | iety,
Care, and satiety.

4. *One foot.*

Chēērfŭlly,
Fearfully.

THE AMPHIBRACH.

"There is a | bleak desert | where daylight | grows weary
Of wasting its smile on a region so dreary."
' With storm-dar | ing pinion | and sun-ga | zing eye,
The gray forest eagle is king of the sky."
"There's pleasure | in freedom | whatever | the season,
That makes every object look lovely and fair."

OBS. 1.—The first syllable of a verse is sometimes omitted.

EXAMPLE.

[ ] "And there | lay the ri | der, distort | ed and pale,
With the dew | on his brow | and the rust | on his mail."

OBS. 2.—A syllable is sometimes added to a line.

EXAMPLES.

"Earth has no | sorrows that | Heaven can not | *heal.*"
"A guar | dian an | gel o'er | my life | presid | ing,
Doubling my pleasures and my cares dividing."

OBS. 3.—The different measures are sometimes combined in the same line.

EXAMPLES.

"I come, | I come, | ye have called | me long,
I come | o'er the moun | tains with light | and song;
Ye may trace,| my steps | o'er the wak | ening earth,
By the winds | which tell | of the vio | let's birth."

OBS. 4.—Sometimes the last syllable of a line becomes the first syllable in the first foot of the next.

EXAMPLE.

"On the cold | cheek of death | smiles and ro | ses are blend | *ing,*
And beau | ty immor | tal awakes from the tomb."

FIGURES.

PRIN.—Language is modified in its structure, style, and utterance, by the use of *Figures.*

DEF. 1.—A *Figure* of speech is a licensed departure from the ordinary structure or use of a word in a Sentence

OBS.—Figures are employed to give *strength, beauty,* or *melody,* to Language.

PRIN.—*Figures* are { Grammatical or Rhetorical.

DEF. 2.—A *Grammatical Figure* is a deviation from the ordinary *form* or *office* of a word in a Sentence.

DEF. 3.—A *Rhetorical Figure* is a deviation from the ordinary application of words in the expression of thought.

I. Figures modifying the Form of Words.

These are called—

Aphæresis,	*Synæresis,*
Apocope,	*Diæresis,*
Prosthesis,	*Syncope,*
Parogoge,	*Tmesis.*

Def. 4.—*Aphæresis* allows the elision of one or more of the first letters of a word.

EXAMPLES.

1. "'Mid scenes of confusion."
2. "And therefore thou may'st think my 'havior light."—*Juliet.*
3. "What! have you let the false enchanter 'scape?"—*Milton.*

Def. 5.—*Apocope* allows the elision of one or more of the final letters of a word.

Examples.—1. "And that is spoke.. with such a dying fall."
2. "Tho' the whole loosened Spring around her blows."
3. "T' whom th' archangel."—*Milton.*

Def. 6.—*Paragoge* allows a syllable to be annexed to a word.

EXAMPLES.

1. "Withouten trump was proclamation made."—*Thomson.*
2. "Nor deem that kind*ly* nature did him wrong."—*Bryant.*

Def. 7.—*Synæresis* allows two syllables to become one

Example.—Extra session—ordinary session—extraordinary session.

Def. 8.—*Prosthesis* allows a syllable to be prefixed to a word.

EXAMPLES.

1. "Else would a maiden blush *be*paint my cheek."—*Juliet.*
2. "Let fall *adown* his silver beard some tears."—*Thomson.*
3. "The great archangel from his warlike toil
*Sur*ceased."—*Milton.*

Def. 9.—*Diæresis* separates two vowels into different syllables.

Examples.—Coöperate—reïterate.

DEF. 10.—*Syncope* allows one or more letters to be taken from the middle of a word.

EXAMPLES.—1. "Or serve they as a *flow'ry* verge to bind
2. The fluid skirts of that same *wat'ry* cloud,
3. Lest it again dissolve and *show'r* the earth."—*Milton.*

DEF. 11.—*Tmesis* allows a word to be inserted between the parts of a compound word.

EXAMPLE.—"*How* MUCH *soever* we may desire it."

OBS.—Sometimes two figures are combined in the same word.
EXAMPLE.—"Ah! whence is that sound which now *larums* his ear!"

II. FIGURES MODIFYING THE OFFICES OF WORDS.

These are called

RHETORICO-GRAMMATICAL FIGURES.

They are—

Ellipsis, *Syllipsis*,
Pleonasm, *Enallage*.
Hyperbaton.

DEF. 12.—*Ellipsis* allows the omission of one or more words necessary to complete the grammatical construction, when custom has rendered them unnecessary to complete the sense.

EXAMPLES.—1. "Thou art perched aloft on the beetling crag,
And the waves are white below [ ]."
2. "Unnumbered systems [ ], suns, and worlds,
Unite to worship thee,
3. While thy majestic greatness fills
Space [ ], Time [ ], Eternity."

DEF. 13.—*Pleonasm* allows the introduction of words not necessary to complete the grammatical construction of a Sentence.

EXAMPLES.—1. "The moon *herself* is lost in heaven."
2. "I sit *me* down, a pensive hour to spend."

DEF. 14.—*Syllipsis* allows a word to be used not in its literal sense.

EXAMPLE.—"And there lay the steed, with his nostril *all* wide."

DEF. 15.—*Enallage* allows the use of one word for another of similar origin.

EXAMPLE.—"A world *devote* to universal wreck."

DEF. 16.—*Hyperbaton* allows the transposition of words in a sentence.

EXAMPLE.—"His *voice* SUBLIME, is heard afar."

III. FIGURES OF RHETORIC.

They are—

Simile,	*Antithesis,*	*Vision,*
Metaphor,	*Metonomy,*	*Paralepsis,*
Allegory,	*Synecdoche,*	*Climax,*
Personification,	*Apostrophe,*	*Anti-Climax,*
Irony,	*Interrogation,*	*Alliteration.*
Hyperbole,	*Exclamation,*	

DEF. 17.—A *Simile* is a direct comparison.

EXAMPLE.—"The Assyrian came down like the wolf on the fold."

DEF. 18.—A *Metaphor* is an indirect comparison.

EXAMPLE.—"There is a tide in the affairs of men,
Which, taken at the flood, leads on to fortune."

DEF. 19.—An *Allegory* is an extended metaphor, by which a narration, real or fictitious, is made to convey an analogous truth or fiction.

EXAMPLE.—"Eternity's vast ocean lies before thee;
There, there, Lorenzo, thy Clarissa sails;
Give thy mind sea-room; keep it wide of Earth—
That rock of souls immortal; cut thy cord;
Weigh anchor; spread thy sails; call every wind;
Eye thy great Pole-star; make the land of life."—*Young*

DEF. 20.—*Personification* represents inanimate things as being endowed with life and volition.

EXAMPLES.—1. "And old *Experience* learns too late
That all is vanity below."
2. "*Joy* has her tears, and *Transport* has her death."

DEF. 21.—*Irony* makes a sentence convey a meaning the opposite of its ordinary sense.

EXAMPLES.—"And we, *brave men*, are satisfied
If we ourselves escape his sword."

DEF. 22.—*Hyberbole* exaggerates the truth.

EXAMPLE.— "With fury driven,
The waves mount up, and *wash the face of heaven*."

DEF. 23.—*Antithesis* contrasts two or more things with each other.

EXAMPLES.—1. "*Zealous* though *modest*, *innocent* though *free*."
2. "*By honor* and *dishonor*, by *evil* report and *good* report, as *deceivers*, and yet *true*."

DEF. 24.—*Metonomy* puts one thing for another—
The cause for the effect,
The effect for the cause,
The container for the thing contained,
An attribute or quality for the thing or person.

EXAMPLES.—1. "Shall the *sword* devour for ever!"
2. "Thy *hand*, unseen, sustains the poles."
3. "His *ear* is ever open to their cry."
4. "I am much delighted in reading *Homer*."
5. "He has returned to his *cups* again."
6. "I'll plunge thee headlong in the whelming *tide*."

DEF. 25.—*Synecdoche* puts a part for a whole, and a whole for a part.

EXAMPLES.—1. "When the tempest stalks abroad,
Seek the shelter of my *roof*."
2. "Oh! ever cursed be the *hand*
That wrought this ruin in the land."

DEF. 26.—*Apostrophe* is a sudden transition from the subject of a discourse to address a person or thing, present or absent.

EXAMPLE.—"This is a tale for fathers and for mothers. *Young men and young women, you can not understand it.*"—*E. Everett.*

DEF. 27.—*Interrogation* expresses an assertion in the form of a question.

EXAMPLE.—1. "Looks it not like the king?"
"He that formed the eye, shall he not see?"

DEF. 28.—*Exclamation* expresses a sudden or intense emotion.

EXAMPLE.—"O liberty! O sound, once delightful to every Roman ear!"

DEF. 29.—*Vision* represents past or future time as present to the view.

EXAMPLE.—"I see them on their winding way,
About their ranks the moonbeams play."

DEF. 30.—*Paralepsis* is a figure by which a main truth is expressed incidentally, or with a professed effort of the speaker to conceal it.

EXAMPLE.—"*Without alluding to your habits of intemperance,* I would ask, how can you attempt to justify your present inattention to business and the neglect of your family?"

DEF. 31.—*Climax* is that form of expression by which the thoughts are made to rise by successive gradations.

EXAMPLE.—"He aspired to be the highest; above the people, above the *authorities*, above the LAWS, above his COUNTRY."

DEF 32.—*Anti-Climax* is the opposite of the climax.

EXAMPLE.—"How has expectation darkened into anxiety, anxiety into dread, and dread into despair."—*Irving.*

DEF. 33.—*Alliteration* is the repetition of the same letter at the beginning of two or more words immediately succeeding each other.

EXAMPLES.—1. "Up the *h*igh *h*ill *h*e *h*eaves a *h*uge, round stone."
2. "He *c*arves with *c*lassic *c*hisel the *C*orinthian *c*apital that *c*rowns the *c*olumn."

QUESTIONS FOR REVIEW.

PAGE

283.—What is PROSODY?
Name the different *mark of punctuation.*
When is a *Comma* properly used?
When a *Semicolon?*—a *Colon?*—a *Period?*
When is a *Dash* properly used?—an *Exclamation?*
When do we use a mark of *Interrogation?*

289.—Name the GRAMMATICAL SIGNS.
What is an *Apostrophe?*—a *Quotation?*—a *Hyphen?*
What is a *Bracket?*—a *Parenthesis?*—*Reference marks?*
What is a *Brace?*—*Marks of Inflection?*—*Measures?*
What is a *Caret?*—a *Dieresis?*—an *Index?*—a *Section?*
What is a *Paragraph?*—How are Paragraphs commonly indicated?
What is *Accent?*—What is *Emphasis?*

292.—What is COMPOSITION?—What are the varieties?
What is *Prose?*—Name the various kinds of Prose.
What is *Verse?*—When properly used?
Name and define the various kinds of *Poetry.*

295.—What is VERSIFICATION?
What are the distinctions of verse?
What is *Blank Verse?*—What is *Rhyming Verse?*
What is a *Verse?*—a *Hemistich?*—a *Couplet?*
What is a *Triplet?*—What is a *Stanza?*
What is a *Foot?*—A Foot may have how many Syllables?
What are the Feet of two Syllables?—of three Syllables?
What is a *Trochee?*—an *Iambus?*—a *Pyrrhic?*—a *Spondee?*
What is a *Dactyl?*—an *Anapest?*—an *Amphibrach?*—a *Tribrach?*
What measures are commonly used in English Poetry?

299.—What is a FIGURE OF SPEECH?—Why are they used?
What is a *Grammatical Figure?*—a *Rhetorical Figure?*
Name the Figures which modify the forms of Words.

APPENDIX.

NOTE A.

REM.—Orthography properly belongs to a separate branch of the Science of Language. The following Synopsis is given, chiefly to present the Author's views as to the proper method of presenting this subject.

DEF.—Orthography is that branch of the Science of Language which treats of LETTERS—their forms, their offices, and their combinations in the structure of WORDS.

OBS. 1.—The English Language has twenty-six Letters, which are distinguished by their *forms* and *uses*.

OBS. 2.—The various *forms* of letters are exhibited in the following table:

ROMAN—*Capitals.*

A	B	C	D	E	F	G	H	I	J	K	L	M
N	O	P	Q	R	S	T	U	V	W	X	Y	Z

Small.

a	b	c	d	e	f	g	h	i	j	k	l	m
n	o	p	q	r	s	t	u	v	w	x	y	z

ITALIC—*Capitals.*

A	*B*	*C*	*D*	*E*	*F*	*G*	*H*	*I*	*J*	*K*	*L*	*M*
N	*O*	*P*	*Q*	*R*	*S*	*T*	*U*	*V*	*W*	*X*	*Y*	*Z*

Small.

a	*b*	*c*	*d*	*e*	*f*	*g*	*h*	*i*	*j*	*k*	*l*	*m*
n	*o*	*p*	*q*	*r*	*s*	*t*	*u*	*v*	*w*	*x*	*y*	*z*

OLD ENGLISH—*Capitals.*

𝔄	𝔅	ℭ	𝔇	𝔈	𝔉	𝔊	ℌ	ℑ	𝔍	𝔎	𝔏	𝔐
𝔑	𝔒	𝔓	𝔔	ℜ	𝔖	𝔗	𝔘	𝔙	𝔚	𝔛	𝔜	ℨ

Small.

𝔞	𝔟	𝔠	𝔡	𝔢	𝔣	𝔤	𝔥	𝔦	𝔧	𝔨	𝔩	𝔪
𝔫	𝔬	𝔭	𝔮	𝔯	𝔰	𝔱	𝔲	𝔳	𝔴	𝔵	𝔶	𝔷

OBS. 1.—Roman letters are in most common use in the English language.

Italic Letters are used in words of special importance, and sometimes in Sentences.

In the Sacred Scriptures, words supplied by the translators to complete the construction of Sentences according to the English idiom, are printed in *Italics*.

Old English Letters are used for variety or ornament—in title pages, etc.

OBS.—The small, or "lower case" Letters, are used in forming most Words, and constitute the appropriate form of letters now used in printed works—with the following EXCEPTIONS, which provide for the use of

CAPITAL LETTERS.

RULE 1.—A word should begin with a capital letter, when it is the first word of a distinct proposition.

RULE 2.—When it is a Proper Name, or a word immediately derived from a Proper Name.

EXAMPLE.—Boston—William—American—Vermonter.

RULE 3.—When it is a name or appellation of the Supreme Being.

EXAMPLES.—God—Saviour—Holy Spirit—Lord—Omnipotent.

RULE 4.—When it is the first word of a line in poetry.

EXAMPLE.—"Twinkle, twinkle, little star,
How I wonder what you are;
Up above the world so high,
Like a diamond in the sky."

RULE 5.—When it is a principal word in a title of a book or office, and sometimes when it is a word of special importance, or used technically.

EXAMPLES.—"Willard's History of the United States."
"Burke on the Sublime and Beautiful."
"The Subject of a Verb should not take the place of the Object."

RULE 6.—When it commences a direct quotation.

EXAMPLES.—"The footman, in his usual phrase,
Comes up with 'Madam, dinner stays.'"
"Wo to him that saith unto the wood, 'Awake.'"

RULE 7.—When it constitutes the Pronoun "I" or the Exclamation "O."

EXAMPLES.—"O, I have loved in youth's fair vernal morn,
To spread Imagination's wildest wing."

RULE 8.—When it is a Common Noun fully personified.

EXAMPLES.—"Sure I Fame's trumpet hear."—*Cowley.*
"Here Strife and Faction rule the day."

OBS.—Letters are of various sizes, and have their corresponding appropriate names. The varieties of type in most common use are the following:

1. *Pica.*—ABCDEFGHIJKLMNOPQRSTUVWXYZ. abcdefghijklmnopqrstuvwxyz.

2. *Small Pica.*—ABCDEFGHIJKLMNOPQRSTUVWXYZ. abcdefghijklmnopqrstuvwxyz.

3. *Long Primer.*—ABCDEFGHIJKLMNOPQRSTUVWXYZ. abcdefghijklmnopqrstuvwxyz.

4. *Bourgeois.*—ABCDEFGHIJKLMNOPQRSTUVWXYZ. abcdefghijklmnopqrstuvwxyz.

5. *Brevier.*—ABCDEFGHIJKLMNOPQRSTUVWXYZ abcdefghijklmnopqrstuvwxyz.

6. *Minion.*—ABCDEFGHIJKLMNOPQRSTUVWXYZ. abcdefghijklmnopqrstuvwxyz.

7. *Nonpareil.*—ABCDEFGHIJKLMNOPQRSTUVWXYZ. abcdefghijklmnopqrstuvwxyz.

8. *Agate.*—ABCDEFGHIJKLMNOPQRSTUVWXYZ. abcdefghijklmnopqrstuvwxyz.

9. *Pearl.*—ABCDEFGHIJKLMNOPQRSTUVWXYZ. abcdefghijklmnopqrstuvwxyz.

10. *Diamond.*—ABCDEFGHIJKLMNOPQRSTUVWXYZ. abcdefghijklmnopqrstuvwxyz.

THE OFFICES OF LETTERS.

PRIN.—Letters constitute the Elements of Words, and, like the Elements of Sentences and Phrases, are distinguished as *Principal Elements* and *Adjunct Elements*.

DEF. 1.—The *Principal Elements* of a Word are the Letters which indicate the principal sound. They are called VOWELS.

EXAMPLES.—*a* in m*a*te—*e* in m*e*—*oi* in t*oi*l—*ou* in s*ou*nd—*ă* in h*ă*t—*ĕ* in m*ĕ*t—*æ* in aph*æ*resis—*œ* in subp*œ*na.

DEF. 2.—The *Adjuncts* of a Word are the Letters prefixed or added to the Principal Elements to modify their sound. They are called CONSONANTS.

EXAMPLES.—*m* in mate, *m*e—*t* in mate, *t*ime—*l* in toil, *l*ame—*c* in cider, *c*ane—*h* in hat, *h*ate—*s* in aphæresis, *s*ound—*v* in vile, twelve—*p* in post, ha*pp*y.

REM.—For convenience in articulation, most words are divided into Parts, called *Syllables*; hence,

DEF. 3.—A *Syllable* is a whole Word, or such part of a Word as is uttered by one impulse of the voice.

EXAMPLES.—Man, man-ly, man-li-ness, un-man-ly.

DEF. 4.—When a Word has but *one* Principal Part, it is pronounced by one impulse of the voice, and is then called a *Monosyllable*.

EXAMPLES.—Hand—fall—me—so—strength.

DEF. 5.—When a Word has *two* Principal Parts, it requires two articulations, and is then called a *Dissyllable*.

EXAMPLES.—Handsome—falling—strengthen—holy.

DEF. 6.—When a Word has *three* Principal Parts, it requires three articulations, and is then called a *Polysyllable*.

OBS. 1.—Generally a Word has as many Syllables as it has Principal Parts.

OBS. 2.—Two Letters may form one Principal Part of a Word when they are placed together, and combine to form one sound.

EXAMPLES.—*oi* in toil—*ou* in sound—*ai* in fair.

OBS. 3.—A Letter, ordinarily used as a Vowel, is sometimes added to a Syllable or a Word, to modify the Sound of other Letters, and is then an Adjunct.

EXAMPLES.—*e* in time—*y* in they—*i* in claim.

OBS. 4.—One Letter is often made to represent the Sound of another

EXAMPLES.—*e* represents *a* in they—*e* represents *u* in her—*i* represents *u* in sir.

OBS. 5.—In *written* Language, many Letters are used which are not sounded in *spoken Language*. Such are called *Silent Letters*.

EXAMPLES.—Hym*n*, thum*b*, ei*gh*t, *ph*t*h*isic.

OBS. 6.—One or more of the Letters constituting a Word, are sometimes used as the representative of that word. These are called

ABBREVIATIONS.

The most common abbreviations are the following:—

A. C.	Before Christ	from the Latin	Ante Christum.
A. B.	Bachelor of Arts	"	Artium Baccalaureus.
A. D.	In the year of our Lord	"	Anno Domini.
A. M.	Master of Arts	"	Artium Magister.
	In the year of the world	"	Anno Mundi.
	In the forenoon	"	Ante Meridiem.
B. D.	Bachelor of Divinity	"	Baccalaureus Divinitatis.
D. D.	Doctor of Divinity	"	Doctor Divinitatis.
e. g.	For example	"	Exempli gratia.
i. e.	That is	"	Id est.
LL.D.	Doctor of Laws	"	Legum Doctor.
L. S.	Place of the seal	"	Locus Sigilli.
Messrs.	Gentlemen	French	Messieurs.
M. D.	Doctor of Medicine	Latin	Medicinæ Doctor.
MS.	Manuscript	"	Scriptum Manus.
N. B.	Take notice	"	Nota Bene.
P. M.	Afternoon		Post Meridiem.
	Postmaster		
P. S.	Postscript	"	Post Scriptum.
S. T. D.	Doctor of Theology	"	Sanctæ Theologiæ Doctor

[illegible]

[illegible] has been [illegible]

[illegible] The snow [illegible] our

[illegible] visited [illegible]

[illegible]

[illegible] the [illegible]

that I [illegible] until [illegible]

[illegible]

[illegible] Reed

[illegible]

[illegible]

[illegible]

[illegible]

CPSIA information can be obtained
at www.ICGtesting.com
Printed in the USA
BVOW06s1223291017
498919BV00026B/193/P

9 781375 705394